Contemporary Studies

Contemporary Studies

By
Charles Baudouin

Translated from the French by
Eden and Cedar Paul

Essay Index Reprint Series

 BOOKS FOR LIBRARIES PRESS
FREEPORT, NEW YORK

First Published 1924

Reprinted 1969

STANDARD BOOK NUMBER:
8369-0002-2

LIBRARY OF CONGRESS CATALOG CARD NUMBER:
75-76892

PRINTED IN THE UNITED STATES OF AMERICA

Table of Contents

Part One : The Liberators of the Mind

Part Two : The War and the Peace

Part Three : Education and Society

Part Four : Art and Criticism

PART ONE

THE LIBERATORS OF THE MIND

TOLSTOY'S DIARY

(" Le Carmel," Geneva,
October 1917.)

THE Genevese firm of Jeheber has begun the publication
of a great book, Tolstoy's diary during the last fifteen
years of his life, i.e. from 1895 to 1910.[1] The French
translation, an excellent one, is the work of Natasha Rostova
and Marguerite Jean-Debrit. The first volume, the only one
as yet issued, contains the diary down to the year 1899.

Tolstoy kept a diary during the greater part of his life.
The main interest in such documents is to be found in the
inward conflicts they disclose ; in the writer's spiritual
crises ; above all, in the manifestations during tense, eventful,
and dynamic periods. From this point of view it seems
probable that the section of the diary now published is neither
so striking nor so valuable as the sections penned in earlier
years, for it dates from a period subsequent to that during
which the author was undergoing extensive moral perturbations. Still, to the end of his days Tolstoy was a seeker, a
restless being, one ever on the march. His flight to the
steppes a few days before his death was symbolical ; it
showed him to be one of those who never find fixed moorings,
and for whom no port can be anything more than a port of
call. Even in the pages we are now considering, his inner
life is in a perpetual flux. Nevertheless, they contain a
fair proportion of static and settled elements, as I shall
be able to show by my quotations. The moral interest
of the volume is supplemented by a historical interest, which

[1] Tolstoï, Journal intime, 1895–1910, Vol. I., 1895–1899, Jeheber, Geneva,
and Flammarion, Paris, 1917.—For English translation, see Bibliography.

it owes to the detailed, accurate, and copious notes added by Paul Birukoff.

The diary shows Tolstoy's inner life to have been a long examination of conscience, a continual struggle to remain severe towards himself while being lenient to others.

This severity towards himself is meticulously and scrupulously displayed. Moreover, it is displayed by a psychologist, by one who pitilessly scrutinises the deeper motives of a feeling or an action :

" I have often longed to suffer ; I have wanted to be persecuted. This amounts to saying that I have been idle, that I have been loath to work, that I have been better pleased to let others work for me while torturing me, what time all I had to do was to suffer."

As for his leniency towards others, this, in like manner, is the outcome of his understanding of others' motives. Being a great novelist, he has the power of putting himself in another's place. As Guyau says, " To understand every- thing is to forgive everything." Tolstoy understands.

" It is foolish to be vexed with those who think that human life is rooted in the flesh ; persons who take this view know nothing of the things of the spirit, and cannot think otherwise."

" You sometimes complain because people think only of your body instead of loving your soul. They may or may not love your body. You, who grow angry and blame them, do you not see that they cannot help it ? Your soul which for you is the most sacred thing in the world, the unique thing which exists and acts, is nothing at all for them, since they cannot see it any more than they can see the ultra-violet rays of the spectrum."

The book is interspersed with thoughts suitable for

separate publication in collected form, like the collections made some time ago by Ossip-Lourié from Tolstoy's other works.[1] Sometimes, these thoughts give a clearer expression to ideas enunciated by the writer elsewhere; sometimes, without making any substantial addition, they give such ideas livelier, more pointed, or more vigorous enunciation. For instance :

" God is not love : but in unawakened beings he manifests himself as selfish love ; and in awakened beings as unselfish love."

Here we meet once more the Tolstoyan distinction between the unawakened or animal life, and the awakened or spiritual life ; the latter is the life of those in whom a true religious sense has developed. Tolstoy does not condemn the animal life. Both forms of life are healthy, natural, " divine." But the animal life is only a stepping-stone on the way to the spiritual. What Tolstoy condemns are the aberrations due to the crisis that occurs during the passage from one life to the other, when all values are confused, when man idealises the flesh, sees a spiritual impetus in the passions, and, conversely, materialises the spirit. Thus he recognises two forms of art : spontaneous, popular art, in which man is presented as a fine and healthy animal ; and religious art (in the widest sense of the term religious), the art which has a sacramental influence on men, and touches them with an exalted emotion. Tolstoy repudiates any intermediate forms of art, regarding them as hybrid, confused, sacrilegious, and deceptive. Of his own greater works, he would retain *The Oossacks*, which belongs to the first category ; and *Resurrection*, the last of his novels, which belongs to the second. He disowns *War and Peace* and *Anna Karenina*.

For the man who has entered upon the second phase of

[1] Pensées de Tolstoï, and Nouvelles pensées de Tolstoï, Alcan, Paris, 1898, etc.

existence, the centre of gravity of the ego has been displaced, and this enables him to abstract himself ever more completely from his animal nature :

" In moments of passion, the only way to conquer is to destroy the illusion that it is oneself that suffers and desires ; to detach the true self from the stormy waves of passion.

" Another important point : reason alone can set love free. I think I omitted this pregnant thought from my exposition of faith."

The animal ego, which daily life jostles and bruises, is not the true ego ; to a great extent we can dissociate ourselves from it and its sufferings. We must interpret Tolstoy's precepts in the light of this fundamental notion. His onslaughts on war are not instigated by sentimentality ; his lamentations are not occasioned by the miseries of war :

" All the misfortunes men suffer, all the evils under which they groan, are the outcome of militarism. But what they complain of is not the chief of their ills. The worst thing is that the service of the State, especially in the army, kills the soul."

A man who has been reborn, no longer fears death :

" We must conquer death—not death itself, but the fear of death, the fear which comes from a failure to understand life. When we understand life, and understand that death is its beneficent and inevitable end, we no longer fear death and no longer resist its coming. And when we have ceased to fear death, we no longer serve our mortal ego. We devote ourselves to the service of the immortal being, the service of God, from whom we proceed and to whom we return."

Tolstoy has nothing definite to say concerning the form taken by this immortality of which he speaks. At times he seems to favour the notion of individual survival, but he has no fixed belief in the matter. Generally, when he speculates concerning the future life, he keeps himself well in hand, and is careful to point out that we can only discuss the topic in figurative terms, which convey no more than an imperfect idea of something we cannot really understand. He is content with this agnosticism. He has no interest in purely metaphysical speculations. His only concern with philosophy is in so far as it can serve as the mainspring of life and as the regulator of our actions. From this outlook, the mere affirmation of the eternal within us suffices :

" For my part, this is all I have to say about the dogma of the soul. The soul is the divine, the spiritual, restricted within us. The restriction gives the soul a form, just as the container imposes a shape upon a quantity of a gas or a liquid. This form is all that we know. If the vessel be broken, that which it contains no longer has any form ; the content is scattered. We may ask ourselves what becomes of the content, whether it assumes a new form, or fuses with other elements. An insoluble enigma faces us here. This much, however, we can be certain of, that the original form is lost when the vessel is broken. Thus with the soul after death ; the soul is no longer the soul ; it becomes spirit, divine substance ; it becomes something different, and something which eludes definition."

Tolstoy is no less agnostic as regards the idea of God. We know that God exists, but we cannot define the notion. He manifests himself in us as love, but we do not know his essential nature :

" It is not because God is personal (I know that he cannot be personal, seeing that he is infinite) that I pray to him as if he were a person. I do so because I myself am personal and finite. If I wear green spectacles, I see a green world, though I know quite well that the world is not really green."

Such an unequivocal spiritualism (a spiritualism reduced to its simplest terms), and such an agnosticism, are integral constituents of Tolstoy's thought. The reading of Spir [1] helped to confirm his outlooks in these respects, and his becoming acquainted with the writings of that philosopher marked an epoch in his spiritual development. We can no longer treat adequately of Tolstoy's philosophy without ascribing to Spir, among formative influences, a place no less important than the place we ascribe to Kant. Natasha Rostova, one of the translators of the diary, writes in a private letter: "No one, hitherto, has pointed out the important change that took place in Tolstoy's mind thanks to the readings of Spir. This disclosed to Tolstoy the non-reality of matter."

The recognition of the non-reality of matter confirmed for Tolstoy the conviction that our animal life is based on illusion. The idea of the non-reality of matter is simple. We are to suppose that the world as we know it does not exist per se, but is created by our senses. Just as touch furnishes us with remarkable rectifications of the errors of sight (perspective), so that we attain thereby to a completely different perception of the world, so a new sense would disclose everything to us from yet another angle. When this conviction of the unreality of matter had become firmly implanted in Tolstoy's mind, it was a revelation to him. It became the indispensable metaphysical substratum of his moral teaching. This was why he could write:

[1] African Alexandrovich Spir, b. 1837, d. 1890. Of Russian birth, he removed to Germany in 1867, and spent the closing years of his life in Switzerland. His German philosophical works, published by Neff, of Stuttgart, have never been translated into English. Available in French are: Esquisses de philosophie critique ; Nouvelles esquisses de philosophie critique (with a biography by Hélène Claparède-Spir) ; and Pensée et réalité. These were published by Alcan, Paris. A brief account of Spir's life and writings, from the pen of F. Max Müller, will be found in the " Nineteenth Century " for June, 1894, p. 942, et seq.—E. & C. P.

" We can neither understand nor know God until we understand the unreality of matter."

But Tolstoy valued Spir quite as much for his agnosticism as for his idealism. It is true that Spir affirms the duality of spirit and matter, but his primary thought is the postulation of a *radical* dualism. He contends that we are unable to grasp the interconnexion between spirit and matter—and that still less are we able to explain one by the other, as the theory of creation attempts to do. To ask what is the origin of evil is, in like manner, an unmeaning question.

Now for Tolstoy, as for Spir, God is not the creator of matter, but " the Father of Life."[1] After he has read Spir, Tolstoy's affirmation to this effect becomes more categorical :

" God finished his work when he gave men intelligent love. Why does he work through man instead of acting himself ? The question is absurd, and no one would ever have dreamed of asking it unless man's intellect had been led astray by the dogma that God created the world."

Again : " to seek for the origin of evil is as absurd as to try to discover the origin of the world. It does not matter where evil comes from ; what matters is that we should know how to fight evil, how to make use of love."

There are two traditional attributes of deity. God is described as being both all-powerful and all-good. Throughout the ages, theologians, confronted with the existence of evil, have fruitlessly endeavoured to reconcile the two attributes. Tolstoy deliberately sacrifices the power to the goodness.

If you understand, if you feel, if you " live " the unreality of matter, you will be aided in your duty to love, which is your most essential duty. As soon as we realise the unreality

[1] My Religion.

of matter—our material body not excepted—all this matter becomes for us no more than a vesture, a transparent veil, and we are impelled to look for the solid reality which underlies it. We disclothe men of the empirical and ostensible self, the self revealed to us by postures and actions ; and we find our way into the depths of being, where the eternal soul sleeps as a vein of metal sleeps in the rock. Tolstoy discerns this buried treasure even in the most debased of mortals. As Zlinchenko has written of him : " His peculiar strength lay in his intimate conviction that the vilest, the most wretched among human kind can triumph over debasement and become aware of a high calling." [1]

The purest love known to us, Christian love, which is the foundation of Tolstoy's wisdom, is this love for the divine that lies at the core of every human being. Such love is all the more fruitful in proportion to the thickness of the rock which conceals the vein, in proportion to the extent of the obstacles that hinder love ; it is more fruitful when, in order that we may love, we have had to win a victory over ourselves, and over the material contingencies whose memory has been a hindrance to love :

" To love our enemies ! How difficult it is, and how rare—like all that is truly beautiful. But how we rejoice when we succeed. There is something marvellously sweet in such love, and even in the expectation of such love. The intensity of the feeling of pure delight is inversely proportional to the attraction exercised upon us by the object of love. To love our enemies is spiritual rapture."

All love is good, but Christian love must be our ultimate goal. When we love our enemies, we may know we have attained that goal. Through the outward personality we shall have penetrated to the inward being, depersonalised and divine, who is no longer our enemy :

[1] " Cœnobium," Lugano, August 1916, " Tolstoï et le mouchard."

" It is a great error to confound carnal love, love for children and friends, with the love of men through God, the love of those who are indifferent to us, the love of our enemies—the love of strayed sheep."

" When we know how to conquer the offence by love, when we have learned to love our enemies, then only can true love arise in us."

In this part of the diary, Tolstoy's interests revolve round the two or three great ideas we have been considering. To conclude my essay, I wish to show how Tolstoy the moralist is still Tolstoy the great writer ; and I shall choose, in illustration, some thoughts whose imagery makes them peculiarly striking. They are little parables :

" Man fancies that animalism is his real being, and that his spiritual life is its work. In like manner, one who is on a moving boat fancies that he is motionless and that the shore recedes."

" We deceive ourselves when we believe our finite personality to be our true being. Our mistake resembles that of the traveller who, at the end of the first stage of his journey, believes himself to be at the end of his journey ; or that of one who mistakes a day for his whole life."

The tone is that of the sages and the apostles, but Tolstoy does not use stereotyped phrases, does not simply retrace the old parables. His imagery is alive. Often, he is content to draw his metaphors from contemporary life ; and will use the most unclassical, the most everyday instances, provided only that they serve to give concrete and picturesque expression to his thought :

" The action upon life which discloses itself to me in this world by an increase of the love within me, and by the fusion of beings in love, simultaneously produces many other actions which I do not see. When I arrange eight

2

little cubes so as to sketch something, another sketch is formed by the sides of the cubes opposite to those I have under my eyes ; but I do not see this other sketch."

It was Tolstoy's way to speak of great things with child like simplicity.

TOLSTOY AS EDUCATIONIST

(" Les Tablettes," Geneva,
June 1917.)

LEONARDO DA VINCI was, upon occasion, a bridge-builder
and a mechanical engineer. Goethe, the imaginative
writer, made important and valuable contributions to
natural science. In like manner Tolstoy offers us the
spectacle of a great artist who works with astonishing
mastery in intellectual fields which he seems to cultivate
merely as a pastime—but where he shows himself to be a
formidable rival to the professional experts. This aspect
of Tolstoy's activities has for the most part been ignored.
Our attention is apt to be monopolised by the more spontaneous, primitive, tempestuous, and tragical manifestations of this soul and this life.

Tolstoy's faculty for methodical study is, I think, preeminently shown in the domain of education. From youth
until the end of his days he was always keenly interested in
educational problems. In 1849, when he was only twenty-
one years of age, Tolstoy opened a school ; and in the
pedagogical field his life perhaps exhibits a more perfect
unity than in any other. Whereas both in art and in
philosophy the day comes when he finds it necessary to make
a holocaust of that which he has hitherto worshipped, his
educational principles show little variation. They develop,
it is true ; they undergo a continuous evolution ; but there
is no crisis, no revolutionary change.

The difference is not difficult to explain. It was in
respect of his ideas concerning education that Tolstoy

first became fully awakened and self-conscious. Here he first recognised the essential importance of love, freedom, and the avoidance of the use of force ; the fallaciousness of a mechanical order, authoritatively imposed from without ; the need for an order that is deep-rooted, that is living, that grows from within—an order that may simulate disorder, but is nevertheless the only true order. *The ideas which, after his spiritual crisis, Tolstoy came to regard as fundamental to the regulation of social life, were but a generalisation, were but an application to the adult, of the ideas he had always advocated where children were concerned.*

Furthermore, Tolstoy's ideas on education, like his ideas in general, have a definite bearing on life. No matter whether he is writing a novel or expounding a theory, this great psychologist, this supreme connoisseur of both grown-ups and children, always displays pitiless realism. His thoughts are the natural outcome of his acute and penetrating observation of life. Yet, with strange inconsistency, some of the critics tell us that Tolstoy is an unrivalled novelist because his knowledge of human nature is without parallel ; and in the same breath these critics say that his moral theories are so utopian that they can only arouse a smile in any one who really knows human nature.

As far as educational science is concerned, Tolstoy's views are directly based upon experience. The fact is obvious.

Tolstoy knows children. Descriptions of the inner life of the child were the first themes of his literary genius. The tale *Childhood and Youth* opened the series of his imaginative writings. The book, moreover, was autobiographical. The author, a man always fond of self-analysis, gave a marvellously accurate account of the minor impressions of childhood and youth—those which in most of us have been forgotten or repressed. He had merely to call up these memories. They sufficed to inform him that the inner life of the child is rich and full and variegated—but also tender and sensitive. Like George Eliot, he was aware that the " happy age " is often a period of unspeakable torment ; he could recall the way in which the child brims over with affection, and how often adults (utterly failing to understand the child's mind) repel these childish proffers of affection.

Aware of this, he always studies children as individuals. The child-figures in his novels are not lay-figures ; he plumbs their souls just as he plumbs the soul of adults.

Tolstoy devoted himself to practical work as a teacher. Faithful to the precept " discat a puero magister," he continued to study childhood in the persons of his pupils, for he was convinced that conventional education is apriorist, and that it is necessary to inaugurate a system of education based on experimental research. A school, he considered, should also be a " laboratory " of child psychology.

Thus Tolstoy, while influenced by other educationists— for instance, by Rousseau ; by Froebel (whose nephew he had known) ; and by Diesterweg—was mainly guided by his personal experience as a teacher. The pedagogical experts just mentioned were all champions of freedom ; he would be faithful to their principles by refusing to accept their authority blindly, as the scholastics had accepted the authority of Aristotle. In fine, his sole master was experience, the direct and careful observation of life.

The school in the grounds of Yasnaya Polyana, where, with a few helpers, he taught the children of peasants, grew like a living organism.

Tolstoy's general aim was to introduce into the school an

increasing measure of freedom, and to do away with punishments. He wanted to place the children under the conditions of concrete life : for instance, lessons were not to be recited at fixed hours, but the pupil, at any moment when he felt both fit and inclined, was to repeat what he had learned from the master ; the living emulation aroused by collective work was to be substituted for the objective and formal emulation aroused by placing the children in order of merit, and by marks. He laid stress, too, upon the educational value of games. If these are banned during school hours, and relegated to the home or to the hours of " recreation," the life is taken out of class work, and the school becomes no more than a dead mechanism.

Let us picture to ourselves Tolstoy, during winter evenings, in the little school at Yasnaya Polyana, when the waning of the light has made the further use of the eyes impossible, and when he is telling his pupils a story, a historical episode, or the life of one of the saints or sages of old. The peasant lads sit at ease on the benches, the tables, or the window-sills ; the girls are together in a corner ; one youngster is crouching at the feet of the master to whom the children are devoted. They have been playing and chattering, but now order has been spontaneously restored, and all have their eyes fixed upon the speaker. He is himself moved at sight of these eyes that gleam in the gathering darkness. When he has finished, they are eager to tell the tale in their turn ; not a word has been lost.

We must read the periodical " Yasnaya Polyana," the literary organ of the school, if we want to realise how clearly, methodically, and logically Tolstoy discussed the data of his educational experience, criticised pedagogical theories, and scrutinised proposed educational laws. These articles are masterpieces of their kind.

After his religious crisis, Tolstoy found it easy to incorporate his educational theories into his general social scheme. Education seemed to him more important than ever, for in his view it must be the chief instrument of social reform. By beginning with children, it would be possible to establish a society founded upon love and the absence of coercion. During the latter part of his life, Tolstoy continued to receive children at his home, and to teach them there. He never abandoned the field of practical experience, for he considered that realist observation must always precede theorising. On the other hand, he never ceased to draw theoretical inferences from his experience, and it was at this epoch that he wrote numerous letters dealing with educational problems—letters of enormous value.

Thus Tolstoy was a great educationist. He loved teaching, believed in it, expected it to give splendid results. His over-scrupulous conscience often made him uneasy—and the uneasiness would spread to his friends. On one such occasion, Paul Birukoff asked him : " Have you never in your life enjoyed a sense of perfect satisfaction ? "— " Oh yes," answered Tolstoy, " when I have busied myself with children."

TOLSTOY AND THE REALIST FAITH [1]

TOLSTOY, being one who lived intensely, had no great love for men of letters or for men of science. He considered that they were out of touch with life, that they were lacking in a wide and deep humanity. He was in the habit of saying that he had learned more from two peasants than from all the scientists or all the wisdom of printed books. These two peasants were Sutayeff and Bondareff. Sutayeff's straightforward Christianity and Bondareff's doctrine of manual work were equally dear to him. It is touching to see how simple Tolstoy himself becomes in his letters to a man of simple mind. He wishes to identify himself with all comers, and is able to do so.

For Bondareff, man's essential duty was found in the nineteenth verse of the third chapter of Genesis : " In the sweat of thy face shalt thou eat bread." Work, physical toil, was the first of the commandments. The supreme interest of the Letters to Bondareff is to learn from them how entirely Tolstoy shared the views of the peasant, and how, in his moral teaching, he assigned to physical toil a role of supreme importance.

Although, in his humility, Tolstoy repudiates the notion, this is a remarkably individual interpretation of Christianity. According to the gospel of Martha and Mary, and according to the parable of the lilies of the field which toil not neither do they spin, it would hardly seem that this insistence upon physical toil is an essential part of Christ's ideal.

[1] This essay was penned as the Introduction to Tolstoï, Lettres à Bondarev, Cahiers du Carmel, Geneva and Paris, 1918.

There are, in fact, two contrasted religious attitudes, one contemplative and the other active. One is compounded of lyricism and ecstasy, the other of labour and struggle. The former ideal is that of those who aspire to forget the material world and to merge into the world of the spirit ; the latter ideal is that of those who strive to mould the world with the aid of the spirit. The two attitudes have always existed side by side.

The East, the South—these are the placid parts of the world, where contemplation flourishes most. In Christ himself, we find the contemplative mood quite as often as the active, That was why Renan loved Jesus. In Tolstoy, who is in all respects so typical of the Russian soul, everything recalls the native of a barren land, the child of a race of toilers whose backs are continuously bent as they till the stubborn soil. He embodies the characteristics which Renan, a Hellene and a votary of the fine arts, would stigmatise as crude, coarse, and barbarous.

Tolstoy is a realist through and through. The actualities of daily life, the actualities which are often harsh and poverty-stricken, are what interest him. His novels were realistic ; and when the artist had become the apostle, his faith was realistic too. There was no lyrical element in it, nothing symbolical or metaphysical ; these qualities were alien to Tolstoy's temperament. Before all, he was a realist, was overwhelmingly active, was concerned to the pitch of obsession with the rude realities of social life—with poverty, with the shivering of those who were cold, with the pinched looks of those who were hungry.

In such matters Tolstoy retains the outlook of a man of a practical turn, one who keeps his affairs in good order, one who always gives his first attention to things of primary importance. Underlying his whole conception of morality we find the problem of urgency, usefulness, the gradations of usefulness in things and actions. These notions are admirably expressed in *What to do?* They find a place once more in Tolstoy's preface to Bondareff's *Le travail*, the preface, dated 1888, being entitled " Le travail et la théorie de Bondareff : " [1]

" The leading thought of the book is this : In all the circumstances of life, the essential thing to know is, not what is good and necessary, but which thing, among those that are good and necessary, is of the first importance, which should come second, which third, and so on. . . .

" Before we provide people with priests, soldiers, judges, doctors, teachers, we should find out whether they are dying of hunger . . .

" No one for whom the significance of life is to be found in the service of others could possibly go so far astray as to believe that he could serve those who are dying of hunger and cold, by writing laws for them, by making cannons, by producing luxuries, or by playing the fiddle or the piano.

" Love cannot be so stupid.

" Just as we do not try to show our love for one who is hungry by reading a novel to him, or for one who is cold by giving him a pair of costly ear-rings, so in like manner it is absurd to suppose that we can display our love for others by amusing the well fed, while we allow the cold and the hungry to perish in their wretchedness."

His realist faith is what makes Tolstoy ascribe so much importance to the physical toil that is essential for the satisfaction of our daily needs.

But this man, whose own inner life was so rich, could not be content with an incomplete outlook. It is well that we should remember how, during his last years, he was again able to find a place of esteem for contemplation.[2]

---

[1] Léon Tolstoï et Timothée Bondareff, Le travail, Marpon et Flammarion, Paris.   [2] Cf Natasha Rostova's article in " Le Carmel," No. 8 for 1917.

This gives us a wider view of Tolstoy, and shows us once more that there is no possibility of circumscribing our account of such a man within a few narrow formulas. The truly great man is too multiform for any framework.

It is true, nevertheless, that the doctrine which usually passes by the name of " Tolstoyism " is a characteristically and uncompromisingly realist faith ; a religion of action, not of prayer ; a religion that takes us by the shoulders and gives us a vigorous push forwards. Does the method seem drastic ? What matter, if it be the expression of something strong, impassioned, and vibrant ? In that case we may prefer even excessive zeal (corrected, later, by the complementary attitude) to the dull counsels of chill reason, which take the fire out of our energies. Even though such realism may not fulfil all the needs of our spirit, there can be no doubt that it fulfils those which are most urgent. The realities of the western world—the modern world— are harsh, oppressive, and cruel ; nevertheless, we must ballast our ideal with realism.

That is why we have need of Tolstoy's message to-day.

December 1917.

NIETZSCHE'S LETTERS

("Le Carmel," Geneva,
May and June 1917.)

THE correspondence between Friedrich Nietzsche and his friend Professor Overbeck has recently been published.[1] I have read Nietzsche's letters with profound interest and lively emotion. They introduce us to the most intimate life of this thinker. When I say "intimate," I am not referring to those petty personal details which critics of a certain order love to record in the case of great men. I mean the innermost workings of mind and heart. My extracts from the correspondence will bear witness to the fact.

The letters perfect the work of earlier documents in that they give us a fuller revelation of the Nietzsche whom we already know : we see a man of sensitive spirit, susceptible and vulnerable, infinitely and exquisitely human, all-too-human ; a very different Nietzsche from that of the crude image set up by those who did not know him, sketched after the model of the ogre in a fairy tale.

" I understand, now, how valuable an asset misanthropy must have been to all anchorites. Unfortunately, I have a different temperament. If only I had a firm faith in myself —but that seems even more remote." (Rapallo, January 1883.)

We understand that the glaring and brutal paradoxes which abound in Nietzsche's writings are the outcome of a defensive instinct, of a wish to " become hard," in one who has too often experienced the pricks of the goad of compassion.

[1] By the Insel-Verlag, Leipzig, 1916.

" I am perpetually remaking the same mistake, incessantly overestimating others' suffering. From childhood onwards I have had repeated confirmation of the truth that to feel compassion was the greatest of my dangers. (Perhaps this is the outcome of the strange nature of my father—a man considered by all who knew him to resemble an angel rather than a human being.) Suffice it to say that my own painful experience of the workings of sympathy has led me to modify, in a way that has great theoretical interest, my estimate of the worth of this emotion." (Sils-Maria, September 14, 1884.)

This passage enables us to understand the bearing of Nietzsche's condemnation of sympathy, and leads us to the conclusion that we are not all entitled to utter the same condemnation. Such a privilege must be reserved for those who have suffered as Nietzsche had suffered, for those to whom the precept " become hard " is a vital necessity. Then only can we be sure, like Nietzsche, that we shall never succumb to the cynical and monstrous hardness which some readers discover in the teachings of Zarathustra.

How far Nietzsche himself was from being hard, is shown by such effusions as the following :

" One who lives so long ' on the heights,' or ' on the mountain top,' or (like the outlaw) ' in the air,' grows sensitive to the least intimation of warmth, grows more and more sensitive. My dear, old friend, such a one becomes so *grateful* [1] for friendship ! " (Leipzig, October 17, 1885.)

Continually he shows us that a certain hardness, a certain impassivity, is for him an unrealised ideal, and an ideal which he has no great wish to realise.

" The *antinomy* of my present position and of my present mode of existence lies in this, that everything which I *need*

---

[1] The corresponding words to those italicised in these citations are thus stressed in the German original.

as *philosophus radicalis*—freedom from occupation, wife, children, society, fatherland, creed, etc., etc.—all these freedoms become *privations* to me in so far as (by good fortune) I am a living man, and not simply an analysing machine and an objectifying apparatus." (Nice, November 14, 1886.)

Thus, in Nietzsche, the thinker is, above all, a " living man." His wisdom is by turns passionate, suffering, enthusiastic, and joyous. It is alive. Its development resembles rather that of a tragedy than that of a theorem—and this is why it is so captivating.

In the letters we are able to follow close at hand the development of the tragedy. We feel that each one of Nietzsche's thoughts has first of all been lived in every fibre of his being.

In a few words, almost in a cry, he expresses the contrast between the optimism he desiderates and the suffering he really feels, a contrast similar to that between his theoretical hardness and his actual sensitiveness.

" No ! This life ! And I am the champion of life ! ! " (Rapallo, February 22, 1883.)

Nietzsche looked upon his " task " as being, in a sense, a mission. The word " mission " must not be interpreted in a mystical way ; but, while abandoning mysticism, Nietzsche retained the fervour of the mystic, retained the mystic's state of soul. In *Ecce Homo* we find him defending the idea of revelation, provided that we are thinking of that which " reveals itself," and not of that which " is revealed." Such is the characteristically original tint of Nietzsche's mysticism. We shall find it once more in his letters. His " task " imposes duties, entails scruples, just like those familiar to persons of a religious bent :

" To teach : yes, that would be congenial (I was still

thus engaged last summer, and I felt how well it suited me). But there is *more important* work to be done, work in comparison with which even the most useful and most effective teaching post would only seem to me a pastime, a recreation. Not until I have fulfilled my first task, could I conscientiously enjoy such an existence as you contemplate for me." (Genoa, April 19, 1883.)

As a " living creature," moreover, Nietzsche understands the superiority of the " living " word to the word that is written in a book. (That is why the prospect of a teaching career holds out certain temptations.) He looks forward to such action as that of which Romain Rolland was to speak at a later date : " the strongest and the only effective form of action, individual action, the action of one man on another, of one soul on another, action by word, by example, by the integral personality."

Thus Nietzsche writes to Overbeck from Zurich at the end of October or the beginning of November 1884 : " I need disciples *while I am still alive.* The best things, the things that matter most, can only be communicated *from one human being to another* ; they neither can nor should be public."

In the life of this thinker there is no intellectual happening which is not at the same time, which is not first of all, an intimate happening, an emotion, a shock :

" I am amazed, delighted ! I have a *forerunner*, and such a forerunner ! I knew hardly anything of Spinoza. . . . Not only is his general trend identical with mine—to regard knowledge as our *most powerful* affect—but I rediscover myself in the five leading points of his teaching. This most unusual and most lonely of thinkers is closest to me in *these* things above all : he denies free will ; final aims ; the moral ordering of the universe ; non-egoism ; evil. If, the differences between us are, none the less, enormous, these differences depend mainly on differences in time, culture, science. *In summa* : my loneliness, which, as when one is in the high mountains, has often made my breathing difficult and has made my heart feel as if it would burst—will at any rate henceforward be a solitude à deux.—Strange ! " (Sils, Engadine, July 30, 1881.)

" To regard knowledge as our most powerful affect "—to contemplate the things of the intellect through the medium of sensibility ; to endow intelligence (whose nature it is to dissect the sentiments) with a higher, an affective value ; to transform it into a sentiment, an affect, advantageously replacing the affects which the intellect has itself destroyed (the " affections " and " passions " of Spinoza)— this is, indeed, Nietzsche's general trend, and nowhere is the fact more plainly disclosed than in this description of the emotional shock he experienced on becoming acquainted with the most abstract of philosophers.

The letters to Overbeck afford glimpses into all the aspects of Nietzsche's personality.

We read of the material organisation of his life, and note how humiliated he is at having to haggle over the charges for board and lodging. We mark the simplicity of his tastes, worthy of a classical philosopher ; and we feel that some of our contemporaries who are pleased to consider themselves Nietzscheans might profit by his example :

" One whose desires in respect of food, clothing, and shelter are as modest as mine, can live easily and cheaply wherever he goes." (Nice, December 1883.)

We are prone to forget that the glorification of the forces of instinct (which is, indeed, an essential part of Nietzsche's doctrine) was for him subordinate to the glorification of self-mastery. The sumptuous life, the " magnificently sensual " life sung by d'Annunzio, is as remote from the

Nietzschean spirit as the "hog of Epicurus herd" sung by Horace is remote from true Epicureanism—which, like all the ancient philosophies, was a discipline in moderation and simplicity. Nietzsche may say harsh things of Socrates and Plato, but nevertheless he exhibits many of the traits proper to the archetype of the Greek philosopher. In one of his letters, having just reread Plato, he expresses his surprise at the way in which his own Zarathustra "Platonises" (πλατονίζει).—(Genoa, October 22, 1883.)

A little later we find him sympathetic towards Pythagoras' rule of silence. Nietzsche writes from Genoa in November 1883 : "I have come to recognise that there is nothing to be prized more highly than a *tenacious will*, for which ten years would not be too long, were they to be ten years of silence."

In actual fact, Nietzsche's discipline, far from being a glorification of instinct in all its forms, implies the establishment of a hierarchy among the instincts, under the supreme guidance of certain primordial tendencies which constitute the true genius of the individual concerned. This is the secret of the individualism that was especially characteristic of the Renaissance.

"To me the Renaissance always seems the *culmination* of this millennium. What has happened since is but the great reaction of all kinds of herd impulses against the 'individualism' of that epoch." (Leipzig, October 1882.)

In another place, beside the philosopher we perceive the poet, sustained by the wave of creative enthusiasm :

"On Friday I wrote the last words of *Also sprach Zarathustra*, and I am now copying the manuscript. . . . The last two weeks have been the happiest of my life. I have never before voyaged with such sails over such a sea ; the immense buoyancy of the whole of this voyaging (which

3

has lasted since you first came to know me in 1870) then reached its climax." (Nice, January 1884.)

Another extremely interesting feature of the correspondence is the light the letters throw upon some of the noted figures of our time ; and the reflex light that is thrown upon the essential nature of the writer's own mind. " Tell me your company, and I will tell you what you are."

A contemporary philosopher who is one of Nietzsche's " associates " is African Spir, the Russian thinker who advocated radical dualism, and denied the possibility of a causal explanation of the universe. Spir, as I have shown in another essay (*supra*, p. 14) likewise exercised a notable influence on Tolstoy.

Nietzsche writes from Sils in September 1881 : " Another book I need very much from among those in the Zurich boxes is Spir's *Denken und Wirklichkeit*. You will find the two volumes among the unbound books."

At one time Spir seems to have been for Nietzsche a bedside companion, as it were. Despite marked contrasts in doctrinal matters, there is an unmistakable kinship between the two minds. Both Nietzsche and Spir cherished the notion of the " Cœnobium," a revival of the lay convent of Pythagoras. We know, moreover, that Nietzsche made abundant marginal notes in Spir's book (as he did, also, in some of the works of Guyau).

Emerson, likewise, was regarded by Nietzsche as a kindred spirit. But he considered there was something lacking to the great American—something which accounted for Emerson's failure to exercise as wide an influence as might have been expected :

" Tell your wife that I feel Emerson to be a brother-soul (but his mind is ill-formed).—(Nice, December 1883.)

" I would give almost anything if I could but retrospectively bring it to pass that this man with a grand and splendid nature, this man rich in soul and spirit, could have experienced a strict discipline, could have enjoyed a *truly scientific culture*. As things are, Emerson is *a philosopher lost to us*." (Nice, December 22, 1884.)

To conclude these examples, I will quote some of the references to a man numbered among those with whom Nietzsche had come into personal contact, Carl Spitteler— then at the very beginning of his career, but now acclaimed by the Swiss as their poet. The influence exercised by *Prometheus und Epimetheus* on *Also sprach Zarathustra* is well known. It may be added that Nietzsche was one of the first to discover Spitteler's merits, and did something to smooth the poet's path. Consider, for instance, the following passage (written at Sils on September 17, 1887) :

" Have you any personal knowledge of Herr Carl Spitteler, now living in Basle (he wrote to me recently from 74 Gartenstrasse) ? Obviously an interesting man, and endowed with a first-class intelligence. What sort of position has he ? He seems to be rather sore about something. I am trying to find a publisher for his treatise on aesthetics. (I have given up the attempt to find a publisher for myself.) "

Nietzsche's good offices for Spitteler were successful :

" Herr Spitteler writes to me with grateful acknowledgments. I was able to help him in a matter where he had given up hope—namely, to find a publisher. His book deals with the aesthetics of the French drama. . . . The little service I have done him is charged with affect ; it was my way of paying him out for an exceedingly tactless article from his pen in the ' Bund ' last winter, one dealing with my writings as a whole.—I have so high an opinion of this Swiss author's talent that I cannot be turned against him. I respect his character." (Sils, July 20, 1888.)

Thenceforward, any differences there may have been

were forgotten.   Spitteler, on his side, came to understand
Nietzsche better and greeted the publication of *Der Fall
Wagner* by writing an enthusiastic article on the book :

" Herr Spitteler expresses his delight, writing in last
Thursday's issue of the ' Bund.' "   (Turin, November 13,
1888.)

A few weeks later, when *Ecce Homo*, Nietzsche's last book,
appeared, Spitteler and Overbeck were among the favoured
few for whom presentation copies were reserved :

" Besides your copy, there are copies for the Library,
the Reading Society, the ' Basler Nachrichten,' and Herr
Spitteler." (Turin, December 22, 1888.)

Not many days after this was written, the darkness of
dementia was to close in on Nietzsche's mind.   We are,
therefore, justified in saying that one of his last lucid thoughts
was devoted to Spitteler.

The onset of dementia was sudden.   But whatever the
superadded cause that led to this final affliction may have
been, we know that Nietzsche had long been ill   One of
the most remarkable features of his trouble was the lucidity
with which he followed the march of the disease.[1]

The first symptoms were those of functional nervous
disorder, and Nietzsche was well aware that the eye troubles
and other bodily symptoms were merely the multiple effects
of a single cause, a cause that was at work in the central
nervous system.

Subsequently there became manifest the first indications
of the persecution complex (and, a little later, the signs of
the megalomania which is apt to be intimately associated

[1] This disease was a psychoneurotic trouble which paved the way for
the onset of dementia.   But it was not the effective cause of the dementia,
cannot be identified with it, and does not justify any apriori argument
against Nietzsche's philosophy.   The censures of hostile critics are invalid,
in so far as they are based on such considerations.   The dementia seems
to have been due to an independent organic cause.

with delusions of persecution). The development of the persecution complex is made especially clear in the correspondence :

" I am suspicious of everybody now ; in everything that I hear, I sense the animus of contempt. . . . Yesterday I broke off the correspondence with my mother ; it had become unendurable, and I should have done well to take this step long ago." (Rapallo, December 25, 1882.)

It will suffice to point out, in passing, that this shows how the origins of the trouble date from long back, and concern Nietzsche's most intimate experiences ; for the *mother* comes into the case thus early, and from the first the " persecuted " man's hostility is concentrated on her.

Next to the mother, the fatherland becomes intolerable, this extension of antagonistic feelings corresponding to the natural bent of Nietzsche's mind.

" I can no longer endure the German atmosphere ; the very persons whom I most esteem among the Germans, have taken a dislike to me ; and the Germans are so inconsiderate in their dislikes that they become tactless— positively rude. I was treated with more respect in my student days, than during the last year." (Rapallo, January 1883.)

The generalisation runs its natural course. In the end, the whole of mankind is involved in it :

" Excepting only my friend Overbeck (and three other persons), during the last ten years every one I know has behaved towards me in some preposterous way, sometimes by the display of offensive suspicions, or at least by showing a hateful impudence (the last to sin in this way was Rohde). The most favourable upshot has been to make me more independent ; but my experience has also made me more callous, perhaps, and more misanthropic than I could wish." (Nice, November 12, 1887.)

The most remarkable feature in the case was the way in which Nietzsche accounted for his trouble. Though the modern methods of psychoanalysis were still unknown, he saw clearly that a " repressed instinct " was at the root of the mischief. The essential trouble was, he considered, the repression of his " individuality "—this meaning the most profound, the most personal, among his tendencies :

" My dear, old Sils-Maria, as I am reluctantly forced to admit, must be consigned ' ad acta,' just like Nice : in both these places I now miss the first and most essential require-ment—solitude, perfect tranquillity, the possibility of living a life apart—in default of which I cannot *get down* to my problems (for, let me tell you between ourselves, I am to a terrible degree a man of the *depths* ; and without this sub-terranean work I should find it impossible to bear life any longer). My last winter in Nice was a martyrdom, and so was my last sojourn at Sils : for I had forfeited that incognito which is the first condition of life for me, and the only road to *health*. From year to year my health grows worse ; and the condition of my health has become for me an infallible sign, how far I am on my own road or on that of others." (Canobbio, April 14, 1887.)

Nietzsche was, in truth, an expert in the psychology of repressed and transformed instincts. The most ingenious among the views expressed in *Human, All-Too-Human*, in *The Genealogy of Morals*, and even in *The Origin of Tragedy*, are foreshadowings of the theories of repression and sublima-tion. Now, Nietzsche, the sick man, analysed himself, just as he analysed others. Though not always able to explain himself to himself, he pushed self-analysis far :

" People had better give up expecting ' pretty things ' from me : just as little as they would expect a suffering and hungry beast to devour its prey gracefully. The en-during lack of a truly invigorating and healing *human* love, the absurd isolation this entails, so that such vestiges as remain of ties with my fellows are the source of little beyond mortifications : all this is extremely distressing, and has only one justification for its existence, that of being inevitable." (Nice, February 3, 1888.)

As we advance through the letters, they make us more uneasy. We feel that we are in the presence of one whose nervous system, strained like an over-stretched bowstring, is on the verge of snapping. We draw near to the arcana of the human enigma :

" Almost every letter that I write, now, begins with the phrase that there is no longer any chance happening in my life." (Turin, December 22, 1888.)

" There are no more chance happenings. If I think of any one, a letter from him presents itself politely at my door." (Turin, Christmas 1888.)

Very quickly, as the last days draw on, his state grows worse. More and more, Germany seems to have become the central object of his defiance and hatred. In one of the last of all the letters (wherein the ineffable calm of the great release can already be foreseen), we find an amazing, terrible, and prophetic utterance concerning Germany :

" I am working at a Promemoria for the European courts. It concerns the establishment of an anti-German league. I want to encircle the ' Empire ' with a ring of iron, and to provoke it to a war of desperation.

" This for your most private ear !—Perfect calm of soul. I have slept ten hours without a break." (Turin, December 28, 1888.)

It is the fashion to dress Nietzsche up as a pan-German. That is why I conclude my review of the Nietzsche-Overbeck correspondence with the foregoing citation.

April and May 1917.

NIETZSCHE AS FORERUNNER IN PSYCHOANALYSIS

(Part of an article entitled " Psychoanalysis as an evolutionary Theory of Instinct," that appeared in the "Revue de Genève," 1922.)

A LOGICAL deduction from the theory of evolution is that the higher sentiments must be derived by evolution from certain elementary instincts. Nietzsche would seem to have been the first, if not to draw this conclusion, at any rate to give it substance, to give it the relief and the emphasis which ideas received in the passage through his mind. Until he turned his attention to the matter, no one endowed with such eager clarity of vision, no one with so coldly impassioned an outlook, had scrutinised the unacknowledged genesis of our sentiments, had disclosed what Nietzsche terms " the fabrication of the ideal." That is why he is entitled to be regarded as the great instigator of the psychological theory of evolution which psychoanalysis is now developing. Even where details are concerned, the explanations he ventured to give have in many instances been rediscovered by the science of the subconscious; and his formulas, far from growing obsolete, seem to-day younger than ever, in their challenging and paradoxical mode of expression.

Human, All-Too-Human embodies Nietzsche's first attempts to scrutinise things in this fashion. The scrutiny is pitilessly turned inwards. We feel that the author has a malicious delight in throwing off all sense of intoxication. He does not make a holocaust of what he has adored (this would be too crude a sacrifice), but he dissects it. With the sardonic laugh of the victor, he affirms that this adoration was human, all-too-human—that, in other words, it was animal. In the opening pages, he blames the philosophers for their " original sin " ; they had " historic sense " (Aphorism 2), the historic sense which is whetted by the adoption of the evolutionary outlook. " All that we require, and which can only be given us by the present advance of the single sciences, is a *chemistry* of the moral, religious, aesthetic ideas and sentiments, as also of those emotions which we experience in ourselves both in the great and in the small phases of social and intellectual intercourse, and even in solitude ; but what if this chemistry should result in the fact that also in this case the most beautiful colours have been obtained from base, even despised materials ? Would many be inclined to pursue such examinations ? Humanity likes to put all questions as to origin and beginning out of its mind." (Aphorism 1.)[1]

The closing words of the foregoing quotation already remind us of the psychoanalytical theory of *repression*, to which Nietzsche draws still closer elsewhere : " How little moral would the world look without this forgetfulness ! A poet might say that God had placed forgetfulness as door-keeper in the temple of human dignity." (Aphorism 92.) This porter wears much the same uniform as Freud's " censor " ! In *The Genealogy of Morals*, where Nietzsche rounds off and synthetises the views expressed in a less finished form in *Human, All-Too-Human*, we find a remarkable theory of active forgetfulness : " Forgetfulness is no mere *vis inertiæ*, as the superficial believe ; rather is it a power of obstruction, active, and, in the strictest sense of the word, positive ; . . . a very sentinel and nurse of psychic order, repose, etiquette." (II, 1.)[2]

---

[1] The English renderings of these Aphorisms are from Helen Zimmern's translation of Part I of Menschliches, Allzumenschliches in Oscar Levy's edition of Nietzsche's works.—E. & C. P.

[2] The English renderings of The Genealogy of Morals are taken from Horace B. Samuel's translation in Oscar Levy's edition of Nietzsche's works.—E. & C. P.

If our shrewdness enables us to elude this supervision, to pass this sentinel, we shall catch a glimpse of things that are far from edifying ; we shall recognise " the possibility of that particular sweetness and fulness which is peculiar to the aesthetic state, springing directly from the ingredient of sensuality. . . . It may be, consequently, that sensuality is not removed by the approach of the aesthetic state, as Schopenhauer believed, but merely becomes transfigured, and ceases to enter into the consciousness as sexual excitement." (*Genealogy*, III, 8.) This implies that there must be a sort of conservation of instinctive energy, with a change of direction : " Every artist knows the harm done by sexual intercourse on occasions of great mental strain and preparation ; as far as the strongest artists and those with the surest instincts are concerned, this is not necessarily a case of experience—hard experience—but it is simply their ' maternal ' instinct which, in order to benefit the growing work, disposes recklessly (beyond all its normal stocks and supplies) of the vigour of its animal life." (*Genealogy*, III, 8.) This change of direction is what psychoanalysts term *sublimation*. The very word is employed by Nietzsche : " Good actions are sublimated evil ones." (*Human All-Too-Human*, Part I, Aphorism 107.)

The fundamental instinct, whose avatars form the most diversified sentiments, is, according to Nietzsche, the will-to power. This lurks even beneath the mask of pity, which is " a consolation for the weak and the suffering in that the latter recognise therein that they still possess one power, in spite of their weakness, the power of giving pain." (Ibid., Aphorism 50.) But Nietzsche reserves his most vitriolic analysis for asceticism : " that was the last pleasure that antiquity invented after it had grown blunted even at the sight of beast-baitings and human combats." (Ibid., Aphorism 141.) In all renunciation he discerns repressed voluptuousness and repressed cruelty. (*Genealogy*, II, 18.) He endorses Novalis' affirmation : " It is strange enough that the association of lust, religion, and cruelty did not long ago draw men's attention to their close relationship and common tendency." (*Human, All-Too-Human*, Part I, Aphorism 142.)

Thus the broad lines of psychoanalysis were already traced by the genius of Nietzsche. Ere long, science, reaching the same goal by a different path, was to grave the lines more deeply, and to fill in the details. The German original of *The Genealogy of Morals* was published in 1887. Breuer and Freud's paper *Ueber den psychischen Mechanismus hysterischer Phänomene* appeared in 1893.

CARL SPITTELER

("Revue de l'Epoque," Paris, October 1920. A first sketch of this essay appeared in " Le Carmel," Geneva, May 1916.)

THE little town of Liesthal, near Basle, the town of Basle, a half-way house between France, Germany, and Switzerland, a humanist centre, long ago the dwelling place of Erasmus and of Holbein, more recently that of Jacob Burkhardt and of Böcklin; the year 1845 (the year following that in which Nietzsche first saw the light)—such was the constellation which presided over the birth of Carl Spitteler.[1]

Meine frühesten Erlebnisse[2] discloses Spitteler as a child endowed with an exceptionally sensitive physiological organisation. Eyes, ears, all the senses, were precociously developed, so that he has retained clear-cut memories of the second year of his life. His nervous system was a most delicate instrument, a lyre ready to vibrate at the touch of the psyche that was about to awaken. An atmosphere like that of a beautiful legend already surrounds his childhood with its radiance. One day when the future creator of myths accompanied his mother on a shopping expedition to Soleure, he had the vision, the persistent vision, of a town where the houses were roofed with gold.

[1] Works on Spitteler in French are the following: P. Desfeuilles, Le poète suisse, Carl Spitteler, "Revue de l'enseignement des langues vivantes," Didier, Paris, 1915; Otto Kluth, Carl Spitteler et les sources de son génie épique, Sonor, Geneva, 1918; J. E. Spenlé, Carl Spitteler, l'homme et le poète, Comité de relations avec les pays neutres, Marseilles, 1916.

[2] "My first experiences"; Carl Spitteler, Meine frühesten Erlebnisse, Diederichs, Jena, 1914; French translation by H. de Ziegler, Premiers souvenirs, Payot, Paris and Lausanne.

Little by little, psyche awakens, in answer to the stimulus of the first impressions of youth, the responses to the manifold beauties with which nature has endowed Switzerland. Spitteler had a painter's eyes, and rejoiced in the magic of light and colour (Licht- und Farbewonne). He had a gift for drawing, and for a time was attracted towards the pictorial arts. But his most decisive impressions date from visits paid to an aunt, a young woman who lived in the little town of Winterthur, in the canton of Zurich. The first of these visits took place when Carl was fifteen years old; the second, when he was seventeen. It was not the dark pine-forests, with their still pools and their running waters, nor yet was it the neighbouring Rhine Falls (described by Goethe as indescribable), which most attracted the lad's attention, when staying at the Maison du Cèdre and at the Pflanzschule. The first visit was rendered notable by the discovery of music, thanks to an aria by Bach which his aunt played on the piano; and that of metaphysics, thanks to a little volume by Feuchtersleben, a present from his aunt. " This," says Spitteler, " was a magic book. A year before reading it I had still found amusement in playing with tin soldiers, but a year after reading it I had become a serious thinker." His second visit was notable for another discovery, that of Beethoven. This was the way in which Spitteler's temperament was moulded, a temperament universally gifted, like that of Leonardo da Vinci. The young man was a painter, a philosopher, a composer—anything in the world, except a poet. But he was seventeen, and it seemed to him that his talents as painter and as musician had been discovered too late for the technique of these crafts to be fully attainable. He had a respect for art, and aimed at nothing less then perfection. He decided to become a poet.

Yet, hitherto, poetry had not aroused his interest. Otto

Kluth goes so far as to say that he had disliked it. Does this mean that he was not a poet ? Let us say, rather, that he was too intensely a poet. Poesy overflowed from his being, as his friends of that date were well aware ; it found expression in his words and actions ; his imagination peopled his surroundings with poetical conceptions. He was poet to excess. Above all, the poesy which germinated within him was alien to contemporary literature. That literature, therefore, did not touch any responsive chords in his nature. By the irony of fate, this creator of myths and epics was born in an age when realism was dominant. He was a solitary, like Nietzsche—the comparison is irresistible. Both these writers were fully aware of their isolation. Their greatness lay in the fact that they were not ashamed of it, but proud. Had they made concessions to the spirit of their time, their fame would have been cried in the market-place ; but they were stubborn, and clung to their isolation as a privilege.

Spitteler's outer life has been uneventful, the life of one who lives remote from petty actualities, and therefore makes little noise in the world. He was eighteen when he chose his course in life. The reading of Ariosto brought self-revelation ; he would be an epic poet. At twenty-four (1869), writes Otto Kluth, " he experienced all the joys of the creator ; his head was full of themes. It was now that his mind, young and vigorous, confident in its enthusiasm, attained its highest levels."[1] Outwardly, during these years, he was the ordinary student, giving his attention first to law and then to divinity. In 1871, he was ordained, but never took up active work as a pastor. Then (this, says Spenlé, is the unexplored riddle of his life), he exiled himself to St. Petersburg, where he was a private tutor. Throughout this epoch, he was working at *Prometheus und*

[1] Op. cit., p. 17.

Epimetheus, the elaboration of which occupied him for thirteen years. They were years of meditation, of a sober and retired life, of a life concerned only with the things of the spirit. *Prometheus und Epimetheus* was published in 1880-81, after his return to Switzerland. The publishing house was a minor one,[1] and the place of publication was the little town of Aarau. The book ruffled all the conventions, but not enough to make a sensation. The upshot was that the work into which Spitteler had incorporated his whole being, passed almost unnoticed. Having to earn his livelihood, the poet accepted a post as master at a girls' school in Berne, working there in 1879 and 1880. In 1881, Spitteler married one of his pupils, a Dutch girl, and settled at Neuveville, on the shore of Lake Bienne. Here he taught in the French language for thirty hours a week, giving lessons at the Progymnasium in German, Latin, and Greek. Then, for a time, he lived at Basle, doing journalistic work. In 1892 he settled at Lucerne, and has lived there in retirement ever since. Here he has been the " genial hermit " described by Spenlé. One of his neighbours is François de Curel, who has published reminiscences of the poet.[2] His house is on a slope overlooking the lake. He has planted pines, liking to have greenery all the year round. The flowers in his garden are for the most part exotics. Curel is perhaps right when he says that this choice of trees and flowers is symbolic of a stubborn individualism, of the mentality of one who is in conflict with his environment, and whose real life is elsewhere.

Though his life has been so uneventful, he has not escaped a misadventure. He became known, at length, in

[1] H. R. Sauerländer.—This edition bore on the title-page the pen-name " Carl Felix Tandem "—doubtless an indication that the publication had been long and eagerly awaited by the author.

[2] Souvenirs sur Carl Spitteler, Mercure de France, 1919.

France, and attained, there, quite the wrong sort of celebrity. On December 14, 1914, in a lecture given at Zurich,[1]
he protested against the invasion of Belgium and against
the insensate cult of Germanism. By this bold step, he
alienated his German admirers ; and the man who, the day
before, had been acclaimed as the greatest among living
German poets, was now descried as a traitor. His works
were banned from the anthologies compiled for use in the
German schools. It was natural, on the other hand, that
the Zurich lecture should have been well received in France.
But the distressing feature in the case was that the enthusiasm of the French for Spitteler was not directed towards
the poet's real personality. It was an enthusiasm for the
man of the moment, instead of for the man of all time. A
number of French translations of his writings were made
at this date, and any honest bookseller would admit that
such success as they had was mainly " political." Spitteler
assures us with a smile that his political career lasted one
hour and ten minutes.[2] It was to this political career
that he owed his celebrity in France. It is useless to kick
against the pricks, for incidents of the kind are familiar.
The same thing happened to Victor Hugo ; and, only the
other day, to Verhaeren. Such is often the pitiful fate of
great men. Assuredly, one of the most unhappy characteristics of fame is the frequency with which it attaches
to heroes for the things which are least truly a part of
them. " Pendant que tu chantais, je regardais tes
pattes,"[3] said the Blackbird to Chantecler. I, too, have
known fame. It was my fate, at one time, to instruct
the son of a farmer in the elements of philosophy. The

---

[1] Unser schweizer Standpunkt, Rascher, Zurich, 1915.—French translation by Catherine Guilland, Notre point de vue suisse, Rascher, Zurich,
1915.

[2] Paroles au jubilée de Genève, " Journal de Genève," October 9, 1915.

[3] " While you were crowing (singing) I was looking at your feet."

worthy farmer complimented me one day on my pupil's progress, saying that the lad had become a past master in knowing one variety of mushroom from another.

Spitteler's misadventure was more serious. Thanks to this sudden fame, some of his works were translated into French, and the translators began at the wrong end. They began with his minor writings. In France, to-day, Spitteler is known by his prose works, by his novels (" je regardais tes pattes "). But these are not Spitteler, or they are very little of Spitteler. He is not a novelist, and has no wish to be one. He has an Olympian disdain for the novel. If he is told that the novel is akin to the epic poem, since each of them tells a story, he answers that there is certainly a resemblance, like that of a slug and a hussar travelling along the same road.[1] He thinks that an author is only entitled to write one novel—the romance of his own life. If, in spite of this, Spitteler wrote *Conrad der Leutnant*, this was one of the paradoxes in which he delights. He wanted to test his powers; and to prove that he, an epic poet, could be a realist if he pleased, whereas a realist writer of novels would find himself incapable of writing an epic poem. But, in his novels, Calliope, the epic muse, lets us hear the rustle of her skirts, and the spirit of myth is always peeping round the corner.

" Processions of supra-terrestrial creatures were moving along the mountain tops; it was like a file of horsewomen clad in gold and silver raiment, riding black or white chargers. He turned to look back from time to time, to see if an angel might not be following him up the mountain."

Who had these visions ? Was it Prometheus ? No, it was Gustav. It is in *Gustav*, too, that we read : " The

[1] Lachende Wahrheiten, Gesammelte Essays, seventh edition, Diederichs, Jena, p. 238.

artist's eye discerns in all these images [of nature] living personalities, each with its own soul. From their finite contours, the artist can detach cosmic symbols."[1]

Is that all? Yes, that is all—" cosmic symbols " in a simple idyl, which is written in a light vein!

Few of Spitteler's prose works can be adequately appraised unless they are regarded as commentaries on his major poems. Particularly does the remark apply to *Imago*,[2] which is puzzling if read without this key. But, as soon as we understand the genetic relationship between *Imago* and *Prometheus und Epimetheus*, the whole of the first-named book is illuminated by the idea, and we see that *Imago* is a great work.

In Spitteler's lyrics, the true personality of the author is more plainly disclosed than in the novels. Wherein lies the chief interest of *Schmetterlinge* [Butterflies]? [3] We learn from this book how a great poet endows everything he touches with greatness ; how he lends greatness to that which, if handled by others, might appear paltry. In Spitteler's verses, the butterfly becomes one of the powers of the woodlands, becomes a fairy, a goddess. This trans-figuration is assisted by the poet's use (for titles to some of his poems) of the mythological names which Linnaeus and others have given to various species : Proserpina, Mnemosyne, Hera, etc. These gracious names, may they not unconsciously have contributed to reawaken in Spitteler, the artist in words, the love of butterflies which had irradiated his childhood? However this may be, some of the poems in the volume assume the form of myths,

---

[1] Gustav, ein Idyll, Müller, Zurich, 1892. A French translation, Gustave, has recently been published by Georg in Geneva and by Crès in Paris. The rendering is by E. Desfeuilles, and is an admirable one.

[2] Published by Diederichs, Jena.

[3] Published by Diederichs, Jena ; first published at Hamburg in 1889, the author still using the pseudonym of Carl Felix Tandem.

legends of the creation. Such verses as the following are
frequent :

Then the Spirit of the World, which travels through space,
Measured with a look the towns, the hills, the vales,
And suffered at heart the universal pang.

Thus it is that Spitteler's native genius, surging up
continually, displays itself, almost unwarrantably, in a
field where there might seem to be no place for mythical
treatment. It is in the domain of the mythical epic that
Spitteler is perfectly at home. When he goes elsewhere, for
a time, it is by way of relaxation—chasing butterflies.

The " mythical epic," we have said. But, really, we are
confounding two distinct things, the myth and the epic
poem. Spitteler, who has notions of his own concerning
the problems of aesthetics, and who is described by
Nietzsche as " the most subtle of all writers when he has
to deal with aesthetic matters,"[1] distinguishes clearly
between them. The myth precedes the epic. It issues
from a meditative contemplation of the world and of life ;
it is the echo of this contemplation in the soul ; it is
austere, and charged with cosmic melancholy. The epic,
on the other hand, has an objective trend ; it is fantasy,
adventure, the joy of creating and of relating ; it is an
act, rather than a passive thing like an echo. In this
sense, *Prometheus und Epimetheus* is predominantly myth,
whereas *Olympischer Frühling* [2] [Olympian Spring], is predominantly epic. If I understand Spitteler's thought
aright, this distinction is closely akin to that drawn by
Nietzsche between Dionysian art (participation in the
mystery and suffering of the world) and Apollonian art
(imposing a plastic form of luminous serenity upon this

[1] In a letter quoted by Kluth, op. cit., p. 48.
[2] Published by Diederichs of Jena, 1900, et seq.

content of mystery and suffering).[1] Spitteler is both musician and painter. The musician rules in the former of these domains, and the painter in the latter ; but they are good neighbours, and are always ready for a chat.

The mention of *Prometheus und Epimetheus* raises the question of the relationship between Spitteler and Nietzsche. It is extremely probable that *Prometheus und Epimetheus* (1880–1881) had an influence upon *Also sprach Zarathustra* (1883), an influence which manifested itself alike in respect of the heroic content and in respect of the quasi-biblical form. Spitteler has himself discussed his relationships to Nietzsche.[2] The two recluses must have come in contact at the University of Basle, where Spitteler was finishing his studies at the date when Nietzsche was teaching. But they did not become acquainted at this time. Later, they corresponded. Spitteler acclaimed *Der Fall Wagner* in an article in which he went so far as to say : " Nietzsche is a giant ; he will therefore not take it amiss if we expect him to be great." [3] In 1912 was published Ragaz's study of the relationships between *Prometheus und Epimetheus* and *Also sprach Zarathustra*.[4] Then came the issue of Nietzsche's letters to Overbeck,[5] and these show how high

[1] A considerable part of Nietzsche's first published work, The Birth of Tragedy (1872), is devoted to an exposition of the contrasted meanings of these terms. The following succinct definition, a note penned by Nietzsche in 1886, is taken from Elizabeth Förster-Nietzsche's biographical introduction to the English version of her brother's book (pp. xxv–xxvi) : " Fundamental psychological experiences : the word ' Apollonian ' stands for that state of rapt repose in the presence of a visionary world, in the presence of the world of beautiful appearance designed as a deliverance from becoming : the word ' Dionysian,' on the other hand, stands for strenuous becoming, grown self-conscious, in the form of the rampant voluptuousness of the creator, who is also perfectly conscious of the violent anger of the destroyer."—E. & C. P.

[2] Meine Beziehungen zu Nietzsche, " Süddeutsche Monatshefte," Munich, 1908.

[3] " Der Bund," Berne, November 8, 1888.

[4] L. Ragaz, Spittelers Prometheus und Nietzsches Zarathustra, Chur, 1912.

[5] Briefwechsel mit Franz Overbeck, Insel-Verlag, Leipzig, 1916.

an opinion Nietzsche had of Spitteler.[1] Whether there was or was not a strong direct influence, there can be no doubt as to the kinship between the two men's minds.

Prometheus is the solitary who stands up boldly against the herd. He is not a prophet like Zarathustra ; he lives and acts, but he is chary of speech. He has some of the characteristics of the natives of the Swiss mountains ; he is surly, gruff, and obstinate. A rugged exterior is the shrine of a lofty spirit.

Prometheus says proudly to Epimetheus, his friend and brother :

" Arise, come ! Let us cease to be like the mass, to be like those who assemble in vast herds. . . ."
They did not go to the market to buy conventional ideas ; and when the others sang, they did not join in the song. . . .
And they placed a beam across the road, to bar the access to their valley ; and they would not accept laws or customs.

But Epimetheus allows himself to be led astray by " the Angel of the Lord," who offers him respectability and fame. He exchanges his " soul " for a well-behaved and mechanical " conscience." On these terms he becomes king of men ; he has bartered the substance for the shadow. Prometheus, in exile, preserves his integrity, and does not wanton with fame. In the solitude of the eternal snows he consummates a mystical betrothal with his own soul, now grown visible to him. He is a mystic of the inner life, " beyond good and evil " ; and to the Angel he seems a hardened blasphemer. He has no other god than the manifestation of the " austere mistress " to whom he must devote his life without receiving any return, without a sign that he does not labour in vain. This is a hero's choice. And the " benediction " of the " austere mistress" sounds almost like a curse :

[1] See above, pp. 35–36.

" And human happiness, human joy will not be yours; but you shall have an abundant share of that which, where men dwell, is termed pain; you shall know privation, mortification, unsatisfied desire, anguish vainly endured in the silences of the night."

Epimetheus proves incompetent to save the three divine children which have been entrusted to his care, and which sleep in the heart of a castle of faëry, in the rosy twilight of an inviolable chamber. At the critical moment the " conscience " which knows only how to say " yes " or " no " gets out of gear. It says both " yes " and " no " at once, or else is silent; it hides under the bed; it refuses to act. Here we have a comic scene showing all the originality of Spitteler's humour; the originality consisting, perhaps, mainly in this, that it, likewise, issues from the genius of myth—a humour which inspires, concretises, and personifies like myth, but does so with an unexpected and genial whimsicality. All this part of *Prometheus* is spiced with a wit founded upon a deliberately ludicrous symbolism, such as is especially applicable for the satirising of human stupidity. Take, for instance, this conceit of the " public flagstaff, surmounted by an invisible bird or else by a whale, towards which every one must uplift the left hand whenever he does anything with his right. An action is good if performed in accordance with the prescribed ritual; and woe to him who neglects it, even in order to save a neighbour's life."

But, with an ease that may bewilder the reader, satire gives place to lyric. Some of the scenes develop in an atmosphere of " pious legend " which (to adopt Spenlé's apt comparison) recalls the canvases of Puvis de Chavannes and of Böcklin. In the light that belongs to another world than ours, and in pigments vivid in their purity, we see lovely and majestic figures moving along tortuous highways, and castles slumbering on visionary hilltops in the torpid silence of noon. Such is the environment of legendary beauty in which Prometheus draws breath— Prometheus the solitary, who will throw off his moodiness and emerge from his retreat in time to avert the ruin conjured up by Epimetheus ; and in time to save the last of the children, the hope of the world.

The reader will have realised that, of the ancient Greek myth, Spitteler preserves little more than the names and the pure essence. Prometheus is still the strong man, the rebel against heaven, the exiled benefactor of mankind. But the tale has been refashioned, so that its episodes are utterly different from those of the old legend of Prometheus. Such a method of treatment undergoes generalisation in *Olympischer Frühling*. Here all the gods meet us bearing the old names—but they are new gods. Spitteler has no respect for mythological tradition. If he utters the familiar Greek syllables, this is only because they charm the ear. His gods are his own ; they are the gods of his own household. Thus, in like manner, the Virgins of the Flemish painters were Flemings, fair and ruddy. Spitteler's Olympus is not on the Greek mountain of that name ; it is in Jura or the Alps.

The procession of the gods, awakened from their sleep in the dark recessus of Erebus, climbs the Morgenberg [Mount Morning], ascending towards the serene beauty of the summit in springtime. But these mountain climbers are of a very different sort from the tourists who visit Switzerland. The latter are not loved by our poet, who exclaims elsewhere :

> Save me from the alpinists !
> They measure beauty by the kilometre.[1]
> [1] Schmetterlinge.

What we witness here is the ascent of the gods, the slow but everlasting redemption of the world by beauty.

The redemption of the world! Though Carl Spitteler is a Swiss, and although his imagery is full of the vital juices of his native land, his inspiration is by no means that of a "national poet." It is human and superhuman; it is metaphysical; it is cosmical. His world is the whole world. Nature, for him, is animate throughout; and this nature speaks to him. Pan is close to him, as to all the great poets; and some of the thousand secret energies of the god are communicated to the artist's soul. For Spitteler, the "universe" is not an empty word from which all the colour has been washed out. In his youth he made acquaintance with "Weltschmerz," with those pangs of the poet and the metaphysician which (for want of a succinct vernacular term) we may describe as "cosmic suffering." He has known the state of mind in which we share the misery of all created beings, and in which we feel that the animals are our brothers in pain. This is the condition in which pity becomes a danger to those who feel it. Nietzsche, affrighted by his seer's vision, said of it: "The farther we see into life, the farther do we see into suffering."

Such were the characteristics of the anguish from which the thought-process took its rise both in Schopenhauer and in Nietzsche. Those who suffer from this anguish are constrained by a vital necessity to seek deliverance from it at any price. The artist will find deliverance in the beautiful. Out of suffering he will create beauty:

Beauty fringes with gold the mourning of the violets.[1]

If we cover suffering with a veil of lovely illusion, we have, ere long, not illusion but creation, a transmutation

[1] Schmetterlinge.

into gold ; for this beauty gives birth to a very real joy. Such is Nietzsche's theme in *Die Geburt der Tragödie aus dem Geiste der Musik* [The Birth of Tragedy from the Spirit of Music]. An analogous thought is the source of Wagner's art (though not, perhaps, of his tragedies in particular) ; and it is the source, likewise of the art of Spitteler. And here we seem to have a metaphysical version of the same idea. Is not the world itself (the world of visible creation) the " maya," the illusion, in which God or the gods, the supreme artists, veil from their own eyes the sight of original sin ? In the beginning was evil. May we not consider the creation to have been a deliverance by the beautiful ? This is the fundamental tone of *Olympischer Frühling*.

The deliverance is progressive, being effected in the course of the eighteen thousand verses of the poem. When the mountain has been climbed, there is an orgy of celestial joy, of free aërial fantasy. The gods are making holiday, and show themselves at times to be in a merry mood. Aphrodite is mischievous, and plays pranks on the men. The action takes place in distinct episodes, each being complete in itself, a poem with a colour of its own.

Take, for instance, the poem of Hylas and Caledusa, the beautiful lovers, who have fallen asleep beneath the tree of fate. Caledusa sees the future in a dream, a future in which she will be forsaken. Wishing to cling for ever to the object of her affection, she transforms herself into a ray of light, thus recalling to our mind the most beautiful among Ovid's *Metamorphoses*. Never did Spitteler's strains sound purer than in the following passage :

> Et fraîche de matin sous l'arc des branches confuses,
> prête au départ, surgit la nymphe Caléduse.
> Bruit d'un baiser, salut d'un rire, et ils s'enfoncent
> dans la forêt, d'un pas semblable,—au rhythme d'ailes.

Leur coeur recrée le jour prodigue en couleurs belles,
les légendes dans l'air et les fleurs dans les ronces
et le regard aimant parmi l'éclair des cils.
Leurs yeux, clairs initiés aux grands secrets du monde,
pénètrent le mystère des êtres et des choses. . . .[1]

Consider, again, the episode of Dionysus, who (like Prometheus) devotes his life as an ascetic to the love of the goddess of pure thought, " Astraia," who appears to him only in dreams. The devotees of the cult of " Ashtaroth " tear him to pieces as a blasphemer. Centuries later, a temple will be built in honour of the martyr; he, in his turn, will have his devotees, ready to tear to pieces other martyrs of a lonely creed. Spitteler detests the " spirit of the herd," and the most pointed among the shafts of his satire are aimed at this spirit.

But, however varied the episodes, through them all vibrates the deep tone of cosmic emotion. Take in witness the idyl of Psyche and Cosmos,[2] she a dumb shepherdess

[1] I am doubtful whether a metrical and rhymed translation is possible. I have attempted one because such a translation seems to me essential in Spitteler's case. There are good reasons, or at least excellent pretexts, for preserving the measures and imitating the rhymes, seeing that Spitteler is pre-eminent among writers of German poetry for long poems written in verses which may be termed Alexandrine. Whereas French poets of the new school think mainly of stress, and tend to ignore rhyme and prosody, Spitteler's aim is to write a syllabic German verse. The respective innovations are in opposite directions, but they are not contradictory.
[In view of the foregoing note, and of the fact that Baudouin is himself a poet, the translators have thought it expedient to reproduce in the text the French translation. Many English readers will gain a better notion of Spitteler in this way than from the line-for-line literal English translation of the German which is here appended :

And, fresh as the morning, there came forth from the trees
The nymph Caledusa,ready for the start.
The sound of a kiss, a laugh in greeting. Then hastened they
Along the path together, through the forest, with winged feet.
They remade for themselves in their hearts the richly hued day,
The tales breathed by the air, the blossoms in the coppice,
Friendship's loving glance from brightly flashing eyes.
And of all things, all creatures, the symbolical meaning
Was plain to their eyes, initiated into the secrets of the world.]

[2] In Part Two, Canto Three, Der erste Weltkampf, Gesang und Sage.

and he a king's son. A simple love story in graceful and
limpid verse ; but something more than this, for Psyche is
the soul and Cosmos is the world, Cosmos the sick prince
whom Psyche hopes to cure. Every movement in this
poem arouses infinite harmonies :

> Au lac le plus profond, le plus calme et cache
> elle apportait chaque matin des fleurs des bois
> et grondait l'eau du doigt : " Tu reflètes la figure
> et le faste des monts et des forêts. Pourquoi ?
> Je veux en ton miroir voir Cosmos fils du roi.
> Mon coeur du moins l'acclame si mes lèvres sont closes."
> Et dès qu'au miroir d'onde apparaissait Cosmos,
> elle lui jetait toutes ses fleurs, tous ses baisers,
> minaudait, se berçait en une danse aisée
> jusqu' à ce que l'image au vent du soir se perde.[1]

But how is it possible, in a few brief extracts, to give
an adequate idea of this stupendous poem ? The verses
just quoted are full of grace and charm. Others exhibit,
rather, strength and greatness. Spitteler's heroes are
instinct with will :

> Entre les forts Titans, Phinée est le plus fort :
> la foi de vaincre bat dans son coeur à grands coups,
> pour lui c'est triompher que d'avoir entrepris.[2]

Moreover, whereas the whole book is transfigured by the

[1] There, to a lake most tranquil and profound,
She came each morning from the forest, bearing flowers,
And, chiding with her finger : " Say, why dost mirror
For me all the mountains and the forest and the lea ?
Cosmos, the king's son, fain would I see portrayed ;
'Tis of him my heart sings, though my lips are silent."
And when, in the mirror of the waters, Cosmos' image appeared,
She blew him kisses, and threw him all her flowers,
And rocked with joy, dancing and preening,
Until the image was effaced by the evening breeze.
[2] In heroic growth, alike of body and of soul,
Phineus was the greatest among all the Titans,
Strength and confidence of victory surged up in him,
So that he could fulfil whatsoever he undertook.

refulgence of Apollo, the last word is given to Heracles,
who comes down from Olympus to feel under his feet the
solid ground of the real world, the world where men live
and suffer. He is Heracles the dogged, the willing, the
strong. The dream must not be a flight into the clouds ;
it must mould the world ; it must not (to quote Zarathustra
once more) lose sight of " the meaning of the universe."

Spitteler is a good French scholar ; he reads and loves
our French classics ; in his own writings he has achieved
a synthesis of two cultures. His thought shows him to be
the kinsman of Schopenhauer and of Nietzsche ; and the
Dionysian reverberation of his writings represents the outcome of the Teutonic tradition. But his Apollonian clarity,
the purity of his versification, the supreme beauty of his
visions—all these are Latin. Hence Spitteler's work is
typically Swiss ; but it is also something wider, it is
European. " A European poet," he wrote to me ; " that
is the best description. I have never been a Swiss poet or
a German poet ; but, rather, a European, an international,
an intertemporal poet. It was only by the accident of
birth that I came to use the German language as my
medium of expression."

It would be premature to attempt a final judgment of
these writings ; but we may certainly say of Spitteler
what Edward Carpenter said of Walt Whitman, that he
is as difficult to overlook as a mountain. Spitteler cannot
be ignored. His fame is of sound quality ; it came slowly,
but has come to stay. Though for a long time the general
reading public failed to recognise his merits, he was from
the first esteemed by a few choice spirits. Nietzsche
valued him duly at the very outset ; so did Gottfried
Keller ; so did Jakob Burckhardt. Later, the critic Carl
Meissner compared Spitteler to Homer and to Dante. His

study of Spitteler ends with the words: " Since Ibsen and Tolstoy died, and since the death of Strindberg, Spitteler has been, among the living poets, the only man of genius." [1] Romain Rolland said of Spitteler: " He was the first great man I saw."

We have to do with a force. But may it not be a reactionary force? Has a primitive man wandered into our day? Were it so, this need not give us much concern. But are there any serious reasons for regarding epic poetry as especially characteristic of primitive times? Spitteler has himself gently ridiculed the assertion,[2] declaring it to be a nineteenth-century invention, a Swabian product issuing from the exaggerated refinement of Vischer. He points out that the eighteenth century, that Lessing and Goethe and Schiller, still considered epic to be the loftiest form of poetry.

Spitteler can hardly be gainsaid in this matter. Moreover, the nineteenth century did much to revive epic poetry. We think of Victor Hugo and of Wagner; to say nothing of the symbolist school, which is continually appealing to myth. But Spitteler's own work, and the way in which our being vibrates responsively to his touch, are the best of all proofs that epic poetry is still a vital reality. Inasmuch as Spitteler's own poems are charged with all the interests of modern thought, epos here displays its perpetual youth, sparkling with the dew of creation and of dawn.

[1] Carl Meissner, Carl Spitteler, Diederichs, Jena, 1912.
[2] Lachende Wahrheiten, seventh edition, p. 32.

ROMAIN ROLLAND

("The Word," The Hague,
October 4 and 11, 1919.)

IT was in the year 1915. I had been invalided from the
army, and was whiling away the time in Paris. In a
bookseller's window, near the Odéon, my eyes were
attracted by a title : Henri Massis, *Romain Rolland contre
la France*. My interest was aroused, and I bought the
pamphlet. Had Romain Rolland been indulging in paradox ? Or had he been uttering some lofty sentiment ?
I was stirred at the thought, for his name meant much to
me. This man—to me he was not an " author," but a
" man "—had been the master and the friend of my
adolescence. Among the great ones, no one else had been
so near. He had seemed an elder brother. I had loved
him for his disquietudes, which were akin to my own,
and stimulated my own, so that I could not sleep soundly
upon the comfortable and cowardly pillow of lazily accepted
convictions. I remember an article which appeared in " Les
Annales " (1913) wherein the writer said that Rolland's
works gave admirable expression to the chaotic uneasiness
of a generation of seekers ; but this uneasiness, the critic
went on, was now drawing to a close. The new developments of the nationalist creed had supplied a straightforward outlet for this ebullient and confused energy.
Military aviation was the fulfilment towards which, for
half a century, all the aspirations of suffering youth had
unawares been tending. These remarks had outraged my
sensibilities. I felt as a young idealist feels when an

uncle—a self-satisfied and pleasure-loving man who has outgrown his " illusions "—prescribes as a remedy for all metaphysical anguish " a night out, a good time with the girls." I would not have it. Military aviation was not the panacea. Rolland was right to fan the flame of our disquietude, the sacred fire of the inner Vestal. I thought of Zarathustra's saying : " He who has a chaos within him, may give birth to a dancing star. Alas, the day draws nigh when you will no longer have a chaos within you, and when you will no longer be able to give birth to a star."

This phamplet awakened memories of two of Rolland's books, *Vie de Tolstoï* and *Jean Christophe*. I recalled the ardent hours in which I had read them. Opening the pamphlet, I turned at once to the appendix, where, to make his reader's flesh creep, Massis had been so simple as to reprint *Au-dessus de la mêlée*. It did not make my flesh creep. It was a stimulus, was something that radiated heat and light. I dropped into a seat on the boulevard Saint-Michel. Oblivious of the turmoil around me, I buried myself in my reading. . . . " The European war, this sacrilegious conflict, which offers us the spectacle of Europe gone mad, mounting the pyre and rending its own flesh, like Hercules ! " Here was the sound of the avenging voice ; here was the message for which I had been waiting.

In the close of this same year 1915, Rolland tied up the sheaf of his articles on the war, a sheaf of golden sunlight and substantial harvest. Need I explain how much this volume (*Au-dessus de la mêlée* gave its title to the collection, the original article bearing that name having been published in the " Journal de Genève " on September 22, 1914) meant to us who were stifling, to us who were hungering for a clear utterance of the loving reason. At a time when all the sheep were bleating with the flock, when slavish thought was in the ascendant, came the voice of this free spirit, the voice of one who was above country and above faction. Rolland spoke plain truths to all—to all the governments, all the moralists, the churches, the intellectuals, the socialist parties, all who had denied their erstwhile faiths. Even to Rolland, the militarist imperialism of Prussia seemed the supreme danger. " But it is not the only danger," he continued. Imperialism was practically universal, flaunting itself in its tsarist embodiment, but no less real under the mask of democracy. The true enemy was within the gates.

There flamed, too, in this book the light of humanist and brotherly sentiment, modest lamps perpetually recharged by the faithful. The work of peace was being continued in wartime ; international aid was being rendered ; enemy prisoners were being succoured. " Inter arma caritas." Some of the German poets, Franz Werfel and Hermann Hesse, for instance, not dehumanised by the war mania, were sounding notes that were all the clearer and more arresting for their isolation.

Rolland's tone grew more poignant when he denounced the tragical " murder of the élite " ; and when he called up the image of Jaurès, the first of the victims. But above these distressing actualities, there brooded ever the simple spirit of eternal truth. What could be more consoling than this profession of faith in the spirit ?

" Elite of Europe, we have two abiding places : our terrestrial fatherland ; and the other, the City of God. We are dwellers in the former, but we are the builders of the latter. To the former, let us devote our bodies and our trusty hearts. Yet, though we love our family and our friends and our country, nothing has any rights over our souls."

After the publication of *Au-dessus de la mêlée*, Rolland's utterances on the war grew rarer. In December 1916 came two articles, no longer in the " Journal de Genève," since they were too advanced in tone for that periodical. *La route en lacets qui monte* [Upwards along a winding Road] was issued in " Le Carmel," Geneva ; and *Aux peuples assassinés* [To the murdered Peoples], dated All Souls' Day, 1916, was published in "Demain." In the former, Rolland begins by saying that, if he has kept silence for a year, it is not because his faith had been shaken. His faith stood firmer than ever, but Rolland felt the futility of speaking to those who would not hearken. A regained calm breathes from these pages. Mankind is moving upwards along a winding road. Even when we have entered a section of the pathway which seems to lead backwards, we are really advancing, we are still climbing. The most notable phenomenon of our day is that, in spite of the war, nay, because of the war, a universal culture is being born. But this universal culture will not necessarily be the blossoming of our European civilisation, which is perhaps in its decay. This universal culture " will perchance, looping the loop of time, return to the thought of Asia." Romain Rolland, who had hitherto been merely the "good European," widens his horizon. In his appeal *Aux peuples assassinés*, he gives expression, more bitingly, to his disgust with sadistic and bloodthirsty Europe ; and his eyes turn longingly eastward, as Tolstoy's eyes had turned in earlier days. He listens to the voice of the great Hindu, Rabindranath Tagore. The essay closes with this apostrophe to a war-mad Europe :

" If the war should not bring as its first fruit a social renascence in all the nations, then farewell Europe, queen of thought, guide of mankind. You have lost your way ; you are marking time in a cemetery. The cemetery is

5

the right place for you. Make your bed there. Let others lead the world."

Now we come to a new phase. That of emotional fervour is followed by that in which the intellect is predominant. Here is a Romain Rolland whom we had hardly known before, and who is not yet known as he should be. We see a philosopher, an encyclopaedist, like the great figures of the eighteenth century. But there is something in Rolland which was not to be found in Voltaire, a tragical force which forms an undertone of the "gay science." [1] Nietzsche knew that tone; so did Beethoven; so did all the great Frenchmen of the Revolution.

In August 1918 there was published in the "Revue mensuelle" of Geneva an article by Rolland entitled *En lisant Auguste Forel* [Reflections on reading Auguste Forel]. Rolland follows the naturalist in his researches concerning the social and fighting instincts of the ants. He shows how these studies indicate that the instincts are modifiable. But since, even in the lower animals, the manifestations of instinct are not inexorably determined, all the more may we hope for modification of the instincts displayed by the members of the great human ant-hill. In "Demain" for November 1917 there had appeared an article which may be regarded as complementary to the foregoing, a study of G. F. Nicolai's work on *The Biology of War*. We are shown how man's reason wins cognisance of the instincts which lead it; how reason wishes to gain control over instinct, and will gain control. The boldness, the logical

---

[1] La gaie science, la gaya scienzia, the term is used here in the sense in which it was revived by Nietzsche. It related to a tragical outlook, overcome by a deliberate cheerfulness.

force, and the science of the German biologist are here brilliantly reflected. Rolland conveys to us Nicolai's encouraging ideas, his pantheist affirmations, concerning the unity of the living substance, the biological fraternity upon which the brotherhood of man is founded.[1]

But Rolland's place as a thinker may be best understood from a study of the pamphlet *Empédocle d'Agrigente et l'âge de la haine*.[2] What Rolland mainly sees in Empedocles is a symbol; a real figure, but that of one who lived at the beginning of the historic age; an incarnation of Rolland's own ideal, assuming here a form more serene and less tense than that of the heroes of modern days, Michelangelo, Beethoven, and Tolstoy. In these quasi-legendary surroundings, he rediscovers " minds and times akin to our own."

" The same cosmic convulsions. The same clashes among the nations. The combats between millions of human ants, white, black, yellow; those of every colour and every religion. Empires which wax and wane."

As for Empedocles, who stands firmly amid this chaos, he is, first of all, the apostle of love in the age of hatred; but he is also, and above all, typical of the harmony of mankind, towards which, in our troubles, we more or less consciously aspire. This is the matter to which I would fain, in especial, draw the reader's attention. Herein is revealed to us a new aspect, less familiar and more integral, of Romain Rolland; and it helps us to understand how this thinker is " representative " (in Emerson's sense) of the needs of our epoch.

[1] The essays mentioned in the text, from La route en lacets qui monte down to the one on Nicolai, together with a number of other writings belonging to the same period, were collected in a volume entitled Les précurseurs. See Bibliography.
[2] Cahiers du Carmel, Geneva, 1919.

Mankind, to-day, is poor because its energies are scattered. No one can assemble its splendid riches, and no one, therefore, can own them, They remain potential riches; riches in the abstract ; unmined ores. They are as if they did not exist. Each one of us is pent within his own restricted world—that of a science, an art, or a creed. Our civilisation is one of specialists, of analysts. The best specimens of our race know nothing of one another, or misunderstand one another. Mankind is a broken god, like the great body of Osiris shattered into fragments. Hence our miseries ; herein lies our tragedy ; but the miseries and the tragedy cannot endure :

" After a lengthy period of patient analysis, the new age is stirred to its depths by an urgent desire for synthesis."

Empedocles, philosopher, poet, scientist, doctor, engineer, apostle, man of action both political and social, is one of those who have harmoniously realised this synthesis, have realized it within their own personalities :

" No one ever realized more effectively than he the ideal of Alberti, of Leonardo da Vinci, and of Goethe—the ideal of the man abreast of all the knowledge of his day. . . . He is an arch of faëry, linking the East with the West and the past with the present."

Manifestly the ideal is Rolland's own. He affirms it ever more clearly, and step by step he conquers it for reality. Thus there arises among us such a figure as the men of the Renaissance wished to create, such a figure as arises from time to time to overawe humanity ; one whose mind has attained serenity and equipoise ; one whose peace of soul, far from being stagnant and impoverished, is the outcome of a balance of opposing forces whose thrust and counterthrust express themselves in beauty, as we see in the double curvature of the pointed or Gothic arch :

> Cathedral established
> Upon the perfect balance of opposing forces.[1]

This matter demands closer scrutiny. Romain Rolland is something different from, something more than, the artist in words who wrote *Jean Christophe* and the conscience that produced *Au-dessus de la mêlée*. He is a man, a synthesis, and therein lies the secret of his strength. He is beyond the confines of parties ; he cannot be pigeon-holed. He is something different from that which fanatical admirers worship and from that which his enemies revile. There is that in him which laughs at them all, eludes them. He is far from being the incomplete and unduly sensitive creature of Henri Massis' fancy—far from being an effeminate intelligence such as Proudhon had in mind when he said of Lamartine : " I would much rather have a real woman." Anything but this ! Rolland has a mind in which the serenity of Hellenic thought is buttressed by modern vigour : he, too, is an " arch of faëry," linking hostile or severed worlds ; he, likewise, is a pathway leading to the East, towards which he would fain direct our gaze. There may be minds endowed with a more savage power, but there can hardly be a mind that is richer and more lucid. Moreover, he knows how to be clear without forfeiting strength, how to be intelligent without the loss of creative fire, how to be splendidly Apollonian and yet at the same time Dionysian— harmonious after the manner of a Greek tragedy.

Now comes laughter, the laughter that drives away

[1] Ara Pacis, written August 15 to 25, 1914 ; published in the " Journal de Genève," Christmas 1915. See The Forerunners (English translation of Les Précurseurs), pp. 11–14.

spleen. Is Romain Rolland, then, on intimate terms with the comic muse ? Indeed he is, though we had not expected it of him. He gets those who love laughter on his side. Though he is a lyricist, though he is a " utopist," he has also common sense and wit ; he has the spirit of a Burgundian and a Frenchman ; he knows how to season his words with coarse salt as well as with fine. This tragedian has laughter in his storehouse. In *Colas Breugnon* [1] the laughter grows boisterous, becomes Homeric. Was the time for this laughter ill-chosen ? [2] Perhaps it was not the time you would have chosen—nor yet the author himself. But the laughter chose its own time. A faun, that asks no leave !

" I feel sure that the readers of Jean Christophe were not expecting this new book. It will not surprise them more than it has surprised me." Rolland declares that, in spite of himself, and in spite of his graver plans, " all the Colas Breugnons under his skin " must have free leave to laugh and swear whenever they like—these Colas Breugnons who are his Burgundian forefathers. If he had wanted to lay stress on this heritage, if (like Goethe in a famous poem) he had wanted to make it plain to his readers which parts of the heritage were derived from his respective parents, he might have said that hitherto his mother's nature, refined, grave, and pious, had found expression. But in *Colas Breugnon* his father and the father's ancestry had claimed their turn—and would claim it yet again.

This is not the time to laugh ? But Colas assures us that no time for laughter can be better than the present.

" Breugnon, you rogue, you are laughing. Are you not ashamed ? "

[1] Ollendorff, Paris, 1918.
[2] As a matter of fact, Colas Breugnon was written before the war, during the summer of 1913.

" Laughter does not drive away pain, but pain will never keep a good Frenchman from laughing. And whether he laughs, or whether he cries, the first thing is that he should see."

After we have been taking things seriously, after we have been contemplating their tragical aspects, it is a welcome relaxation—and perhaps a spontaneous and organic defensive reaction—to look at them from the humorous side. Faith itself, like suffering, perhaps needs an occasional release of tension, for it is (at any rate, the faith of Jean Christophe is) a tense force, a tightly strung bow, which suffers from the strain.

Colas Breugnon is a good fellow who loves life, is fond of good cheer, and delights in the generous red wine of Burgundy. As he saunters through life, everything interests him, and everything arrests his attention. He is a glutton ; he devours life ; he devours things with his eyes. He has no dislike for a whiff of intoxication, no matter whence it comes—from the wine out of the cellar, or from the wine of a heady illumination. Moreover, he is a sage. He makes the best of everything he has, and he does not covet the things that are not his. Loving all things, he is content with very little :

" Everything is good, comrade, everything is good ; the world is nicely rounded. If you can't swim, you will drown. Enter, world, by my five senses, for I throw all the windows wide. Enter, and circle with my blood. Am I to sulk in a corner, because life is not all I should like ? "

He laughs, he rallies life. For him life is a show in which there is always a spice of comedy. He is full both of good sense and of good blood. Though he laughs at all that happens, his laughter is never sneering or ill-natured ; it is hearty, cordial, sanguine—and fundamentally genial. A sensitive emotion is hidden behind the laugh and the oath.

Often the roguish eyes are moist with tears—these eyes which have been surrounded by crow's feet through the passing of the years. But always he has an animal and eager love of life, and more life, and yet more :

" I might never have lived. . . . Good Lord, a cold shiver runs down my back when I think of it. This jolly little universe, this life, without Brugnon ! And Brugnon, without life ! What a wretched world that would have been."

This is the way in which Colas monologises, from one end of the book to the other. He is writing his diary. But he is a poet as well. Artist by profession, a wood-carver, he loves to caress the figures that shape themselves under his chisel, or the images his fancy calls up, the fauns and the dryads he fashions out of the trees. He has a parent's love, a father's love and a mother's, for the work of his hands, his heart, and his brain. Among his manifold troubles, he makes light of the plague, of war, of having a shrew for his wife, of a broken leg ; but what really cuts him to the heart is that when his house is burned down the work of thirty years perishes in the flames. Thenceforward his laughter lacks the old hearty ring. A tragical shadow has passed, and we recognise Jean Christophe.

In other respects we have Montaigne, or, even more, we have Rabelais—the latter's rough and truculent wisdom. Colas Breugnon is Rabelais' contemporary. He has been nourished in the same soil of Old France ; has ripened under the same sun ; is swelling with the same sap.

Again, as a typical Frenchman, Colas has plenty of faults to find. God is beginning to put up with heretics, and his halo has therefore lost some of its splendour. Nor are the great ones of the earth, the kings and the dukes, in better case. Breugnon certainly lacks the bump of veneration. He tells us that St. Peter, seeing a beggar-woman who was suffering from tedium, supplies her with a hundred lice, just to give her something to occupy her mind :

" It is from kindness, no doubt, and to provide us with a little distraction, that heaven has been good enough to send us these two-footed beasts who fleece us. Let us rejoice, therefore ; let us lift up our hearts. We are told that it is a sign of good health to be well supplied with vermin ! (Vermin—these are our masters.) Rejoice then, brothers ; for in that case who can be in better health than we ? "

Consider, too, the style of *Colas Breugnon*. It is that of Rabelais, with a dash of Paul Fort ; extremely original, a metrical prose, packed with rhymes and assonances. The result is succulent as well as truculent, a feast for epicures of words. We have to read this book out loud, in a good round tone ; we must chew the phrases well, and must not be finical about big mouthfuls. Some of the pages recall the fleshly and brawny imagery of Verhaeren's *Les Flamandes*.

But *Colas Breugnon*, despite the racy humour of the book, falls short of the brilliancy of *Liluli*. Colas still had some restraint in his laughter, but Liluli's very name (" l'illusion ") is a catcall. Irreverence and unconventionality reach their climax here.

What is *Liluli* ? A Comedy penned by an Aristophanes who has studied farce in the French school and in modern warfare. A drama which forms an undivided whole, like a mad laugh, disregarding the classical separation into acts and scenes, and recking naught of stage difficulties—for in these respects it is as unconventional as in all others. It is a satire, beautifully terrible and elegantly cruel ; the prank of a gutter-snipe turned loose in our heroic times ; a pin-prick into all our sacrosanct bladders, which we mistake

for splendid lamps ; something which bursts all the asses'
skins of our most sonorous drums.

Two nations encounter one another on the acclivity of the
future, and after a time come to blows. Their respective
identities shine clearly through the transparent names of
the Gallipoulets and the Hurluberloches. Their queen
Liluli, the goddess of illusion—she rules over both the
nations, this embodiment of levity and bird-song—humbugs
them through their devotion to " love " or " the ideal,"
to " peace " or " the fatherland." The war-cry " Onwards,
children of Liluli " leads them all to a common doom.
Individual caricatures show themselves from time to time
against the background formed by the agitated and chaotic
swarm. These prominent personalities lead the crowd,
but Liluli leads the leaders by the nose. It is she who pulls
the strings that move all the puppets.

God is one of the quaintest figures on the stage. He has
the airs and graces of an Arab carpet-pedlar ; he sells amu-
lets by the gross. Turn about, he wears the military uniform,
now of the Gallipoulets and now of the Hurluberloches,
preaching in the same strain to both. He is on excellent
terms with all the Powers and all the States, and his passports
have the proper visas. His dear friend Truth is not naked
as in simpler days ; she is habited like a harlequin, in
rainbow-tinted spangles—but for the most part she is
gagged and in the pillory. When she bares her bosom, the
peoples are told to hide their faces, overcome with shame.
Reason wanders about with her eyes bandaged, and knocks
her nose against a tree ; but Reason was all right, and the
tree is blamed for the mishap. All the modern idols make
their appearance, one after the other : Liberty, carrying
a horsewhip ; Equality, with pruning-shears ; and, of
course, that fine fellow, Fraternity. This last is a negro
in a tall hat, and he walks arm-in-arm with a clergyman ;

he is still a cannibal, " but he uses a fork, and always says grace before meat."

All these characters are the slaves of Liluli. The only exception is Polichinelle, the supreme master of laughter, who holds his own in the world for the very reason that he is a laugher. "Laughter is armour against illusion." He has plenty of common sense, and enough wit to stuff his hump full. Own brother to Colas, he differs from the latter in that he is not so much a person of flesh and blood as laughter personified—the " gay science " embodied and given power of articulate speech. He is as wise as a sensible and witty peasant, as wise as a philosophic sceptic free from sarcasm ; he is disillusioned without having lapsed into despair (man may be a bad lot, but life is all right) ; he knows how to find fault, and yet he does not revolt. In a word, he is a sage who lacks heroism. Dame Truth exclaims against his cowardice :

" You can laugh, you can mock ; but you do it furtively, like a schoolboy. Like your forbears, the great Polichinelles, like Erasmus and Voltaire, the masters of free irony and of laughter, you are prudent, prudent in the extreme. Your great mouth is closed to hide your smiles . . . They are handsome fellows, my lovers . . . But you don't love me. . . . When will the lover come, the great Victorious Laugh, the roar of laughter which will set me free ? "

Despite his shortcomings, Polichinelle can hold his own in argument against Liluli. But he does not escape the crowning disaster, engineered by Liluli. At the close, the nations and their impedimenta all collapse—fall in upon Polichinelle :

> Und das hat mit ihrem Singen
> Die Lorelei getan.[1]

[1] And that, with her singing,
The Lorelei has done.

When, as a last defiance, he says : " Nothing can hurt me. Laughter is safe ! " by the irony of fate he is more hopelessly flattened out than all the rest. He lies beneath the rubbish, and Liluli is on the top—the sole survivor. Let those laugh who win.

Such is this sparkling and motley extravaganza, this fantasy which moves as lightly as a rope-dancer, which is as heedless as a practical joke. Add that the style fits the matter like a glove. In *Colas Breugnon*, packed with rhymes, the touch is lighter ; there is a quaint and lively rhythm based upon little periods of four or eight syllables, flying and rebounding like shuttlecocks :

"Allons les bûcherons, cognez ! Et les charpentiers, sciez ! Nous les autres, en attendant, sur les deux bords asseyons-nous et banquetons ! Qu'en dites-vous ? Mangeons —mangeons ! quand il s'agit d'un gueuleton, gens de cœur n'ont jamais dit non . . . Et qu'avez-vous dans vos paniers ? Des andouilles, du cervelas . . . Des saucisses, du boudin gras." [1]

What a delight to see an author exempt from the taste for posing. It is a pose to wish to remain faithful to the image the public has formed of us. It is a pose to remain for ever a writer of tragedy or of lyrical verse because we have made our first bow in such a capacity. That way lies the path towards unction, towards sermonising, towards humbug. But how many authors walk along this path—preserving at all hazards the pose which has come to be accepted as typically their own ! Mannerisms, original mannerisms, are

[1] The rhythms, the rhymes, and the assonances of Colas Breugnon are untranslatable ! Here is a literal rendering of the passage in the text : " Fall to it, woodmen, wield your axes ! And you, sawyers, saw away. We others, while we are waiting, let us sit on either side and feast. What do you think of that ? Let us eat, let us eat ! When a blow-out is in prospect, no good fellow ever refuses to eat his fill. What have you got in your baskets ? Chitterlings, saveloy ? Sausages, white pudding ? "

not easy to acquire. The small fry of the literary world take a lot of pains to this end ; and, once they have become known as the exponents of a particular style, they are loath to take any new departure. People might think they had no originality after all. That would be a pity when they have taken so much trouble.

But the tritons pay no heed to these perplexities of the minnows. The great ones know that, whatever they do, they will still be themselves ; they know that their personality is strong enough to impress its own stamp upon any avatar they may assume. The gods may adopt various mortal forms, but something will always reveal the presence of the divine. So is it, too, with great men. When Victor Hugo, after his sublime *Contemplations*, his stinging *Châtiments*, turns to humming his jolly *Chansons des Rues et des Bois*, he knows there is no decline to a lower level. " I am putting Pegasus out to grass." This relaxation of genius is one of the characteristics of genius.

At the close of *Liluli*, the wisdom to which Rolland had, some years before the war, given expression in his *Vie de Tolstoï*, recurs, in a strange parody of itself. In the biography, he had quoted Sophocles' saying that no man should be called happy until his destiny had been played out to the end, Liluli sums up the episode of Polichinelle in a caricature of the same thought :

> Attends pour faire le malin,
> Et rire du destin, la fin.[1]

Thus it is that Romain Rolland's spirit finds expression in *Liluli*. Thus does he amuse himself by studying his own reflection as Polichinelle—a grotesque image in a distorting mirror.

[1] Before being confident that you have the laugh of destiny, you had better wait till the end.

But the most intimate bond between the various writings, so amazingly different, which Rolland gave to the world during and just after the war, is to be found in the passion for liberty. The spirit of liberty has but few weapons for use in the fight against the dogma of the nationalist state, against the beast-idol which has us under its feet, and which crushes us even more effectually than do any of the superstitions that have come down to us from the past. Liberty's weapons are : the fervour of *Au-dessus de la mêlée* ; the serene intelligence of *Empédocle* ; the hearty and sensible laughter of *Colas Breugnon* ; the biting and satirical laughter of *Liluli*. The laughter of *Liluli* is the sharpest weapon, and perhaps the strongest of the four. Freedom of thought brings freedom of art in its train. This is the secret of Rolland's changing and multiform art, which is not bound by the fetters of tradition, and is even free from the shackles of habit, from those ties of habit which, for persons of conventional mind, seem to become obligations. Nevertheless, in his love of freedom, in his unconventionality and in his irony, Romain Rolland is always the Frenchman. He has not been uprooted from his native land ; he is Colas, the Burgundian ; on occasions he can be as much of a particularist as Barrès. Though the tree-top may respond to all the breezes, may receive all the messages that are wafted from the vast freedoms of space, the roots of the tree are firmly fixed in native soil. What if to-morrow, or the day after, Rolland should come to be regarded as the most typical Frenchman among the writers of our own day ? He would have the laugh of us all !

HAN RYNER

(This essay was originally written for " The Word," published at The Hague, but that periodical became extinct in 1919, and the account of Han Ryner first saw the light in " Les Primaires," Paris, June and July, 1922.)

" In those days, two men were trying to live a *human* life. One of them was named Tolstoy, and dwelt in eastern Europe ; the other, named Han Ryner, dwelt in western Europe." I quote from Pierre Larivière, whose book *Au temps des sous-hommes* [In the Days of the Submen] is, as the title suggests, a castigation of our own time. Recognition came late to Han Ryner, and it was not until a year or two before the war that a group of young Frenchmen began to consolidate as his admirers. In 1912, on the occasion of his fiftieth birthday, he was hailed as the Prince of Story-Tellers, just as Paul Fort had been acclaimed the Prince of Poets. Despite these labels, Paul Fort is an admirable teller of tales, and Han Ryner has written some splendid poetry. Thus it is that all specifications, even the most harmless, impose limits upon man while defining his qualities. Ryner himself expresses the same idea when he says that all words are liars : " Fixity is an error created by words which, being themselves unchanging, believe that they describe immutabilities. Names, you are always falsehoods. For this reason, even if I could, I would not name you. O mystery, O ineffable one, O beauty as fluctuating and indefinite as life, or as the light that trembles amid foliage shaken by the wind." [1]

This man who passes such strictures upon words is a

[1] Les voyages de Psychodore.

master of words. As a sculptor loves the statue he carves, so Ryner loves the word he fashions and wields. What he objects to is that the word, made to be the servant of man, should become the master, as it does day by day in the lying press. In a world where most people are the dupes of words, Han Ryner is an exception. He does not believe in the idols of the age ; and without growing too wrathful because of human folly, he smiles. He has reached the stage when wisdom smiles. Has not his good and strong face been described as " a smile in the midst of a beard " ? Even before the war, this smile had conquered free spirits and had charmed profound thinkers, but its realm was greatly extended during the reign of the bloody idol. The smile brought healing. Unwittingly, it gave expression to Nicolai's motto : " Don't take war seriously." In fact, Han Ryner, being a sage, does not take the perturbations of his own time too seriously. The most violent convulsions of history, like storms at sea, affect no more than the surface. The depths of humanity are practically untroubled, for here other laws prevail. When either for good or for evil, we are inclined to exaggerate the importance of what is happening, Han Ryner's smile recalls us to wisdom. He is not much inclined to think that there are either great epochs or futile epochs.

" It is hard to say, when we admire an epoch from a distance, what we should think of it were we to see it close at hand. Two things, at least, are certain : all epochs are ugly so long as we contemplate them in the swarming stage ; but every one of them contains a few beautiful individuals. It is difficult to say why we are so unjust, but we judge some generations by the hideousness of the crowd, whereas we admire others for the beauty of the heroes who were persecuted in them. We say that the age of Pericles was magnificent. Yet Pericles was the object of all sorts of accusations.

Pheidias was prosecuted ; Anaxagoras was exiled ; Socrates drank the hemlock."[1]

Nothing can be more wholesome than this " backward glance " upon the vehement passions of the present ; nothing can be more substantial and more essential than this unsubstantial view of things. We must not deceive ourselves, however. Ryner's smile is, perhaps, melancholy ; but it is not disillusioned. He is not negationist or sceptical, for he has a heart as well as a mind, he is a poet as well as a sage. He might say of himself what he has written of Pythagoras' teacher :

"Anacreon and Ibycus said of him : ' He is not a poet ; he is only a sage.' But Pittacus, under whom he had studied at Mitylene, said with no less disdain : ' He is not a sage ; he is only a poet.' "

Han Ryner, unquestionably, has been the victim of this twofold contempt. We have passed through an age of excessive specialism, in which artists were prone to despise thinkers, and thinkers to despise artists. Those whom Nietzsche described as " amphibious " could not find a home in either camp. But the world seems to be entering a new phase, in which the human mind is endeavouring to assemble its scattered energies. This is because we are living in a time of need and of anguish ; because art and thought are not, can no longer be, mere Alexandrian luxury, nothing more than the pastime of a pundit ; because, henceforward, they must aim at the service of man and of life, and therefore at synthesis. Romain Rolland has been the herald and the embodiment of such a synthesis of art and thought. Han Ryner has a like aim, and that is why his day is now dawning. Ryner speaks of Heracles as the only one of the gods to be virtuous—" because at first, and for long years, he was a man." [2] Thus art and thought are

[1] Les chrétiens et les philosophes. [2] Ibid.

only divine because they are human ; and in their humanity
they are unified.

Ryner is one of the " humanists " who think that mankind
can best be served, not by preaching to the crowd or by
legislating for the cities, but by beginning with the cultivation of the individual.   He is hostile to all forms of political
activity, considering that " to command is just as slavish
as to obey."[1]   When humanity and the city are in conflict,
we must not doubt as to our allegiance : " Civic interest
cannot annul natural right.   We are men before we become
citizens.   If we are forced to choose between mankind and
the city, we shall not hesitate.   The sage will repudiate the
city if he must do so in order to affirm humanity."

Han Ryner is an individualist like Nietzsche, but he wears
his individualism with a difference.   To the will-to-power
he counterposes what he terms the will-to-harmony[2]—the
harmony which is an internal force.   The individual is to
secure self-realisation, not by dominating others, but by
self-mastery, by the difficult task of effecting a balance
between the conflicting tendencies at work in us all (and
especially in those whose natures are most richly endowed).
Thus there is no taint of selfishness in this individualism.
Far from it, the harmony of which Ryner speaks has the
aspect of love.   Permeated with the thought of the philosophers of the stoic and of the cynic school, with that of
Pythagoras " the son of silence,"[3] and with that of Jesus
whose " Fifth Gospel " he proclaims, Han Ryner comes at
last into communion with Tolstoy, so that Pierre Larivière's
approximation of the two figures is justified.   His mind is
much occupied with the problem of social injustice : " In
those days, the Nile distributed its waters much as

[1] Les chrétiens et les philosophes.
[2] La philosophie, " Revue de l'Epoque," Paris, 1919.
[3] Le fils du silence.

wealth is distributed to-day. There are regions barren from excess of poverty ; and regions swampy from excess of riches."

Like Tolstoy, however, he is far from looking to force as a remedy for these evils. He looks to individual action and to love. The sage who is able to sacrifice his own life is a contagious " fire." His sacrifice will kindle seven other fires, and each of these will in turn kindle as many more :

" When they see us, men will say : What is this love which is worth more than life, and for which they give their lives ?

"And they will acquire a taste for our love, and will refuse all other food."

These are the words which Han Ryner puts into Jesus' mouth in the Fifth Gospel, and such is Ryner's own inmost thought. Having given a brief sketch of the author's personality, I now propose to undertake a more detailed examination of his later works, to study the Han Ryner of wartime. The war was a touchstone to distinguish pure gold from base metal. Han Ryner was one of the rare spirits that triumphed over the test.

Could a book entitled *Les pacifiques*[1] have been published at a more unfortunate hour than in June 1914 ? Within a month or two, the general mood was to be anything but pacific ! At another date, the book would have made more noise in the world, gentle though the music is which sustains it throughout. Now, when the tumult has been stilled, let us incline our ears and listen to this soft and harmonious voice.

It is a story, beginning like an ordinary account of travels, but leading us insensibly into dreamland. We set out on a solidly built vessel, and after a night's sleep we awaken

[1] Figuière, Paris.

in the island of Utopia. We took our ticket for America, and find ourselves in Atlantis.

Atlantis, the fabled continent which of yore stood where now no land shows above the waters of the Atlantic Ocean. In Han Ryner's geography, a part of this mainland has escaped engulfment, to remain as a wondrous isle hidden away amid the tangle of the Sargasso Sea—so difficult of access that Ryner's hero was the first bold navigator to reach the lonely spot. In this land of Cockaigne, nature is bountiful, and men's hearts are attuned to the sweetness of paradise. Goodness and peace are in the very air. We wonder which seems most lovable : the tropical trees, heavy with golden fruits, made lively by many-hued birds ; or the well-behaved monkeys which, at a sign, gather for the human inhabitants any fruit the latter may wish to eat ; or the human beings themselves, as harmonious and richly-endowed as their environment. Ere long, however, our interest is concentrated upon these admirable specimens of humanity. We feel that it is through the goodness of the men that the beasts have been converted to gentle ways ; and later it becomes clear to us that the radiation of goodness from human beings has evoked the cordial and kindly qualities of the trees. All the rest is no more than the emblematic setting of the spirits of these Pacifics. The golden fruits and the celestial warmth are within them.

They have remarkable customs. Centuries ago they repudiated the use of force. That had been outgrown ; they could no longer believe in it. They do not make war ; they do not resist attack ; and, as Tolstoy declares, non-resistance is perpetual victory. Like water, they yield before the sword-thrust ; but they are uninjured, and their integrity is restored the instant the blade has been withdrawn. No one compels another, and no one exploits another. They have no State. Each for himself, and each for all. They lead wonderfully simple and natural lives. Long since, they abandoned their towns, the reason for this desertion being piquant. Since the use of force was tabu, it became more and more difficult to recruit persons willing to undertake the unsavoury work needed for the upkeep of towns. There were no street-sweepers, no dustmen, no nightmen. The cities became uninhabitable, and there was no choice about leaving them.

The Pacifics are simple folk. The most elaborate explanations fail to convince them of the complicated beauties of our modern civilisation.

" They shook their heads and fancied I must be making fun of them, when I told them that in my country the tiller of the soil often lacked bread to eat ; and that the man who had been building houses all his life might very likely be shelterless in his old age."

They have no sense of decency, but go about naked. Their fashions of speech are remarkable. In their tongue, the same word is used for " brother," for " friend," and for " man." One of their classical authors, in the old days when war was still known in the land, wrote : " War is a lightning conductor attached to the temple in which the well-to-do dwell."

Various other peculiarities may be mentioned. They never eat meat, and they speak of the lower animals as their cousins. Their sexual partnerships have no legal sanction. They are a strange medley of the savage and the ultra-civilised being. They have made some remarkable inventions : the pantoscope, which enables them to see all that is going on throughout the world ; and the oneirogen, an engine which supplies them with beautiful dreams. Thus they do not disdain the marvellous gifts of science, but they commit the blasphemy of adopting only those that contribute to their welfare.

We see, then, that the Tolstoyan notion of non-resistance forms the core of this book. But Han Ryner weds to it ideas of his own, so that his work has a synthetic originality. First of all, there is the ingredient of his uncompromising and yet supple individualism. Irony is another element; and thus the story, though Tolstoyan in its thought, is almost Voltairian in its style. It is a classic, typically French, sometimes recalling one of Perrault's fairy-tales, being chatty without losing distinction. It displays scepticism in tone and temper; and yet at heart it is inspired by a faith which frees the scepticism from all bitterness.

" If by religion you mean a mobile and tender dream which flutters over the surface of things, . . . and which, knowing how all things are interdependent, yet chooses to ignore this interdependence, and to conceive the unity in a thousand different fashions, fluctuating and emotionally tinged—then, indeed, we are deeply religious ? "

" Fluctuating and emotionally tinged." Of such a character are the fancies called up again and again as we read this book. The atmosphere is one of a gentle, dewy morning. There is mischief in it, doubtless, but much more of kindness.

The war seems to have given rise to a breeze of biblical inspiration. Dujardin, in a recent study[1] would actually have us regard the movement towards writing in the style of the Bible as embodying the pure essence of poetry, for he contrasts this style with that of the Graeco-Latin tradition, which was preeminent in straightforward prose. Biblical thought in fact, being presented in brief verses, finds expression in jets. Dependent and interlocking propositions are exceptional; the grammatical structure is extremely simple; the writing conveys pulses of emotion.

[1] De Stephane Mallarmé au prophète Ezéchiel, Mercure de France, Paris, 1919.

Dujardin shows how the poetry of our day is striving to become biblical in this sense. Moreover, contemporary writers are returning to the themes of the Bible. In " Le Carmel " (April and May 1916), Stefan Zweig gave us *La tour de Babel.*[1] Here, the old image has a new meaning. The Tower is European civilisation; its downfall is the war. In a sort of prologue, Zweig pointed out how aptly biblical themes symbolise the dramatic movement of all epochs in which force is predominant. We may say that both the symbols and the rhythms of the Bible are endowed with such comprehensiveness and such tragically human truth, that the whole great drama of mankind can be moulded upon them, and is subject to their lure.

Han Ryner, likewise, makes use of the legend of the Tower of Babel ;[2] but, for his part, he leaves the story in the red-and-gold mist of mythical fancy. The peoples are very numerous and strangely diversified. We see black men and white ; men wearing priestly vestments and men with Assyrian beards ; some clad in skins, some overburdened with clothing and ornaments, and some totally nude ; men with straight noses and waxen-tinted skins, men with aquiline noses, and men with oblique eyes. All are on the way to build the Tower of the Peoples, a storeyed pyramid like the ziggurats of Chaldea,[3] but not, like these, to be consecrated to idols. This Tower will belong to the human brotherhood. The procession reminds us of the numbering of Xerxes' army in Victor Hugo's *La légende des siècles.* Both writers, perhaps, are inclined to dwell at too great a length on the interminable enumeration. But if Ryner

---

[1] The German original, Der Turm zu Babel, appeared in the " Vossi-che Zeitung " on May 8, 1916.

[2] La tour des peuples, Figuière, Paris, 1919.

[3] See Zénaide A. Ragozin, Chaldea, " Story of the Nations " series, Fisher Unwin, London, 1887, pp. 278 et seq.—E. & C. P.

errs in this respect, it is as we see, in good company. Should we, indeed, find fault with the poets who thus take delight in being prodigal with their treasures ? There is joy for all the senses ; joy of form, of tone, and of colour—a Rabelaisian joy. Such superabundance is the good health of art, and no matter if it leads us away from the main path of action. The poet, we are told, is a child. We must not grudge children their playthings.

The episode of the loves of Riphat and Tel-Loh is not, as might appear at first sight, a side-show. Riphat is of Aryan stock ; Tel-Loh is a Chaldean woman, a Semite. Their love is but part of the general wedding of the peoples. The episode gives concrete expression to the main thought of the book. The notion is somewhat abstract, but in the love episode it takes human form. Tel-Loh is the West ; analytical intelligence ; the cult of science and industry. Riphat personifies oriental nonchalance ; leisurely contemplation of the Universe as it passes. His wisdom smiles at Tel-Loh's science :

" You cannot count things at all. You count falsely, even if you count only up to two. The date I am eating differs from the date you are eating. It is smaller, and it is not so ripe. . . . Indeed, he whose mind is truly open to things, cannot count even up to one. A thing changes. The name, which is the father of number, is already a falsehood, for the changes in names never keep pace with the changes in things."

Thus do Riphat and Tel-Loh learn from one another ; the spirits of their races undergo mutual interpenetration. What ideal can be more actual than that of the fusion of the East and of the West ? The Russian and Asiatic East, the Anglo-Saxon and "Allied " West—have we not in these two souls and two bodies between which a conflict is impending. Would not their interpenetration, their mutual understanding, be the supreme guarantee for the future Tower of the Peoples ?

For Han Ryner, moreover, this love which expresses the clash and the harmony of two races, is not an arbitrary product. It wells up out of the depths of his own psyche. He has expressed the same idea in other fantasies, and *L'homme-fourmi*[1] is the most typical of these. In every one of us, the paternal heritage and the maternal, jostle one another more or less violently. In Ryner the jostling is forcible, but nevertheless he feels the vital need of harmonising the two heritages. It has been currently reported that Han Ryner is a child of two races ; gossip has even supplied him with a Spanish mother and a Norse father. This is pure mythology ; but, like all mythology, it has a symbolical truth. Ryner has a twofold nature, and the confluence in him of the poet and the thinker is merely one aspect of this duality. Now, such duplex beings, striving for inner harmony, are also desirous that harmony shall prevail in their outer world. They are tolerant and conciliatory for the very reason that in the inner man there are contraries which love one another.

Thus the objective activities of Han Ryner draw their energies from the wellsprings of a subjacent internal drama. Maeder, in his work on Hodler, contends that this is a general rule of artistic creation, and that the strength of the objective manifestations depends upon the robustness of the subjective drama.[2]

The Tower, then, is being built. The peoples work ardently at their joint task, under the leadership of their prophets But when the Tower has been built as far as the red storey, the one which in the ziggurats is consecrated to Nergal the war-god, the spirit of discord is breathed into the prophets.

[1] Maison d'art, Paris, 1901.
[2] Maeder, F. Hodler, etc., Zurich, 1916;

Those who wish to build upon love come into conflict with those who wish to build upon justice. Thereupon, both factions are animated by hatred and injustice. They take to blows, and, stone by stone, the builders break down their work, using the fragments as missiles with which to slay one another.

But the spirit of Nergal is not the chief culprit. The trouble has really arisen out of the alliance between the kings and the priests. For a long time these have been aiming to turn to their own base uses the League of Nations—the phrase slips from my pen ; I should have written, the Tower of the Peoples—which the brotherly workers have been trying to build.

" What took place was a massacre of foreigners. This is always pleasing to gods, kings, and patriots."

Han Ryner has an inextinguishable hatred for kings, theocrats, rulers of all kinds ; and he denounces " the crime of obedience, the parent of so many other crimes."

But the kings and the priests are victorious. They cleanse the tower (an unfinished attempt, now fallen in ruins) of the vestiges of love and harmony. They consecrate it to their idols and to their own sway over the peoples. There is a triumphal banquet, to celebrate the victory.

" The entranced elders bubble over with delight. The wine flows freely, into their mouths, and sometimes elsewhere."

The huge abortion of the ruined tower stands there to shame mankind.

This prose epic runs its course in spacious cantos ; is sketched in bold frescos, in fanciful images that are rich with colour. No longer do we have the light, sportive, and honeyed tone of *Les pacifiques*. The later work is one in which a swarm of sturdy and muscular figures, brightly tinted, stand out against a sombre background.

Justice and love—these were the two forces a conflict between which had brought about the ruin of the tower. A discord between these same forces is the central feature of *Les apparitions d'Ahasvérus*.[1] This is what Han Ryner writes about his own book : " I regard Ahasuerus as the representative of inexorable justice, the justice that takes its stand upon the law of retaliation, the justice that denounces pity. He is the revolutionist. He is the enemy of Jesus, because the forgiveness of injury, and the careless or benevolent surrender of our cloak also to one who would rob us of our coat are the expression of a spirit which makes revolution impossible."[2]

Ahasuerus is the Wandering Jew who, for the offence committed against Jesus on the road to Calvary, has been doomed to wander eternally throughout the world. He traverses the ages with giant strides, conversing by turns with persons widely separated in time ; with Seneca, Marcus Aurelius, Galileo, Kant, Nietzsche, and others. In each case, we have a philosophical dialogue, penned, as it were, by a Plato endowed with the vision of a seer and gifted with the stern Hebraic imagination. Ahasuerus is the embodiment of an insatiable craving for justice, which makes him, century after century, the tormentor of mankind ; he is eternal aspiration ; he is unceasing disquiet to such sages as Marcus Aurelius and Boethius, who might otherwise have died with minds at peace. His greatness lies in this perpetual disquiet. At times he plays the part of an active revolutionist, as when, in a jacquerie, he aids the oppressed peasants to fire the strongholds of their oppressors.

However, his greatness notwithstanding, he suffers from an ineradicable blemish. His offence against Jesus, the embodiment of love, has brought a curse upon his flesh,

[1] Figuière, Paris, 1920.
[2] " La Revue de l'Epoque," No. 9, 1920

which has been turned to bronze. The touch of it is like the touch of cold metal ; and the living heart within his breast has ceased to beat.

The principle of justice, which is either an arid mathematical reasoning power, or else a dull revengeful hatred, does not suffice to support life. And what are we to think of the principle of wisdom, with its unemotional concern as to the welfare of society, its being content to strive after an inward perfection, to achieve the moral adaptation of the individual to the cosmos ? In fact, the combat between Ahasuerus and the sages is a drawn battle. There are neither victors nor vanquished.

We are not thinking here of the pseudo-sages of whom Ahasuerus speedily gets the better—of Seneca, for instance, whose wisdom is no more than window-dressing, and a mask for ambition. " You joined a party in the hope that it would make your fortune, as it has done. You espoused its doctrines as a man eager to secure a dowry espouses the woman without whom the dowry is unobtainable."

Marcus Aurelius is a philosopher of a very different stamp. Still, Ahasuerus has some unpalatable truths to say to the emperor. Antoninus had tried to reconcile incompatibilities ; and had been forced, in the end, to sacrifice philosophy to power. " Well do I understand your despair. At once emperor and philosopher, you were always being rent in sunder . . . As an emperor, you had to slaughter the Sarmatians ; as a man you knew it was your duty to respect human life. Your doom was that you were compelled to choose ; you had either to renounce being Antoninus, or being a man. You threw your philosophy and your principles overboard, and you remained Antoninus."

The case of Marcus Aurelius shows the failure of the principle of wisdom when this principle is supposed to be valid beyond the limits of the individual, and is asked to furnish solutions for the problems of society. But is the principle of pure justice any more serviceable ? Its solution of the problems of society is no more than an approximation ; is, in a word, illusory. Mathematics, rigidly applied to life, always culminate in illusion. Who speaks of justice, speaks of equality ; but strict equality is a pure abstraction in the mobile sphere of life. As Bergson shows, mathematics can only be applied to inert matter. Like words, and like numbers, justice is a liar.

"As for justice, when she promises peace, she is the most artless of liars."

But if she be a liar in her abstract reality, yet more is she a liar on account of the passions which animate her as soon as the many speak in her name.

" It is futile to talk to the people. A just people would not become the victim of injustice. The only way in which you can move the crowd is by appealing to its worst passions. . . . When I said ' Justice,' what those to whom I spoke heard was ' Vengeance.' "

Thus a revolution based upon strict justice cannot solve the social problem. One who wishes justice to be effective, must be able to get beyond his own point of view, must be able to put himself in another's place. Otherwise, how can he judge fairly between himself and another ? But one who does this, does more than a simple act of justice ; he does an act of sympathy and love. We see, then, that the justice which puts itself in another's place, ceases to be justice in order that it may become love.

That is why Ahasuerus, at last, meets Jesus once more. By Jesus, he is moved to tears, the tears he had ceased to know during the centuries in which his flesh had been turned to bronze. Now his heart begins to beat once more.

Are we to regard Han Ryner as the advocate of a definite

doctrine ?   He himself rejects the idea.   In *Comment tc bats-tu?*[1] he repudiates the right to preach.   A consistent individualist, he says, is not entitled to be an apostle. Doubtless, Ryner might be an apostle, for he has the apostolic spirit.   But, like his master Socrates, he would fain be the midwife of souls, and not supply souls " with children of unknown parentage."   He would gladly help others to find their own truths, but does not wish to force his truths on others.   Still, the temptation to do this latter is strong, and a man must be a hero to resist it.   Han Ryner forbids himself what is commonly termed action, for " action is a treacherous wine,"[2] and he is too wise and too clear-sighted to yield to the seductions of this intoxication.   We may apply to him the words he has used of Plato :

" Plato's thought is comprehensive, vigorous, individual ; and, despite the legislative mania by which he is sometimes seized, it is too full of wisdom ever to pass on into action. In invocations to Plato, amid a hundred flaming eulogies, we might mingle the smoke of this reproach : O thou who, with a small quantum of the mania for action, might have become a maker of converts, a builder of cities, and the founder of a religion." [3]

But is not such a " smoke " inseparable from such a " flame " ?

[1] An article published in " Le Symbole," a short-lived review, August 1917.

[2] Les chrétiens et les philosophes.   [3] Ibid.

PART TWO

THE WAR AND THE PEACE

APPEAL FOR THE FOUNDATION
OF "LE CARMEL"

(April 1916.)

IT would be, in a sense, monstrous that men who, for various reasons, are not taking part in the great struggle now in progress, should retire to Mount Carmel, should muse with shaded eyes and deafened ears, surrendering themselves to private meditation, ignoring the cries of horror which arise from the lowlands.

But each one of us possesses a Holy Mountain, a Carmel within his own soul. It is thither that we desire to withdraw, whether we live peacefully or whether we are under arms. Even for those among us who are actively engaged in the combat, this inward sanctuary has not been obliterated.

Our cathedrals are crumbling, and in this they are symbols of our faiths. That which was regarded as immortal, disappears in a rapid blaze like a fire of straw. Of how little account, amid this incendiary devastation, now seem our literary, political, and other sects, the various formulas in in which our vanity has been accustomed to patter its " credo." Let us forget our " credo," our sects, and our places of literary worship. We are of those who have preserved, not this or that faith, but Faith, the simple and essential faith in the spirit which is in us all, and in the human race, its guardian.

Amid the crumbling of the ephemeral temples, we give utterance to our faith in the temple everlasting. We are a few human voices, nothing more. Above all, our Carmel is not a stronghold of insensibility, for we are well aware that it is upon the summits of the mountains that one can most plainly perceive all the noises of the valleys.

But we believe that, while listening to the voices from below, we are doing useful work by listening also to the voices from above, the voices of that heaven in the mind where peace still reigns ; we believe that we do well to give plain expression to the utterances of these voices.

Our message is : Take hope, for life still continues. Beneath the roar of the cannon, be they distant or near, you will be able, in this solitude, if you listen, to hear the murmur of mounting sap and the rustle of germinating fruit.[1]

[1] The foregoing translation was originally published in " The Socialist Review " for August–September 1916.—E. & C. P.

NICOLAI AND THE BIOLOGY OF WAR[1]

(" The Word," The Hague,
October 11, 18, and 25, 1919.)

AT the outbreak of the war, Nicolai was a professor at the university of Berlin and physician to the imperial household. He had the rare courage of fidelity to conviction, and thus brought on himself, at first disgrace, and subsequently persecution. He adopted a stalwart attitude from the start. His feelings and his reason were alike outraged by the famous (if not infamous) manifesto of the ninety-three intellectuals, published in the beginning of October 1914. Though, of course, he had not signed it, it seemed to him that silence might be taken for approval. During the same month, therefore, in conjunction with Albert Einstein and Wilhelm Foerster, he launched a counter-manifesto, an *Appeal to Europeans*. In this document, the unity of the great European fatherland was boldly affirmed. Nicolai (the actual wording of the manifesto was his) drew the parallel which had many years earlier been drawn by Victor Hugo between modern Europe and ancient Greece ; saying that we are born Frenchmen or Germans as a man might be born an Athenian or a Corinthian, but that the Frenchmen and the Germans are Europeans just as the Athenians and the Corinthians were Greeks. Europe had been rent in sunder like Hellas ; Europe, like Hellas, was in danger of utter

---

[1] G. F. Nicolai, M.D., sometime professor of physiology at Berlin University, Die Biologie des Krieges, Betrachtungen eines Naturforschers den Deutschen zur Besinnung, Orell Füssli, Zurich, 1917 ; English translation by Constance A. Grande and Julian Grande, The Biology of War, Dent, London and Toronto, 1919.

ruin ; were it simply for self-preservation, Europe must come to realise her own unity. The duty of the intellectuals was to assist Europe towards this realisation. It was not their part to fan the fires of nationalism ; to intensify these parochial disputes which, to a sane mind, were even more absurd than they were tragical.

Goethe, and after him Nietzsche, had with the same sure touch outlined the notion of the " good European." They had not been actuated solely by that humanitarian sentiment at which cold reason sometimes mocks ; but by the simple straightforwardness of those who see clearly what is needed and do not hesitate to utter their thoughts. However, Goethe and Nietzsche had been promoted to the rank of idols. Their utterances were falsified. They were made out to have sung the national glory, to have extolled the might of empire. Even Kant, the author of the scheme to establish perpetual peace, the founder of the idea of a federation of free states, had been forced into an official livery. It is so convenient when people are dead; their utterances can be recast in an official mould, and the dead have no power to protest.

Live dissentients are less easy to deal with.

Is there anything more to say about *The Biology of War* after Romain Rolland's masterly exposition ? [1] Were Nicolai's book less prolific, doubtless there would be nothing more ; but it is so full of thoughts and facts that any one who wishes may draw freely from this source. My own chief purpose is to show its historical significance, to point out the doctrines it develops and modifies, to indicate its place in the curve that represents human science and human reason.

[1] Cf. Romain Rolland, The Forerunners, Chapter Twenty, A Great European : G. F. Nicolai. The article of which this is a translation was originally published in " Demain," Geneva, 1917.

Nicolai studies war as a natural phenomenon, but as one belonging to the biological sphere, not to the physical. Consequently, though it is a natural phenomenon, he regards as fallacious the familiar comparison of war to an earthquake, to some irresistible cataclysm independent of the human will. Natural phenomena belonging to the biological sphere are capable of undergoing an evolution. Nay more, evolution is the law of biological phenomena, and the human brain is one of the factors in this evolution.

Himself permeated with the Darwinian spirit, Nicolai protests against the crude but fashionable interpretation of Darwinism. The year 1859, when *The Origin of Species* was published, marks a turning-point in scientific and philosophical ideas; since then, everything has been impregnated with Darwinism. But most people pattered the new terms without understanding them, and the phrase " struggle for life " was in every one's mouth. The idea of the struggle for existence became dominant in sociology. Even politicians and journalists, whose knowledge of science and philosophy was not worth a rap, were ready to describe the competition between the nations as a form of the struggle for existence, and there can be no doubt that this pseudo-Darwinism played a considerable part in intensifying the nationalist fever of recent years. Was not a nation a living creature ? Had not living creatures to struggle for life ? Had they not to show their teeth and their claws ? Those who held such views were naturally inclined to regard pacifist ideas as causes or as symptoms of degeneration.

In this development, one half of Darwinism was hypertrophied at the cost of the other half. Darwin had shown that, side by side with the instinct of struggle, there is a social instinct, and that this latter plays a no less important part in the evolution of species. Some of Darwin's successors, notably Kropotkin and Novikoff, have been at pains to expound the neglected social side of Darwinism. Kropotkin spoke of the law of mutual aid.

At the time when Darwinism was stamping its imprint on psychology and sociology, and was inviting us to regard man as a bundle of instincts, there was a general tendency to look upon instinct as a sort of higher power, as an infallible guide, to whose promptings we ought to abandon ourselves with a mystical trust. This had been the attitude of Rousseau and the romanticists. But the instincts which Darwinian teaching has disclosed in mankind are far from being divine instincts such as Rousseau assumed to exist ; on the contrary, they are animal instincts which have undergone evolution. No matter ; those whose minds were charged with romanticist presuppositions were ready to worship the instincts none the less, were ready to deify the beast. But since misunderstood Darwinism leads us to regard man as a creature animated solely by the more bestial instincts (the higher instincts being ignored), it is these bestial instincts which are extolled, sanctified, endowed with the romanticist halo. Romanticism, with its passion for the warlike Middle Ages, its poesy that glorified slaughter, was already prone to take this trend. When pseudo-Darwinism became the vogue, the mystics who were panegyrists of war appeared upon the scene.

We must try to get rid of these misleading passions, which make us see red. We must learn to understand the instincts of man for what they really are ; we must learn the good side of instincts as well as the bad—their diversity, their strength, and their evolution.

Certainly, our instincts are strong. They are the mainspring of our strength. Our energies can be tamed and guided by reason and by will, but the motive force is derived from the instincts. We must not underrate their importance; but it is no less essential to avoid putting a blind and mystical trust in them.

We have a fighting instinct; but an instinct may have been beneficial in earlier days and may now have lost its utility. In animal life, there are plenty of examples of instincts that have become harmful to their possessor. But man has the power of canalising his instinctive energies by voluntarily assigning new aims for them (the war on behalf of ideas). "Whole species have become extinct because they *could* not change; is man to become extinct because he *will* not change?"

Furthermore, man is preeminently a social being, the ζῷον πολιτικόν of Aristotle. There can be no doubt that, in the human species, the social instinct is primitive; whereas the fighting instinct is in large part acquired. Monkeys, which we have good reason to regard as closely akin to our own ancestors, live in hordes. (The reference here is not to the anthropoid apes, which are merely the "cousins" of the human kind, but to the lower types of monkey, from which all the "primates," including man, are descended.) It follows that the social instinct of humanity is older than humanity—much older than the family, from which some are wrongly inclined to derive that instinct. Our children display the social instinct markedly. Their imitativeness is a simian characteristic, and is one of the aspects of the social instinct. "What requires explanation is, not how man, a murderous animal, has become peace-loving, but how man, a social animal, has become bellicose."

There is also a genuine instinct of the fatherland. We see it in the lower animals, as a part of the adaptation to certain soils and climates. In mankind it shows itself as love of the native land, love of a particular corner of the world, and of a familiar horizon. This love is perfectly legitimate, but it is a very different thing from the State patriotism of which a cult is made to-day, and which, in modern times, has become one of the causes of war. This State patriotism is a product of suggestion. It induces a militant hypnosis, which in its turn reinforces State patriotism. Sifting the elements of the notion of fatherland, Nicolai shows how elusive they are—history, language, and race. Our " country," as it actually exists, can only be regarded as a voluntary association, as " the daily plebiscite " of which Renan speaks. But there is no justification for the passive obedience which the State-Country demands to-day.

Thus, the study of our instincts fails to justify war, fails to show the biological necessity of war.

But Nicolai goes further. He shows that biology, like sociology, condemns war.

Flatly contradicting the pseudo-Darwinians who regard pacifist ideas as factors of degeneration, Nicolai stigmatises war as " a product of degeneration." Whereas the pseudo-Darwinians look upon war as a valuable selective factor, and whereas they find a biological justification for club-law by insisting that the victory of the strong and the elimination of the weak improve the breed, Nicolai shows that a less superficial study, one which criticises these vague generalisations, leads to the opposite conclusion. War, as Forel pointed out some time ago, achieves a " reversed selection." The nation is not an individual ; the victory of a strong nation has nothing to do with the selection of strong individuals. But what we have to consider in selection is the selection of the individuals who will perpetuate the species. War picks out the most vigorous individuals and condemns them to death, while leaving the weak alive. Moreover, physical force is not the only thing to consider when we are appraising the value of a human being. A long war, like the recent great war, injures the brains of those whom it does not kill. It is not difficult to imagine what would become of the human race if war were chronic and universal. Certain animal qualities promoting success in the struggle—cunning, camouflage, skill in the construction of lairs and ambushes—would probably be developed at the cost of the higher qualities of the mind. Man would regress towards the lower animals; the reversal of selection would bring about the reversal of evolution.

We see, then, that war has become purposeless at the level to which mankind has now ascended. The true direction of contemporary evolution must be that which cultivates the life of the mind. War is antagonistic to mental cultivation; jingo propaganda is likewise antagonistic. The recent history of Germany offers a crucial example. In that country, the life of the spirit attained its climax in days when Germany did not exist as a nation, in the golden age of Goethe, Schiller, and Beethoven; whereas the spiritual life of Germany was stifled during the days when the nation was strong, victorious, imperialist, and militarist. Nicolai goes even further, for he shows that, not only in the present phase of human evolution, but even among the lower animals, war is far from being the powerful and valuable evolutionary factor it is commonly supposed to be. The animals which have attained a high degree of mental development, the animals whose brains have become potent weapons in the struggle for existence, are vegetarian and peace-loving, and not beasts of prey. He refers, specifically, to elephants and monkeys.

War enfeebles the race, that of the conquerors no less than that of the conquered. The war of 1866 led to a slight fall in the Prussian birth rate, and the war of 1870 to a much sharper decline (the birth rate falling suddenly from 40 to 30). Similar considerations apply to the economic life of the nations. Here, too, the victors suffer no less than the vanquished. There may be an absolute increase as far as the figures of business done are concerned ; but the figures are misleading, and when we compare them with the general movement of business enterprise prior to the war, we see that there has been a relative decline.

(We may add, in passing, that when a war seems to have promoted economic interests, close examination will show that the interests thus favoured are those of a caste, and not those of the community-at-large. If might be instructive to draw graphs showing this.)

Another extremely suggestive curve is that which depicts the growth of armies. The steep ascent of this curve begins with the nineteenth century. During the twenty centuries down to the opening of the Napoleonic episode, the curve rises gradually from 0 to 1 ; during the nineteenth century it rises steeply from 1 to 20. But, while the appearance of Napoleon on the stage marks a turning-point, regarded as a whole the curve is almost horizontal from 0 to 1815, as compared with the nearly vertical rise from 1815 to 1915. If the amazing increase of the last hundred years could continue, we should soon have more soldiers than the total human population of the world ! Something will have to break under the strain. We are confronted with a thing even more formidable than biological and sociological necessity ; we are confronted with mathematical necessity. During the last hundred years, war has entered upon an unprecedentedly critical phase.

The law of growth is one of the laws of evolution ; but all growth has its limits. (Helmholtz has proved this as regards the size of birds, the limit here being a mechanical one.) The species which have tried to exceed this limit, have perished ; this sums up the history of the paleonto-logical monsters ; it is the tragedy of the death of the giants, giganthanasia. War seems to have become one of these monsters, a frog trying to blow itself out to the size of an ox, and destined to burst like the frog in the fable. The death of this monster may be near at hand. Hugo de Vries has taught us that we must not put implicit faith in Leibnitz' adage " Natura non facit saltum." He has corrected and amplified Darwin by showing that evolution may take place by " brusque mutations," that a species may evolve of a sudden out of a different species.

As far as war is concerned, since the curve showing the increase of armies demonstrates that we have reached a critical phase, there is good reason for supposing that we are on the eve of some such mutation in the human species. A peace-loving humanity must arise. Doubtless, when a mutation is imminent, we cannot learn from an examina-tion of the species the direction in which the mutation is likely to occur. In a plant, for instance, when a new species with narrower leaves is about to be formed, individual specimens will vary every year from the average type. Some will have comparatively narrow leaves, and some will have comparatively broad leaves. But we cannot tell whether the narrow-leaved plants or the broad-leaved plants are " right." We do not know which are forerunners (" geniuses"), and which are merely abnormal. But as regards the anticipated mutation of the human species, prediction is possible. We know that war must be con-demned on biological grounds, that in existing circumstances war has become definitely injurious to the human species. On the other hand, we know that evolution, that mutation, occurs in the direction of enhanced adaptation to environing conditions. As far, then, as mankind is concerned, the mutation must be in a pacific direction. The extant types which diverge from the normal in the bellicose direction, as Moltke diverged, are mere abnormalities. Those, conversely, which diverge from the normal in the pacifist direction, a Tolstoy for instance, are " geniuses " ; they are the forerunners of the mutation.

No extensive physiological changes are needed to bring about such a mutation, which is preeminently a moral phenomenon. As Pavloff's work has shown, the potentialities of the brain are far more extensive than our actions indicate. The brain may be conceived as a network in which a number of unused paths intersect one another, so that there may be suddenly displayed new and unexpected aptitudes. This happens in the case of certain monkeys which can be rapidly educated by man, and come to exhibit, without any physiological evolution, aptitudes which are not obviously possessed by their congeners. Here is an additional reason for hope ; for not taking a gloomy view of the destiny of man ; for not taking war " too seriously."

From the biological outlook, from Nicolai's evolutionary standpoint, moral progress is of the same nature as physical progress. Both are phenomena of evolution, of adaptation.

It is upon this fusion of the physical and the moral, upon this monistic principle, that Nicolai founds the philosophical conclusions of his work. The ancients were aware of the profound unity of things, were in sympathetic contact with the soul of the world. All Greek mythology, all the presocratic philosophy of the Hellenes, disclose a mankind steeped in cosmic sentiment. But the intelligence is analytical in its nature ; and in proportion as it wishes to understand clearly that which before was only felt, it divides experience, and thus breaks up the unity. This is what happens in the case of the postsocratic philosophers. Plato and Aristotle still speak of human society as if it were an organism. Aristotle continues to talk of " the soul of plants." The Stoics are the most cosmically inclined among the later Greek philosophers ; they are always permeated with the sentiment of the unity of the world, the one great being of which we are the limbs. Nevertheless, the analytical movement takes its course. The leading Christian theologians insist upon the duality, nay, the antagonism, of the flesh and the spirit. For a brief space, the thinkers of the Renaissance were endeavouring to put man back into nature, to make him feel anew his kinship with nature ; but the reaction upon the Christian side was all the more violent. Descartes, with his doctrine that animals were automata, a doctrine which denied them anything that resembled the human soul, established a watertight partition between man and nature. The Church scented heresy in any doctrine tending to break down the partition. Francis of Assisi, with his chanting of love for birds and for wolves, was barely tolerated. Owing to this dualism, we find in the modern world a cleavage between moral progress and economic and material progress. The former is regarded as the search for a supraterrestrial world ; the latter is solely concerned with the most concrete interests. Progress along one line does not assist progress along the other. On the contrary, they are conflicting trends, and those who devote themselves to the one despise those who devote themselves to the other.

Nevertheless, after the classical thesis, and after the medieval and modern antithesis, there comes to-day a new attempt at synthesis. Three or four centuries back, there were forerunners on the road towards this synthesis. We think, here, of some of the great figures of the Renaissance ; of Cardan, Paracelsus, Bruno, Campanella. The whole of modern science, and in especial biology as revolutionised by Darwin, is tending to reestablish the ruptured unity of the world. The kinship of living creatures is once more manifest. The link between the physical and the moral has been renewed. The unity of physical progress and moral progress is again recognised.

Not only do we find that man must not be isolated from nature, and that mind must not be isolated from matter. Furthermore we realise that the individual cannot be isolated from other individuals ; we realise that individuals are closely banded together, precisely in proportion as we realise the extent to which the individual mind is attached to the organism and participates in the tangible unity of matter. In former days, when individual minds were regarded as impenetrable and absolute units, it was the aim of metaphysics to establish the bonds of morality and right in a supraterrestrial world. These attempts to provide a metaphysical foundation for right were not futile. They were pregnant with meaning when natural science was in its infancy. They had the advantage of keeping alive the sentiment that there existed something that was common to all human beings, even though they made that something too mysterious and too remote. Right has always been felt to be a " universal," a quality overstepping frontiers and embracing all the nations ; great philosophers, from Socrates to Kant, spoke of it as sublimely international. But to-day, right, morality, have secured a biological foundation. The tie between individual minds is a scientific fact.

In the first place, the mind is the self-awareness of a living organism, and we know that living organisms are the fruits of the one great tree of life. Every human being has in his body two kinds of living matter : he has the somatic plasm, which is foredoomed to death ; and he has the germ plasm, which exists for the purposes of reproduction, and circulates like a unitary and immortal sap in all the individuals of a species.

This fact, which has long been known, takes on a new meaning as soon as a monistic philosophy has established a close tie between body and mind, for thenceforward minds are regarded as participating in the intimate unity of bodies. Egoistic sentiments may be looked upon as the consciousness of the soma plasm, and altruistic sentiments as the consciousness of the germ plasm. Herein we discover a physiological explanation of the kinship which psychologists have recognised between sexual sentiments and altruistic sentiments in general. Altruism is an evolution, an expansion, of sex feeling. In everyday speech, this kinship finds expression in the use of the word " love " to denote all our altruistic feelings. We are one.

" How foolish art thou who thinkest that I am other than thou ! " wrote Victor Hugo.

From the outlook of the evolutionist, this unity of substance extends to all living creatures. Thus we reach a new cosmic sentiment, a new pantheism. But, as between man and man, we realise that the bonds are exceedingly intimate. Modern science, in the form of sociology, tends more and more to revive the idea of the social organism. In mankind everything is action and reaction ; there is persistent solidarity. Can this be regarded as justifying the notion that mankind is an organism ? If doubts arise in our mind, this is because we should like to have a *material* bond between human beings, and because we are not content with a simple *dynamic* tie of solidarised reactions. Yet nothing can be more illusory than such a distinction in an epoch when science has dissolved matter, has reduced it to " centres of force," has transformed the conception of the material into the conception of the dynamic. It is of little consequence that we cannot see an actual cord connecting one man with another, that we cannot lay an investigatory finger upon a nerve or a telegraph wire stretching from heart to heart. Let us rid ourselves of this childish need for materialisation. Matter is but one kind of actions and reactions. Other actions and reactions, those which assume a different form, are none the less real for that. Humanity is in actual fact an organism ; a being whose members are linked together ; a being whose functions and organs constitute a coordinated whole. Thus there is a solid foundation for " the religion of humanity," which is the religion of the future. Though built upon a substratum so different from that of the religions and the philosophies of former days, it establishes by rigorous demonstration that which these had intuitively divined. Furthermore, the great precepts of this religion are identical with those of Buddha, Jesus, and Kant.

This " religion of humanity " was the religion of Auguste Comte. Nicolai, however, offers us something more than a reissue of Comte's positivism. What dominates Nicolai's mind is the Darwinian spirit. Or, we may say, it is the monism of Haeckel, but a more consistent monism ; for, when war came Nicolai was better advised than Haeckel, and did not think it necessary to break the unity of the world in the name of the German fatherland.

Nicolai proclaims the unity of all mankind, and he puts human beings back into nature. Throughout he re-establishes the continuity of the world. Thus his religious sentiment, though primarily concerned with humanity, has a cosmic undertone. Comte's positivism was somewhat stuffy and confined ; Nicolai opens the windows to give us fresh air and distant views.

Long views are the characteristic of Nicolai. Though

he never ceases to be a man of science, his eyes are continually turning towards remote horizons. To-morrow, or
the day after perhaps, he may be convicted of errors of
detail, may be shown to have entertained risky hypotheses ;
but there can be no doubt that his is one of those intuitive
minds that are enabled, by flashes of insight, to secure
sound and comprehensive views. He was, indeed, well
fitted to undertake the synthesis attempted in his book.

His thought is clear, bold, forcible. Objective though
it be, it remains individual ; it is characteristically Nicolai's.
In his writings I find the man whose whole personality is
firmly fixed in my memory ; I find the man to whom I
listened when he was recounting his departure from Graudenz,
and his final escape from Germany in an aeroplane ; the
man who described how his heart beat at sight of the sea
washing the shores of the land where freedom was to be
found ; the man who said to me : " They have destroyed
my manuscripts ; no matter, I shall rewrite them all the
better." A frank and dauntless spirit, the spirit of one who
is at home in danger, one who delights in defying fate, in
outwitting stupidity, in suddenly escaping into the free outer
world, in playing, as it were, with lofty ideas. Such dare-
devils are unusual types in Germany, though Nietzsche was
one of them, saying as he did, " We, the aeronauts of the
mind." Nicolai is one of those who can understand the
passionate joy of Pascal's wager.

8

IN FAVOUR OF PEACE (1916)

(First published in Magyar in " Vilàg," Budapesth, on January 6, 1917. The French original appeared in " Cœnobium," Milan, December 1917.—" Vilàg " had planned, at the end of 1916, to publish a Christmas number specially devoted to peace propaganda. It had commissioned articles from Auguste Forel [Switzerland], Prince Hohenlohe [Germany], Enrico Bignani [Italy], and the present writer [France]. The Austrian censorship forbade the joint demonstration, and the articles were only allowed to appear successively, though at brief intervals.)

CONFRONTED by the spectacle of this war, I have come more and more to be dominated by one feeling—that the problems it presents are extremely complicated. I admire the courage of those who believe it possible to find dogmatic solutions. Talking matters over with my friends, I have again and again said that the only reasonable position to take up towards the war is that it is impossible to have any definite position !

And yet, by applying this formula rigidly, it becomes possible to generate an affirmation out of the very hesitancy itself. Just as Descartes' " doubt " is the corner-stone of subsequent certitude, so a *theoretical doubt* concerning the question under discussion results in a *practical affirmation.*

This is the case with all theoretical doubts relative to vital issues. He who has become sceptical in the realm of metaphysics because he has realised the complexity of the riddle of life, nevertheless builds upon his scepticism a system of conduct and of action. I, likewise, have come to understand that, in face of the European war, a purely negative attitude of mind is not possible if one wishes to pass over from theory to practice. Here are my conclusions :

Objectively, it is impossible to form an opinion as to the consequences that may ensue upon the victory of one or other of the adversaries, or upon a fight to a finish, or, conversely, upon an immediate peace.

But we have to adopt some definite line of action. If, on the one hand, the prolongation of the war, or, on the other hand, an immediate peace, is equally incapable of guaranteeing the future, then it is obviously incumbent on us to choose immediate peace. Such a choice would at least curtail the sufferings and put a stop to the slaughter. To choose otherwise would be to relinquish the substance for the shadow.

Nevertheless, even here we must have our reserves : " The formal conclusion of a peace does not furnish a guarantee for peace." [1] Now, without venturing into the realm of the problematical, or, in a word, into the realm of the unforeseeable, we may distinguish between a genuine peace, and a spurious peace pregnant with revolt. The former is alone admissible. The latter would be no more than an armistice, a bending at the knee preparatory to a more impetuous leap.

What is the minimum of conditions that will ensure a genuine peace, a peace that may not be definitive but will be at least fairly durable ?   I feel that there are two equally dangerous shoals to be avoided.

First, there must be no " crushing " of one of the adversaries. A nation can only be crushed for a time ; it becomes like a volcano which is apparently extinct, but which is preparing for an eruption that will be all the more violent because it has long been repressed. Not only is this wholesale crushing sure to have disastrous consequences ; even a partial crushing, as by annexations, is an indefensible measure. Every nation, great or small,

---

[1] F. W. Foerster of Munich, in " Le Carmel," April 1916.

must have the right of self-determination. The revolt of a small, oppressed nation may be the spark which sets the world on fire.

Secondly we have to avoid, under pretext of preventing one nation from crushing another, the maintenance of vast standing armies, like those of late years. It is foolish to expect the enemy to disarm so long as one of the adversaries continues to be armed to the teeth; but it is a grave menace to maintain a system of general arming of the nations. Granted that function creates structure; still, structure induces function to become active. To be armed to the teeth is not a guarantee of peace, but a perpetual threat of war. Recent experience should suffice to prove the truth of this.

Partial disarmament, a limitation of armaments, presupposes an international organisation, not on paper merely, but as a concrete fact. In order that at least the skeleton of such an organisation may be set up at the conclusion of peace, in order that the first foundation of a world-wide confederation may be laid, we must immediately turn our minds to the consideration of such possibilities. Doubtless, the full realisation of this ideal may not be achieved for centuries. Fresh cataclysms may befall our race ere our children reach the haven of desire. But our task is to find the best possible solution for the problems that face our own time.

To sum up. The preliminary conditions of an acceptable peace are :

1. no " crushing " of the conquered ;
2. no annexations ;
3. limitation of armaments ;
4. the framework of an international organisation.

I am not misled into believing that the advocates of a

reasonable peace are anything but the merest handful. We can do no more than voice our hopes. May some of those who have power on their side, hear our feeble voices.

However weak our material effect upon the march of events may be, there is another sphere of action in which we can exercise our influence. In the everlasting realms of thought, of art, of science ; in all purely human and humble endeavour ; in the loving hand held out to help those who are suffering around us—here it is that we can work. That is what we wished to affirm at the beginning of 1916 when we founded " Le Carmel " at Geneva. This periodical is no pacifist review, but it has tried to link up in every land those men, be their names Romain Rolland, Paul Brulat, Han Ryner, or Emile Verhaeren, F. W. Foerster or Stefan Zweig, Carl Spitteler or Otto Borngraeber, who, though separated by the conditions of war, are united still on the holy mount.

I believe that we should do our utmost in favour of peace. But also I believe it to be even more important that we, who are not powerful in the world, should continue to raise on high the chalice of spiritual communion. This is our greatest duty.

A MESSAGE TO THE BERNE CONFERENCE OF 1917

(" La Voix de l'Humanité," the organ of the Committee for the Preparation of the Society of Nations and of the League for the Defence of Humanity. Lausanne, December 8, 1917.)

SINCE I am unavoidably prevented from being present at the gathering in Berne, I venture to sum up in these few lines the thoughts I should have liked to voice in person from the floor of the conference hall—thoughts I deem essential. It is a question of tactics. I am certainly not the father of these tactical ideas, but they are so important that I do not consider they can be reiterated too often, and it is essential that they should always take a front place at such conferences as you are holding to-day.

International organisation is one of the conditions of peace and yet it is a question which is independent of the question of peace. It is necessary to emphasise this independence ; the consideration of the subject from two distinct points of view is of the utmost tactical importance. We must be guided by Descartes' rule : " Divide the subject under as many subheads as possible in order the easier to solve the difficulties."

This subdivision is all the more important in the present case, seeing that the question of *international organisation* has rallied around it many men who are by no means agreed upon the question of *peace*.

Statesmen both from among the Entente powers and from among the Central powers have publicly adhered to the idea of a League of Nations ; and many of the in-

118

tellectuals belonging to the belligerent nations are likewise its ardent supporters. But the idea of working here and now for peace, encounters lively opposition—especially in Entente countries, and on the part of numbers of those who are the most ardent advocates of an international organisation. Many governments and many eminent men regard the mere mention of the word " peace " as " unpatriotic "; whereas the same governments and the same eminent men look upon the work of immediately laying the foundations of an international organisation as thoroughly commendable.

If we confound the two questions, if we find it impossible to speak of an international organisation without at the same time speaking of peace, we shall render the former proposal as suspect as the latter. Thereby we shall alienate much valuable support from the idea of an international organisation. This would certainly retard rather than expedite matters.

The most practical, the most precise, and the most straightforward thing to do would be to form two separate committees, to assemble two kinds of conferences absolutely independent one of the other :

1. Conferences in favour of forming an international
   organisation.
2. Conferences for the study of the conditions of peace.

To the first kind of conferences should be admitted *both the advocates and the opponents of an immediate peace ;* nay more, a special invitation should be sent to all those who have taken a definite stand *in favour of international organisation though they are no less definitely against peace.* The initiative for such conferences should be in the hands of really neutral persons, say Swiss, persons whose neutrality cannot be in any way suspect in Entente lands.

As for conferences of the second category having for their object the discussion of peace (which is only attainable through the governments), such conferences will not be efficacious until the time when all the governments can be represented at them either officially or semi-officially. Nevertheless, it is possible to assemble such conferences on neutral soil, in order that the discussions may react upon the governments and lead them to disclose their war aims with greater precision—a most desirable achievement if we are to see things clearly.

Above all, let the two kinds of conference not impinge upon the domains one of the other. This would only serve to confuse the issues. Let them be absolutely distinct one from the other.

A MESSAGE TO THE BERNE
CONFERENCE OF 1919

(International Conference for the League
of Nations, March 1919.) [1]

THE future is full of menace. The League of Nations, in
the guise in which it has been presented to us, is a two-edged
sword. It is impossible to say on which side this sword
will fall.

We live in a veritable nightmare. I see the two young
republics, the Russian and the German, excluded from the
League of Nations, rising up and organising their forces
with all the enthusiasm of the France of 1792. I see the
former, strong in its active mysticism, inspired by a splendid
dream which transcends the bounds of Russia itself, a dream
which is being fulfilled by stages ; I see Russia in the full
vigour of its ardent youth and backed by its inexhaustible
reserves of men. I see, too, the Germans strong in wrath,
in eagerness for revenge, and strong also in virtue of
that iron discipline beneath the yoke of which they have
bowed their heads for half a century. I see in the East
the great Chinese people, goaded on by rivalry with Japan
and a dumb desire to awake, joining hands with Russia and
Germany. I see the teeming and multiform world of
Hindustan turning for aid to Lhassa, the centre of religious
life, in order to shake off British dominion and to forestall
China, what time, at the other extremity of the globe, the
turbulent republics of South America, fretting under the
ancient jealousies against North America, likewise join the

[1] This article was published in the " declaration of sympathy " issued
by the conference, and printed by Bolliger & Eicher, Berne, 1919.

coalition. I see two Leagues of Nations : one gyrating in the orbit of the Allies ; the other, sweeping along in its socialist wake the prodigious East of Confucius and of Buddha, and the Red Guards who are opening the gates for the passage of the yellow races. Now I see the few remaining neutral countries caught in the whirl of one or other of these maelstroms ; I see the world in flames ; and I see war, world-wide war, a war of which the one from which we are just emerging will have been no more than a dress rehearsal, the paltriest of imitations.

With all the strength of our reason, with all the ardour of our heart, let us sound the alarm. Wilson must hear us. For, in the deliberations of the Allies, if one voice alone makes itself heard it may carry a decisive weight on our side. It is not in our power to say whether the Allies desire the liberation of the world, or, on the contrary, whether they pursue selfish aims. The truth is that a council is a beast with a hundred heads and a hundred wills : a council is composed of idealists, mystics, hypocrites, brutes. Under cover of a phrase, such as the League of Nations, each one pursues a beautiful or a despicable quarry. In such a con- fusion, one voice may suffice to turn the helm to starboard when it was previously turned the other way. Let us raise the alarm signal, and see to it that Wilson hears us.

Moreover, let the whole world hear us. The world must organise. The peoples must arise, for the peoples are ready for the genuine League of Nations. Let the peoples refuse to be robbed by the governments and the diplomatists. The peoples must demand that the League of Nations shall represent a federation of peoples and not a council of diplo- matic pontiffs. In every country, let men seek the suffrages of their constituents on a program of " the federation of the peoples," and when such men are elected to parliament let them uphold this program. Let them insist upon the creation of an international government directly elected by the suffrage of the peoples and not by a cartel of the cabinets. In this distinction there is the huge abyss which separates salvation from disaster.

I speak as a man. But it is also borne in on me that I speak as a Frenchman.

THE EAST AGAINST THE WEST

(" La Feuille," Geneva,
January 16, 1920.)

BOLSHEVISM in Asia ! Among the many sensational news-items with which we have been regaled of late, this one deserves further attention. Conquest of Siberia by the Soviets, risings in China, in India, in Persia, affirmations, denials ! . . . It is hard to sift the true from the false. Nevertheless certain facts emerge whose significance is great. Such news-items are in the order of things ; and if among them there are many fairy tales, we know that some fairy tales are more real than history itself, in that they express the essential spirit of facts and the imminence of the possible. It would not take much to link the vast Asiatic continent with the communist movement of Europe. There are two reasons for this ; one is psychological ; the other political. The psychological reason consists in the inherited predisposition towards communistic ideals which has been developed among Asiatic races by primordial religious beliefs. The political reason rests upon the antagonism between China and Japan, upon the growing revolt against British dominion in Hindustan, and upon the anti-British movement in Persia ; in a word it rests upon the wholehearted hatred felt by the Asiatic world for the British world and its dependents.

In my Message to the Berne Conference of 1919, discussing the possibilities of formidable developments that might lead to a conflict between the East and the West, I used words to which—a year later—I need add little. The prediction seems to be attaining realisation ; facts are coming to substantiate theory ; to the peoples of Asia we may now add the peoples of Egypt. There seems to be a clear indication of a balance of powers which is no longer restricted to a balance of powers among the nations of Europe—a neat and innocent plaything—but a world-embracing balance of powers, a balance of powers as between one hemisphere and the other. The strength of one and of the other consists in the fact that each is the embodiment of an idea.

The Anglo-Saxons form the axis of the western coalition. They were predestined to play this part. They are not instinct with communism, this ideal is not in their very bones. On the contrary they are instinct with individualism. Havelock Ellis, in a recent essay [1] has traced the cause of this fundamental tendency. He ascribes it to " insular selection." The Anglo-Saxons, the descendants of diverse peoples, have a common heritage from their sea-loving and adventurous ancestors, from their pirate forbears. They are as far removed as possible from what Nietzsche has termed " the spirit of the herd." Havelock Ellis perceives in the sublimest products of the British poetical muse, in the fields of British scientific discovery, and in British philosophy, the " sublimation " of a piratical instinct. It is this instinct which makes them successful colonisers. Ellis' notion is more than ingenious, it is profound. If it does not account for everything, it accounts for a great deal. The British have been selected, by their insular position, so as to develop in themselves, to a very special degree, the love of personal risk, and the instinctive detestation of things communal, of communism. We need but compare the social life of the British with that of the Russians. They are two extremes. The Russian will

[1] The Psychology of the English, " Edinburgh Review," April 1916.

enter your room without knocking, settle himself in your chair, and hold forth to you for three hours at a stretch. It will never enter his head that he may be an inopportune visitor. He will borrow from you, lend to you, speak to you without being introduced, will at once begin to treat you like an old friend. The Englishman is straitlaced, waits to be introduced, stands face to face with you and ignores you. He respects your plans for the day, does not interrupt your work, and desires that you treat him with equal respect. The strict etiquette with which he surrounds himself guarantees his personal freedom, and his independence from tiresome interruptions. He finds this perfectly natural, and is horrified if the rules are infringed.

Other nations occupy various planes between those two extremes. One of the most amazing things in history was the alliance between Great Britain and Russia. On the other hand we need not be surprised to find England at the centre of the individualistic world, and Russia at the centre of the communist world. These are the actual facts we are witnessing today. Nor need we be astonished because, at the recent congress of socialist students held at Geneva, the British delegates distinguished themselves by their opposition to the Third International.

The two coalitions which we see concreting under the inspiration of these contrasted outlooks are due in each case to a compromise between deep-seated affinities and political circumstances. Political circumstances are mainly responsible for drawing into a common planetary system of the West all the allies of yesterday. Some of the countries thus drawn in may possess a soil which is fertile to communism, but the power of cultivating it for the growth of such ideas is curtailed because of prepotent historical and political trends. Certain countries may hesitate between the Russian East and the British West. But the two worlds are there ; they cannot be ignored.

What concerns us most vitally in the affair is that the line of demarcation between the two worlds passes athwart the old countries of Europe. France seems to be carried along in the wake of one, whilst Germany is sailing in the wake of the other. It is true that no final decision has yet been made ; but everything seems to point to the coming of such a decision. The frontier between the coalition of the East and the coalition of the West will run along the Rhine. The dividing line will traverse the marches of Lorraine and Alsace ; and it will run through Switzerland, doomed by its racial make-up to be perpetually torn between opposing sympathies. But the anguish which such opposing sympathies necessarily entails has its compensations. For the Swiss people will have the privilege of understanding the gravity of the hour, of sifting the reasons which the two adversaries may bring forward in support of their actions. It may devolve upon them to propose a solution—a solution which will be difficult to find, though urgently required. Will Switzerland be able to rise to the heights demanded by such a privileged position ? Shall we witness the rise of such spirits as shall be capable of warding off the most terrible of the *wars of religion* ? For it is truly two souls, two antagonistic conceptions of life which are standing face to face. Are they irreconcilable ?

PART THREE

EDUCATION AND SOCIETY

BAHAISM, A MOVEMENT TOWARDS THE COMMUNITY OF MANKIND [1]

(" Cœnobium," Lugano and Milan,
June 1917.)

WE westerners are too apt to imagine that the huge continent of Asia is sleeping as soundly as a mummy. We smile at the vanity of the ancient Hebrews, who believed themselves to be the chosen people. We are amazed at the intolerance of the Greeks and the Romans, who looked upon the members of all other races as barbarians. Nevertheless, we ourselves are like the Hebrews, the Greeks, and the Romans. As Europeans we believe Europe to be the only world that matters, though from time to time we may turn a paternal eye towards America, regarding our offspring in the New World with mingled feelings of condescension and pride.

Nevertheless, the great cataclysm of 1914 is leading some of us to undertake a critical examination of the inviolable dogma that the European nations are the elect. Has there not been of late years a demonstration of the nullity of modern civilisation—the nullity which had already been proclaimed by Rousseau, Carlyle, Ruskin, Tolstoy, and

[1] Cf. H. Dreyfus, Le Béhaïsme, son histoire, sa portée sociale ; also Dreyfus, Le livre de la certitude de Béha-Oullah ; and, Dreyfus, Les paroles cachées de Béha-Oullah—all published by Leroux, Paris.—Among notable books on Bahaism available in the English language are the following : Isabella D. Brittingham, The Revelation of Baha-Ullah, Bahai Publishing Co., Chicago, 1902 ; Myron H. Phelps, Life and Teachings of Abbas Effendi, Putnam, New York and London, 1903, second edition, revised, 1912 ; Hippolyte Dreyfus, The Universal Religion, Bahaism, Cope & Fenwick, London, 1919 ; J. E. Esslemont, Baha'U'llah and the New Era, George Allen & Unwin, London, 1923 (contains an excellent bibliography).—E. & C. P.

Nietzsche ? We are now inclined to listen more attentively to whispers from the East. Our self-complacency has been disturbed by such utterances as that of Rabindranath Tagore who, lecturing at the Imperial University of Tokio on June 18, 1916, foretold a great future for Asia. The political civilisation of Europe was " carnivorous and cannibalistic in its tendencies." The East was patient, and could afford to wait till the West, " hurrying after the expedient," had to halt for want of breath. " Europe, while busily speeding to her engagements, disdainfully casts her glance from her carriage window at the reaper reaping his harvest in the field, and in her intoxication of speed cannot but think him as slow and ever receding backwards. But the speed comes to its end, the engagement loses its meaning, and the hungry heart clamours for food, till at last she comes to the lonely reaper reaping his harvest in the sun. For if the office cannot wait, or the buying and selling, or the craving for excitement, love waits, and beauty, and the wisdom of suffering and the fruits of patient devotion and reverent meekness of simple faith. And thus shall wait the East till her time comes." [1]

Being thus led to turn our eyes towards Asia, we are astonished to find how much we have misunderstood it ; and we blush when we realise our previous ignorance of the fact that, towards the middle of the nineteenth century, Asia gave birth to a great religious movement— a movement signalised for its spiritual purity, one which has had thousands of martyrs, one which Tolstoy has described. H. Dreyfus, the French historian of this movement, says that it is not " a new religion," but " religion renewed," and that it provides " the only possible basis for a mutual understanding between religion and free thought."

[1] Rabindranath Tagore, Nationalism, Macmillan, London, 1917, pp. 59, 64, and 65.

Above all, we are impressed by the fact that, in our own time, such a manifestation can occur, and that the new faith should have undergone a development far more extensive than that undergone in the same space of time nearly two thousand years ago, by budding Christianity.

In 1844, a young Persian reformer, the Bâb, began to attract attention. The established authorities, both ecclesiastical and civil, were inclined to regard him as nothing more than a disturber of the peace. He made no attempt, indeed, to spread his teachings by force. But, like Christ of old, he promised the kingdom of God on earth, and to the great ones of this world such promises always seem subversive. The whole country was soon in a ferment, the inhabitants taking sides for or against the Bâb. Breaches of the peace occurred. The Bâb was arrested, confined in one prison after another, and on July 9, 1850, was executed in Tabriz. Large numbers of his disciples suffered the same fate. But these repressive measures served only to stimulate the movement by giving it the glory of martyrdom. In 1852, after an attempt on the Shah's life, there was a fresh outbreak of persecution. By an agreement between the governments of Persia and of Turkey, the Babists were exiled to Bagdad, where they were to live under Turkish supervision. It would, however, have been necessary to exile at least half the population of Persia in order to check the Babist movement in that country.

Mirza Husain Ali Nuri, reverenced to-day under the name of Baha'u'llah (the Splendour of God), was born in Muharram 1233 (November 1817). A disciple of the Bâb, he was imprisoned at Teheran in 1852, after the attempt on the Shah's life, although there was no evidence of his complicity. Subsequently, he was sent to Bagdad with the other exiles. Shortly afterwards, being able to leave Bagdad and

the Persian colony there, he lived for two years as a hermit
in the mountains to the north of Sulaimanyiah. His first
wish had been for a retired and peaceful existence, but an
irresistible inner impulse forced him to action. During the
two years of his retirement, while he lived in communion
with nature, he was collecting his forces for the work he had
to do. Returning to Bagdad, he was accepted by his fellows
as chief and master. The Bâb had regarded himself (like
John the Baptist) as the humble forerunner of a greater to
follow, and the Babists were awaiting their prophet.

In 1862, the Persian government again became uneasy.
Arrangements were made with the Sultan that the Babists
should be transferred to Constantinople, and the caravan
of the exiles set out from Bagdad. At first, as usually
happens in these cases, the march was a slow one. The
preparations for such a journey are tedious, and the main
body has to wait for the stragglers. The procession, therefore,
rested ten days or more in the " Garden of the Rizwan,"
only a little way out of Bagdad. On the first evening
here, a hot spring evening just before sunset, the exiles were
looking back towards Bagdad, and were grieving over their
lot, the loss of their martyred friends, the slaughter of their
master. Then Baha'u'llah rose among them and announced
his mission. With the confidence of inward conviction, he
uttered his thoughts uncompromisingly.

From that evening they must cease to stigmatise any as
unbelievers, for there were no unbelievers.

God had made all men as drops of water drawn from the
same sea, as leaves of the same tree. All the races were pure.

The Bâb had given his life for something more than Persia
and Islam ; he had given his life for humanity-at-large. The
day of " religions " had passed, and the day of Religion
had dawned.

Thus, by the Declaration of Rizwan, the cause was widened

beyond the range of dogma and ritual. Hitherto the movement had been nothing more than a Persian revolution, nothing more than a Mohammedan reform ; now it became world-wide in its scope.

Forsaken by the fainthearted, and by those who clung to the tradition of Islam, driven from town to town with his family and a few hundred followers, Baha'u'llah continued his work. In the mountains he had conceived *The Book of Certainty* (Kitabul-Ikan). He now penned epistles addressed to many of the great ones of the earth. From Adrianople he wrote to the Pope, to Queen Victoria, to the King of Prussia, and to Napoleon III.

Some of these letters have become famous, owing to the prophecies they contained. In 1868, for instance, Baha'u'llah announced to Napoleon III that the fall of the Third Empire was imminent, and told the Pope that the loss of the temporal power of the papacy was at hand. From Adrianople, the Babists or Bahais were sent to Acre, and there Baha'u'llah wrote his later works, *The Most Holy Book, Hidden Words*, etc. The Acre community consisted of men of all races, originally holding the most diverse creeds, who lived a brotherly life apart from the world, and set an example to the rest of mankind ; the Ottoman authorities never had occasion to intervene in their affairs.

Thanks to the exemplary life of its adherents, and owing to the fact that the exiles dwelt in this historic spot—in " the white city on the waters " at the foot of Mount Carmel, in a place so full of biblical memories—Bahaism became endowed with the joint characteristics of simplicity and solemnity, and the influence of the movement was thereby enhanced.

Baha'u'llah died in Acre on May 28, 1892. His son Abbas Effendi, later known as Abdul Baha, succeeded him as chief of the Bahaist movement. Abdul Hamid gave

an amnesty to the Bahaists as to all other political offenders.
At the present time, the majority of the inhabitants of
Persia have, to a varying extent, accepted the Babist faith.
In the great towns of Europe, America, and Asia, there are
active centres for the propaganda of the liberal ideas and the
doctrine of human community which form the foundations
of Bahaist teaching.

Bahaism is not a metaphysical system. It has neither
priests nor dogmas. Mirza Husain says that it is intellec-
tually incumbent upon each one of us to follow in all things
his own reason and the guidance of his natural lights. Thus
the theoretical elements of the religion are of the simplest
possible character.

Still, there are theoretical elements. At any rate,
Baha'u'llah, like every thinking man, has certain general
outlooks. Not being dogmas, these are likely in the future
to undergo a supple evolution. But, for the nonce, they can
be regarded as the articles of the Bahaist faith.

An idea which plays a leading part in Baha'u'llah's teaching is that of the " prophets " which was likewise dominant
in Jewish and in Mohammedan teaching. But the Bahaist
conception of the prophet is wider and freer in scope than
that characteristic of the earlier creeds. The prophet, the
inspired sage, is not made known to us by the material signs
which, according to the credulous, bore witness to the
prophetic mission of Moses, Jesus, or Mohammed. He is
a man, and one who, because of his past life and his social
position, is likely to be despised by the proud. " Such a
man as Jesus is unhesitatingly treated as an unbeliever, and
is speedily put to death . . . Though a hundred thousand
voices proclaim it, still most people will deny that the son
of an unknown man can be the Messiah."

Socrates is said to have declared that philosophy came

to earth from heaven. Baha'u'llah makes the same claim for religion. He insists that the great revelations of the past can be renewed to-day. The miracles related in the sacred writings are of a spiritual nature, and they are no less miraculous now than of yore.

The prophet, then, is not disclosed as such to the peoples by signs obvious to all.[1] Far from it, the prophet is a protestant and an innovator, and this inevitably makes him hated by those who are under the dominion of traditional views. Mirza Husain has an eye on his own possible fate when he recalls what has happened to prophets throughout the ages.

By a sort of natural law, he tells us, priests are the born enemies of prophets, for a priest's interest is in the letter of religion, and not in its spirit. No European freethinker has ever used harsher expressions concerning the clergy than those used by this Asiatic prophet.

" So great, alas, is the ignorance of men, that they accept the will and the desire of priests, while turning away from the will and the desire of God . . . When the light of the stars disappears, it is because the sun is rising ; in iike manner, the light of the doctors and the priests is dimmed when the sun of reality swings into the sky . . . By the Creator's orders, the waves of fecund seas break on the shores of paradise ; and yet, like dogs round a carcase, men assemble round their priests, content with a bitter draught of brackish water ! "

Lamartine said that the poet was more of a man than the common herd. Baha'u'llah thinks the same of the prophet. His conception of God, quite undogmatic, breathes an

[1] Nevertheless, Baha'u'llah would seem to accept in its literal sense the belief that new stars show themselves in the skies to herald the coming of the prophets. Here is a matter in which he is inclined towards beliefs which disconcert us, towards beliefs which our western scientific training inclines us to reject forthwith

atmosphere which recalls that of pantheism on the one hand and that of Leibnitz' monadism on the other. God is present in every atom : " Everything that exists is a place for the manifestation of the King of Reality, and the rays of the sun are reflected in the mirror of all beings." But there are, so to say, degrees in divinity (this recalls the Platonic " participation "). Man is the most divine of all the creatures known to us. When man, through reflection and collectedness, penetrates to the depths of his own nature, he meets God there and identifies himself with God. Prophets, therefore, are nothing more than men who have found their way into the depths of themselves. It is equally true to say that they are men and that they are God ; that they are distinct personalities or that they all have one and the same soul. Mohammed speaks in a like sense when he says : " I am all the prophets " ; and when he says, " I am Adam, Noah, Moses, Jesus."

" If you look carefully, you will see that they all dwell in the same garden, soar to the same heights, are seated on the same carpet, speak the same language, proclaim the same laws."

Thus the great events recorded in the sacred writings must not be relegated to a legendary past, and the expectation of them must not be postponed to an indefinite future. That which is wondrous is in the soul of men ; and, since it exists for all time, it exists also to-day. The " resurrection " of which the Scriptures tell us is not something that will happen only at the end of the world, or only at the close of our mortal life. Beyond everything, it is an inner happening ; immortality is our participation henceforward in the essence of eternal things. The prophet is one who " resurrects " souls. " The indifferent, shut up within their own bodies as if in tombs, receive from the prophet the new mantle of faith. Through him they come to live a new and wondrous

life . . . As Jesus said : ' Ye must be born again.' "[1]
The resurrection is the entering into our higher nature,
the breaking away from the passions of our animal
nature.

Contemporaneously with the Babist movement in the East
there occurred in certain European minds a parallel evolution. The conception of Religion as contrasted with
religions, and the idea that prophets and " magians "
have a role which runs counter to that of priests, recall
the ideas of Victor Hugo. (Scant attention has been paid
to Hugo's religious development. He himself regarded
his little-known book *Dieu*[2] as the most important of
his writings.)

The Persian prophet's theories concerning immortality
and the " resurrection " are closely akin to Tolstoy's. It
would seem that the tendency which found expression in
the Bahaist movement was in conformity with a general
need of our age.

We shall not grasp the full significance of this tendency
until we pass from the description of Bahaism as a theory
to that of Bahaism as a practice, for the core of religion is
not metaphysics but morality.

The Bahaist ethical code is dominated by the law of
love taught by Jesus and by all the prophets. In the thousand and one details of practical life, this law is subject to
manifold interpretations. That of Baha'u'llah is unquestionably one of the most comprehensive of these, one of the

---

[1] This and the foregoing quotations are from The Book of Certainty.

[2] *Dieu* is an unfinished poem, posthumously published. It may be
obtained separately in various editions, or in the Collected Works. Swin-
burne writes : " Dieu and La Fin de Satan are full to overflowing of such
magnificent work, such wise simplicity of noble thought, such heroic
and pathetic imagination, such reverent and daring faith, as no other poet
has ever cast into deathless words and set to deathless music " (Enc. Brit.,
eleventh edition, Vol. XIII, p. 864).—E. & C. P.

most exalted, one of the most satisfactory to the modern mind.

The law of love is something more than a precept for the regulation of the individual life ; it is essentially social, for it aims at regulating the whole development of social life.

That is why Baha'u'llah is a severe critic of the patriotism which plays so large a part in the national life of our day. Love of our native land is legitimate, but this love must not be exclusive.   A man should love his country more than he loves his house (this is the dogma held by every patriot) ; but Baha'u'llah adds that he should love the divine world more than he loves his country.   From this standpoint, patriotism is seen to be an intermediate stage on the road of renunciation, an incomplete and hybrid religion, something we have to get beyond.   Throughout his life, Baha'u'llah regarded the ideal of universal peace as one of the most important of his aims.

But his opinion was that it would be absurd to forbid the nations to make use of armed force against one another if human society were allowed to use force in other circumstances.   Mohammed, and even the Bâb, held that armed force might be used on behalf of the faith, but Baha'u'llah said to his disciples : " It is better to be killed than to kill."   The Bahaists, therefore, answered persecution by non-resistance.   The whole history of their movement bears witness in favour of this attitude.   Prior to 1852, Persia had been devastated by wars of religion ; but since the Bahaists became non-resisters these wars have ceased, and the material development of Bahaism has been all the more extensive.

Nevertheless, Baha'u'llah, being an oriental and therefore having a more supple and less logical mind than Tolstoy, did not draw the extreme consequences that the Russian moralist drew from the principle of non-resistance.   If we carry this principle to its logical conclusion, there is no place left for government, seeing that organised government necessarily presupposes the right to use force. Now, Baha'u'llah's social theories have nothing subversive about them ; the Persian prophet commands us to respect the laws, and desires to maintain personal property. Nay more, Baha'u'llah was himself a legislator. Like so many of the mystics, from Moses to Ignatius Loyola, he was likewise a man of a practical turn, was an organiser. He prescribed the functions of a council, the Baitu'l Adl, or House of Justice,[1] which was to supervise the maintenance of order in the Bahaist city. It is expedient to point out here that the main functions of this council are educational rather than political. Baha'u'llah is in this respect enunciating a novel and fruitful idea. There is a better way of dealing with social evils than by trying to cure them after they have come to pass. We should try to prevent them by removing their causes, which act on the individual, and especially on the child. Nothing can be more plastic than the nature of the child. The government's first duty must be to provide for the careful and efficient education of children, remembering that education is something more than instruction. This will be an enormous step towards the solution of the social problem, and to take such a step will be the first task of the Baitu'l Adl. " It is ordained upon every father to rear his son or his daughter[2] by means of the sciences, the

[1] Esslemont (op. cit., pp. 157 et seq.) calls this body the " Spiritual Assembly." He writes : " In every centre where Bahais exceed nine in number it is recommended that a ' Spiritual Assembly,' or Council, should be elected to guide and coordinate the activities of the friends in the district."—E. & C. P.

[2] This implies the emancipation of woman, which is a bold innovation for Islam.—[As regards the position of women among the Bahaists, the following passage in Esslemont's book (op. cit., p. 158) is of interest. He is describing the election of the Spiritual Assembly : " The friends elect representatives to the number of, say, 38, as a Selection Committee, and this Committee appoints the Spiritual Assembly, the members of which should number not less than nine. In Persia, the women still have a

arts, and all the commandments; and if any one should neglect to do so, then the members of the council, should the offender be a wealthy man, must levy from him the sum necessary for the education of his child. When the neglectful parent is poor, the cost of the necessary education must be borne by the council, which will provide a refuge for the unfortunate." [1]

The Baitu'l Adl, likewise, must prepare the way for the establishment of universal peace, doing this by organising courts of arbitration and by influencing the governments. Long before the Esperantists had begun their campaign, and more than twenty years before Nicholas II had summoned the first Hague congress, Baha'u'llah was insisting on the need for a universal language and courts of arbitration. He returns to these matters again and again.

" Let all the nations become one in faith, and let all men be brothers, in order that the bonds of affection and unity between the sons of men may be strengthened . . . What harm can there be in that ? . . . It is going to happen. There will be an end to sterile conflicts, to ruinous wars; and the Great Peace will come ! " Such were the words of Baha'u'llah in 1890, two years before his death. [2]

While adopting and developing the Christian law of love, Baha'u'llah rejected the Christian principle of asceticism. He discountenanced the macerations which were a nightmare of the Middle Ages, and whose evil effects persist even in our own days.

In contrast with these morbid aspects of Christianity, Bahaism is a doctrine that insists upon a healthy and

separate Spiritual Assembly, but Abdul Baha says that in the West both men and women should be associated in the same assembly. Members are elected for a period of two or three years." Then the Spiritual Assembly has to resign en bloc.—E. &. C. P.]

[1] Kitabu'l Aqdas, quoted by Dreyfus.

[2] A conversation with Professor E. G. Browne of Cambridge, who, in April 1890, visited Baha'u'llah in prison at Acre.

joyous view of life. We are told, indeed, to make the best
possible use of our reason, which of old was under the
tyranny of dogma ; but we are also told to use all the other
energies which nature has implanted in us. In these respects,
Bahaism is akin to pantheism. Whereas the Christians have
their doctrine of original sin, the Bahaists refuse to believe
that nature is radically evil. We must not despise matter,
for matter is only another aspect of spirit ; when we have
ascended to a certain level, we shall perceive the unity of the
world. But there are degrees in divinity, and nature is not
equally good throughout. He who would live well, must
avoid giving free rein to all the instincts alike. He must
control and coordinate his instincts ; must bring them
under the guidance of the spirit. Thus he will be enabled
to direct all his activities towards the ends which nature
has revealed to him as the highest.

Bahaism, then, is an ethical system, a system of social
morality. But it would be a mistake to regard Bahaist
teaching as a collection of abstract rules imposed from without. Bahaism is permeated with a sane and noble mysticism ;
nothing could be more firmly rooted in the inner life, more
benignly spiritual ; nothing could speak more intimately
to the soul, in low tones, and as if from within.

Mirza Husain is a poet. Like all the great mystics, he
uses a language packed with imagery, and his symbols,
with their exotic flavour, give what he has to say an added
charm.

" Verily, I have heard the song of the Lark of Wisdom,
upon the branches of the tree of your soul, and I have
heard the cooing of the Dove of Certainty on the branches
of the tree of your heart, becoming aware of the perfume of
the garment of your love . . ."

Such are the opening words of *The Search*. Here is the

moment of ecstasy : " I can tell you no more of this, for now day is dawning, and the wayfarer's lantern is extinguished."

A wondrous life opens for him who dies to himself : " Blessed is the heart which is taken in His nets, and blessed is the head which falls in His path. Friend, become a stranger to yourself, that you may become an intimate of the Well Beloved."

Sometimes the symbolism is organised to constitute a myth endowed with an intangible, environing, and mysterious poetic force : " We are told that, for many years, a man, seared by the fires of distance, had been suffering the torment of separation from the woman he loved . . . He had become so thin that he seemed as unsubstantial as a puff of wind ; and the sadness of his heart had worn him to a shadow. He would have given a thousand lives for a drop of the wine of meeting. But the wisest leeches were powerless to cure him, and his friends had given up the attempt to help him. No doctor can minister to the sickness of love, for nothing can relieve it but the touch of the well beloved . . . One evening when, weary of life, this man walked abroad, he suddenly encountered a night watchman who began to dog his footsteps. He tried to escape, but the watchman pursued him, and called for help, so that ere long the man was surrounded. Terror-stricken, he said to himself : ' Is it Azrael, the Angel of Death, who thus pursues me, or is it some wicked enemy of the human race ? ' At length, this victim of love, after many adventures, came to a garden wall, which he scaled with great difficulty. Wishing to make an end of himself, he threw himself into the garden from the top of this high wall. But what a wonderful sight awaited him there ! His beloved, lamp in hand, was searching for a ring she had mislaid. He, who had lost his heart, and she, who had bereft him of it, were reunited . . ."

Thus, like other great mystics, Baha'u'llah derives from the experiences of human love the symbols that express divine love. Like them, too, he finds at times that all symbols are futile, and that ecstasy is ineffable : " These examples are for the vulgar. Those who are exalted above the need of such comparisons, those who are seated upon the magic carpet of detachment, those who have pitched their tent in the world of the absolute—have made a bonfire of all such comparisons, and have obliterated all words . . . Language is incompetent to express the splendours of the last three valleys through which the traveller passes. No pen can do justice to them, and to attempt their description is to waste ink and paper. The nightingale of the heart sings another song, and it is another mystery which moves the soul ; but only the soul can say them to the soul, and the heart to the heart."[1]

Nevertheless, Baha'u'llah is continually finding it necessary to return to the use of symbolic language, as the only instrument of exhortation and the only road of persuasion. He multiplies warnings and appeals, that he may keep people on the alert ; for, as the ancient books tell us, the spirit breathes on us when it pleases, and we must be ready to receive it. Now, perchance, is the appointed hour ; to-morrow may be too late : " The day will come when the nightingales of paradise will fly away from the pure garden towards their divine nests. No longer will you hear their song ; no longer will you see the beauty of the rose ! "[2] . . . " How many mornings, coming towards you from the east of the Infinite, have I found you stretched upon the bed of negligence, concerned with another than myself ; and I have turned away, as the spiritual lightning-flash turns away from the images which portray the splendour of God."[3]

[1] The foregoing extracts are from The Seven Valleys, in Hidden Words.
[2] The Book of Certainty.   [3] Hidden Words.

Such is the new voice that sounds to us from Asia ; such is the new dawn in the East. We should give them our close attention ; we should abandon our customary mood of disdainful superiority. Doubtless, Baha'u'llah's teaching is not definitive. The Persian prophet does not offer it to us as such. Nor can we Europeans assimilate all of it ; for modern science leads us to make certain claims in matters of thought—claims we cannot relinquish, claims we should not try to forgo. But even though Baha'u'llah's precepts (like those of the Gospels) may not fully satisfy all these intellectual demands, they are rarely in conflict with our scientific outlooks. If they are to become our own spiritual food, they must be supplemented, they must be relived by the religious spirits of Europe, must be rethought by minds schooled in the western mode of thought. But, in its existing form, Bahaist teaching may serve, amid our present chaos, to open for us a road leading to solace and to comfort ; may restore our confidence in the spiritual destiny of man. It reveals to us how the human mind is in travail ; it gives us an inkling of the fact that the greatest happenings of the day are not the ones we were inclined to regard as the most momentous, not the ones which are making the loudest noise.[1]

[1] Abdul Baha died at Haifa on November 28, 1921. His grandson Shoghi Effendi thereupon (by Abdul Baha's will) became " Guardian of the Cause," i.e. spiritual chief of the Bahaist movement. Shoghi Effendi was at this time twenty-five years of age, and was studying at Balliol College, Oxford.—E. & C. P.

LA CHAPELLE SUR CAROUGE NEAR GENEVA.
    April 1917.

THE LINGUISTIC INTERNATIONAL
(ESPERANTO)

(" La Feuille," Geneva,
February 19, 1920.)

THOUGHT, and its expression, language, are so intimately interconnected that it is hard to conceive of an international thought without an equally international language. In theory, the two things can be separated ; in practice, they are one. Again and again it has been recognised that when the workers of different nations come together, what separates them more than anything else is the insurmountable obstacle of the diversity of tongues. We meet one whom we call " brother " or " comrade," and we urgently desire to come into intimate contact with him ; but if we find it difficult to understand what he says, he remains a stranger. We should learn to speak one another's languages ? Excellent advice, but advice hard to follow since life is short. Even if we confine ourselves to the most widely spoken languages of western Europe, to English and French and German, we have worlds to conquer. The manual worker, who can spare so little time for such studies, may, at a pinch, learn how to read these languages, but he will hardly ever learn to speak them. And there are so many other languages, of which he cannot learn even the alphabet. The value of an international language is made obvious by these considerations.

There are several international languages of long standing, languages which function admirably. To say nothing of the natural expression of the emotions by means of cries and gestures, we have the marvellous tongue of music, competent to express the whole gamut of human feeling. In another domain there is algebra, as a universal expression of abstract thought. These examples give sufficient proof that an international language is possible. But music expresses nothing more than sentiments and emotions; algebra is restricted to the domain of pure abstraction. There is an intermediate domain, that of everyday life, where abstract intelligence is continually mingled with sensibility—the domain of language in the ordinary sense of the word. Every language is simultaneously emotional and logical; that is why languages are, in general, the most adequate expression of what we wish to say. In a word, a language is nothing but a synthesis of these two forms of expression. Its logic is given by its grammar, and its emotional content by its poetry. Now, inasmuch as an international language can exist for logical expression and for emotional expression taken separately, it is difficult to see what apriori objection there can be to a complete international language.

Besides, apriori objections are out of court, seeing that the international language lives and works. Esperanto answers all the requirements of a complete language. What we might dread in the case of an artificial language would be to find its music sacrificed to its algebra. This has, in fact, been the trouble with most of the international languages manufactured of late years. That is what is amiss with Ido and with the other heretical varieties of Esperanto. Romain Rolland, a great artist, saw at a glance the essential difference between Esperanto and these jigsaw puzzles. Esperanto, says Rolland, is a " literary language." Ido, on the other hand, is " the perfect but cold product of mathematical skill." The distinction is admirably drawn. The difference between Ido and Esperanto is the difference between mechanism and life, the difference between talent and genius. Esperanto is alive, viable ; it is the discovery of a man of genius ; and it is simple, like every work of genius. Ido is the arbitrary product of a scientific board, which can work satisfactorily enough when the aim is to produce, let us say, a chemical nomenclature. Esperanto is the output of one man and one life. While still at school, Zamenhof had conceived his great idea and had·decided to devote all his energies to it. He discovered his language "by continually thinking about it," as Newton said when speaking of his own discoveries.[1] That is why Esperanto does not give the impression of being an arbitrary product. It is like a force of nature, something that wells up spontaneously. That is the explanation of its suppleness, of its spontaneous success, of its increasing vitality. That explains why it is possible to produce in Esperanto such excellent translations of the masterpieces of all languages.

Suppleness and vigour are admirably wedded to ease, to the simplicity of a grammar which is extremely logical and in which there are no exceptions. Any one who is already acquainted with one of the Latin tongues and one of the Teutonic tongues, can learn to read Esperanto in a few days. Even if he lacks this groundwork, a few weeks' study will suffice. Esperanto gives us the impression of being a work of art ; of being a splendid piece of architecture, with clear outlines, unembarrassed by excess of ornament ; so that we ask ourselves how anything so beautiful can be constructed out of such scanty materials.

It is a pleasure to see that Esperanto, whose development was, of course, hindered by the war, has taken a fresh

---

[1] "His discoveries were . . . the fruit of persevering and unbroken study ; and he himself declared, that whatever service he had done to the public was not owing to any extraordinary sagacity, but solely to industry and patient thought." David Brewster, Memoirs of the Life, Writings, and Discoveries of Sir Isaac Newton, Edmonton & Douglas, second edition, 1860, Vol. II, p. 324.—E. & C. P.

stride forward. We note with delight, too, that the Esperantists and the internationally organised workers are joining hands. Edmond Privat is about to give a lecture at the Workers' University in Geneva, on the Workers and the International Language, It may be hoped that this will mark a new departure, and that henceforward there will be an active interchange of ideas and energies between the representatives of the international spirit and the representatives of the international language. To its other advantages, Esperanto will add that of being a means by which straightforward persons can secure direct information as to what is going on in foreign lands, without being dependent upon the untrustworthy translations of a dishonest press. The international language will make for the diffusion of truth as well as for the diffusion of sympathy and mutual aid.

WILLIAM JAMES' "TALKS TO TEACHERS ON PSYCHOLOGY" [1]

("La Feuille," Geneva, September 5, 12, 26, and
October 3, 1919.)

THE name and the writings of William James have become
widely known outside the land of his birth. He was professor at Harvard University, at first of physiology, then of
psychology, and finally of philosophy. It was as a psychologist that he became famous, for he made many important
contributions to psychological science, and had the rare
faculty of being able to write on this subject without pedantry.
Having an intimate sense of the meaning of life, in his scientific work he always maintained close contact with life.
He had an admirable and very unusual capacity for ridding
himself of the abstractions and presuppositions which are
apt to intervene between the observer and the object of
study. Thus he entered into direct relationships with
phenomena, contemplating them with that simplicity of
outlook which is characteristic of the truly scientific genius.
His intimate communion with reality led him to some
very remarkable discoveries.

Like most of the Anglo-Saxon philosophers, he is an
"empiricist" by temperament. Abstract ideas, ratio-
cinative processes, do not seem to him to offer sufficient
guarantees. He wants direct experience, first, last, and all
the time. He finds experiment and observation indispensable. His own powers of observation are remarkably
acute, and they are aided by the sympathetic intuition

[1] Talks to Teachers on Psychology and to Students on some of Life's
Ideals, Longmans, London, 1899.

without which there can be no genuine science of the human mind. Now, the first thing which observation reveals to James is that the mind is not an assemblage of clear-cut facts of consciousness, juxtaposed like chemical atoms Consciousness is a flux, a complex and elusive continuity, which language and thought artificially break up into fragments. Where a more superficial science sees everything as fixed, sharply defined, and cold, James reintroduces life and movement.

Another of the guiding lines of his thought is his inclination to regard the mind from what he terms a "biological" outlook. This rounds off his substitution of the dynamic for the static. Where others have seen only mental "phenomena," isolated mental "facts" lacking intimate connexion with antecedent and subsequent facts, he sees the manifestations of mental "functions" which are themselves related to bodily functions, and he holds that the functions of both kinds are subject to the law of evolution and to the law of adaptation to the environment. This biological outlook, new in psychology when it was first advocated by James, has now been universally adopted, and has given an entirely new orientation to the science.

Another of James' leading trends is "pragmatism"—to use the term commonly applied to his philosophy. This pragmatism has a natural kinship with the biological and evolutionary outlooks. The mind, being a bundle of functions, is an organ by means of which the organism is enabled to adapt itself to its environment. The mind has a practical part to play, even more than a speculative part. A thought is not completely understood unless we look upon it in the light of the "active" consequences which result from it sooner or later. The significance of thought is its tendency towards action—πρᾶγμα. This philosophy may be regarded as typically American, but it is American in the best sense of the word. For the " action," the " practice," of which James is speaking, must itself be understood in a comprehensive and lofty sense.

The three guiding trends of James' thought, the empiricist, the biological, and the pragmatist, influence all the educational ideas which he expounds in his *Talks to Teachers on Psychology*. These give the stamp of originality to this little book, which is simply and clearly written, so that it can easily be understood by every one who has educational work to do. It is not a difficult treatise compiled for pedagogical experts. The " talks " should be read by parents as well as by professional teachers.

James' *empiricism*, being very much alive and anything but pedantic, could not find complete satisfaction in " experimental psychology," which its introducers (especially in Germany) looked upon as signalising a revolution in psychological science. James did not repudiate this laboratory psychology, with all its ingenious apparatus for recording " reaction time " ; for measuring memory, attention, work, and imagination. But he had no superstitious faith in the new method. He thought that these laboratory experiments were only of use when their results were coordinated with those secured by the customary methods of direct observation, and that the latter could not be superseded by reaction-time experiments, etc. From an educationist's outlook, in especial, he insisted that we should err if we were to base our judgment of a child's intelligence on laboratory measurements of its faculties.

His first criticism of the reaction timers is that their work is done under conditions remote from those characteristic of normal life. If the experimenter wishes to measure the strength of a child's memory, a series of drawings, more or less trivial, may be shown to the subject at fixed intervals.

The child, perhaps, has no interest in these drawings, and its memory is recorded as poor. But the same child would be found to have an excellent memory if matters arousing its lively interest were in question :

" This preponderance of interest, of passion, in determining the results of a human being's working life, obtains throughout. No elementary measurement, capable of being performed in a laboratory, can throw any light on the actual efficiency of the subject ; for the vital thing about him, his emotional and moral energy and doggedness, can be measured by no single experiment, and becomes known only by the total results in the long run."[1]

On the other hand, and from a more general outlook, the human mind is a living synthesis, whereas measurements of the faculties are necessarily analytical. When we have measured this or that faculty, the synthesis, which is something very different from a simple mathematical total, will have escaped us. However great the theoretical value of such measurements, educationists must not be misled by their fragmentary exactness. What the teacher has to deal with is a child, a living organism. The child can only be understood and appraised by one who sees it living and working, by one who lives in company with the child.

James tells us that, while psychology is a science, teaching is an art. We must not imagine that a good knowledge of psychological science is all the equipment required by the teacher. The latter has still to cross the frontier which separates science from life.

" Sciences never generate arts directly out of themselves. An intermediary inventive mind must make the application by using its originality."[2]

Psychological science is to pedagogy what the science of tactics is to the art of warfare, what the science of

[1] Op. cit., pp. 134–5.   [2] Op. cit., pp. 7–8.

perspective is to the art of the landscape painter, what logic is to the reason when actually at work, what the abstract theory of ethics is to the life of the good man.

The part which a knowledge of psychology has to play in pedagogy is substantially negative ; the role is one of limitation, of safe-guarding from error. From the study of psychology, the educationist may learn that there is a definite field of action within which he must work if he is to avoid making mistakes. But, inside these boundaries, everything is left to his personal initiative.

James' *biological* outlook gave him an especial aptitude for the study of the instincts. He came to look upon many of the phenomena of consciousness as fugitive manifestations of deep-rooted and persistent instincts. To an evolutionist, moreover, instinct, which the psychologists of an earlier day regarded as immutable, must necessarily seem subject to change. Indeed, if we believe extant species to have grown out of other forms, inasmuch as the instincts differ in different species, we are forced to conclude that the instincts, no less than the organs, have become what they are thanks to a process of transformation.

The recognition that instincts are malleable, completely modifies the educationist's attitude towards them. It used to be supposed that the only way of dealing with instincts was to repress them. Instinct must either be subjugated or forcibly repressed. In either case, the teacher had no need to learn much about the instincts. To-day, however, we know that it is necessary to gain an intimate knowledge of instinct, in order that we may be enabled to modify it and educate it, in order that we may learn how to graft derived instincts upon crude and primitive instincts. In-stinct, which was looked upon as an enemy, has become an ally. That is why James devotes some of the most important of his *Talks* to the topic of instinct (Chapters V-VII, on " Reactions ").

He lays considerable stress upon a law based on Spalding's experiments on chickens. If newly hatched chicks are hooded directly they emerge from the shell, they never develop the " following instinct." When the hood is removed after the lapse of a few days, they do not follow the mother hen like an ordinary brood. The inference is that this follow-ing instinct, which seems to persist in the young birds for quite a long time, is in reality no more than transient ; its persistence is not instinctive, but is merely the outcome of habit. The instinct normally appears immediately after hatching, but if it is prevented from becoming operative at this time, the " following habit " is not formed, and the " instinct " passes into abeyance. Spalding's discovery as regards chicks would appear to have its counterpart in the case of many other instincts. We infer that, if they are to become active, most of the instincts must enter into play at a definite phase of development. Where we are dealing with a desirable instinct, we must encourage its practice at the favourable time. When the instinct is an undesirable one, the educator's business is to see that, at the critical moment, it does not become operative.

Thus, the instinct of curiosity (which is extremely active in the child, and upon which all instruction is based) has phases which are so different that we may almost speak of different instincts of curiosity. Each of these has its appro-priate epoch, and the educationist must know how to take advantage of the fact. First of all the child develops a curiosity of the senses, then a curiosity of the intellect, and of diverse fields of intelligence. We shall economise labour if we know how to grasp the favourable moment. Here James comes back by a new route to something which Rousseau had intuitively perceived. Like Rousseau, he advises us, as far as young children are concerned, to pay special attention to the education of the senses. Intellectual curiosity has not yet ripened ; and when it does ripen, the phase of sensual curiosity will have been surpassed. There is in early childhood a vivacity of the sense organs which cannot be won in later years. During the years of adolescence, again, we must acquire the art of handling certain tools, must win facility in particular kinds of manual work. If we do not put our hands to such matters until after we are grown up, we are not likely to become deft. One who has failed to exercise his senses during childhood and to train his hands during adolescence, is likely to be characterised throughout life by an incurable detachment from the real and the practical.

James devotes special attention to the imitative impulse, which the teacher must know how to utilise to the best advantage. He also refers to the fighting instinct which, in the form of emulation and a struggle to overcome obstacles, gives children hardiness and zeal. James is of virile type. Like so many thinkers of the New World, he has the spirit of the pioneer, of those who explored the virgin forests of America, and made clearings in which to dwell. He criticises modern methods of education in so far as they tend to make things too easy for the child, to stimulate interest unduly, to bring about a hothouse development of all that the teacher expects from the child. There is good in these methods, but sometimes their aim is impossible of attainment ; and at other times, when they are pushed too far, they tend to sap the energies. The invigorating ozone has vanished from this stuffy atmosphere. James is moved to enter a protest against Rousseau's censure of emulation. He is a follower of Darwin, and is full of the idea of the struggle for life. This struggle is a source of energy. It can be, and should be, sublimated ; it can become something very different from a brutal and hate-inspired struggle. Nevertheless, life must remain a struggle.

" Constructiveness," which is especially active up to the age of eight or nine must be encouraged at the appropriate time. The instinct of ownership, rooted in human nature is, like the fighting instinct, a potent source of energy, and must not be indiscriminately condemned. It must be given an intellectual turn, and will then be particularly fruitful in instruction ; it should be encouraged to become the collector's instinct, which is already far on the way to being an instinct for science. " Probably nobody ever became a good naturalist who was not an unusually active collector as a boy."[1]

Here we have an example of the art of grafting, which must be one of the talents possessed by the " gardener of children."

James' *pragmatism* has likewise had its effect upon his educational theories. His inclination to look, on every occasion, for the continuation of thought into action, leads him to lay especial stress upon the motor reactions which are the normal results of the impressions we receive from without. The empiricists of earlier days used to say : " Nihil est in intellectu quod non prius fuerit in sensu." (There is nothing in the intellect [thought] which has not previously been in the senses.) James, as a pragmatist empiricist, would add : " Moreover, there is nothing in thought which does not subsequently find expression in action." For him, the prototype of all the processes of life is the reflex action, wherein an impression coming from without is conveyed by an afferent nerve to a nerve centre, and is " reflected " therefrom in the form of a motor reaction transmitted along an efferent nerve.

[1] Op. cit., p. 58.

Educationists, says James, must never ignore this point of view. They err whenever they hinder normal reaction. Nay more, it is their duty to assist and cultivate such reactions.

" One general aphorism emerges which ought by logical right to dominate the entire conduct of the teacher in the classroom : *No reception without reaction, no impression without correlative expression*—this is the great maxim which the teacher ought never to forget."[1]

In fact, when we have to do with the cycle " sensation —thought—reaction," we find that no one term of the cycle is complete unless it be as a function of the two others. The three are inseparable. Thus thought is not fully itself if it has no outward reaction. An impression which has merely entered by the eye or the ear does not leave a well-marked trace upon the memory. The fixation which converts it into a valuable experience comes through its reaction in words, or better still, in deeds. We must, therefore, encourage the child to talk ; to tell us what it has seen, heard, and understood. Even more valuable is the result of encouraging the child to act, to apply what it has just experienced. Deeds are a fuller reaction than words. The child's answer may seem above criticism, and may nevertheless be purely verbal ; the words have been retained, but in the child's mind they are represented by nothing more than self-created fantasies remote from the real meaning. Action is the touchstone. One who has to act, can no longer hide ignorance or gloss over vagueness of thought.

This is why manual work, the application of theoretical knowledge, is also the most satisfactory test of that knowledge, and its natural crown. James considers that practical work of this kind cannot be too highly esteemed.

" The most colossal improvement which recent years

[1] Op. cit., p. 33.

have seen in secondary education lies in the introduction of
the manual training schools ; not because they will give us
a people more handy and practical for domestic life, and
better skilled in trades, but because they will give us citizens
with an entirely different intellectual fibre."[1]

This principle of reaction is good for the teacher as well
as for the pupil. It is a familiar fact that the pupil is always
more interested in what the teacher does than in what the
teacher says. When experiments are going on, the class is
spontaneously disciplined. The teacher, therefore, must,
as far as possible, illustrate his words by practical work,
if it be only by drawing or writing on the blackboard. This
practice of encouraging reaction both on the part of the
teacher and on the part of the pupil, ensures the pupil's
attention, and relieves the teacher of a great part of his
task as disciplinarian.

Finally, as we might expect, James' pragmatism makes
him attach extreme importance to the education of the will.
All his educational theories converge towards this point.
Just as a particular action is always the natural climax of
a particular thought, so, generally speaking, the will is the
complement and the crown of the intelligence. But, conversely, the " will " as James understands it, is permeated
with intelligence ; its most fundamental element is attention
rather than muscular effort. This is an extremely important
notion, and is closely akin to the conclusion towards which
the study of suggestion has recently led the psychologists
of the New Nancy School. James speaks most emphatically
upon this subject, showing us once more that his pragmatism
is catholic in its scope, and that he is far from being inclined
to sacrifice (as he has sometimes been accused of sacrificing)
thought to action, mind to muscle.

" If then, you are asked, ' *In what does a moral act consist*

[1] Op. cit., p. 35.

when reduced to its simplest and most elementary form ? ' you can make only one reply. You can say that *it consists in the effort of attention by which we hold fast to an idea* which, but for that effort of attention, would be driven out of the mind by the other psychological tendencies that are there. *To think*, in short, is the secret of will, just as it is the secret of memory."[1]

A little later he expresses the same idea in a yet more incisive form :

" The power of voluntarily attending is the point of the whole procedure. Just as a balance turns on its knife-edges, so on it our moral destiny turns."[2]

These *Talks* leave upon the reader's mind an impression of virility and energy. But the energy is not of the kind which spends itself in violent and disorderly action ; it is calm, self-contained, throned upon thought. It is a characteristic product of American philosophy. Upon a lower plane, and voiced from the pulpit of those who preach to the crowd, this philosophy reiterates assertions concerning " the power of thought." Upon a higher plane, it secures living expression in the forceful parables of Emerson.

Indeed, James seems often to speak with Emerson's voice, so that we wonder whether we are listening to James or to Emerson :

" We are spinning our own fates, good or evil, and never to be undone."[3]

Again, like Emerson, James makes use of everyday images, which simultaneously recall ancient parables and modern life with its press of business and its hum of machinery.

" Be systematically heroic in little, unnecessary points. Do every day or two something for no other reason than its

[1] Op. cit., pp. 186-7.　　　　[2] Op. cit., p. 188.
[3] Op. cit., p. 77.

11

difficulty, so that, when the hour of dire need draws nigh, it may find you not unnerved and untrained to stand the test. Asceticism of this sort is like the insurance which a man pays on his house and goods. The tax does him no good at the time, and possibly may never bring him a return. But if the fire *does* come, his having paid it will be his salvation from ruin. So with the man who has daily inured himself to habits of concentrated attention, energetic volition, and self-denial in unnecessary things. He will stand like a tower when everything rocks around him, and his softer fellow mortals are winnowed like chaff in the blast."[1]

Could we finish on a better note ? Or rather, not " finish." Following James' advice, we shall allow the " reaction " to follow. Let us be up and doing !

[1] Op. cit., pp. 75-6.

FATHER CHRISTMAS

("La Feuille," Geneva,
December 19, 1919.)

FATHER CHRISTMAS, poor, old chap, I am going to undertake his defence. That of all his family, too : the Infant
Jesus ; Saint Nicholas wearing a mitre and carrying
a golden crozier ; Easter Bells which lay coloured eggs.
I seem to hear voices raised in protest : " You are on
dangerous ground ; it is always dangerous for parents to
tell lies to their children." Are not these tragedy airs
somewhat out of place ? The matter is not so serious as you
imply. Such little marvels are quite harmless ; they may
even make for good.

In Father Christmas and his companions we are merely
confronted with a particular case of a general problem
(what learned words about a ¡retty piece of imagery !).
The problem—for indeed there is a problem—is : Should
we or should we not banish fiction from the lives of our
children ? Are fairy tales unwholesome ?

Let us first agree, without claiming to be original dis-
coverers, that children love fairy tales. Their eyes sparkle
as they listen to such tales, and all marvels are a delight
to children. There can be no doubt that these things answer
to an instinct of the child. Now, the newer science of
education leads us to believe that a child's instincts ought
to be satisfied. They must be guided, of course ; but we
should not simply repress them. Repression was the method
of the pedagogy of former days. The schoolmaster was an
autocrat, and issued a ukase regarding the instincts, like

the ukase which forbade the Poles to use their own language. The autocrat made a mistake, for the Poles were Poles all the more; and the instincts were all the stronger. Or, if they were, indeed, effectively annihilated, there was a corresponding loss of energy.

In actual fact, the child's love for fairy tales and marvels is of precisely the same nature as its love for games. Play, too, is fiction. When playing, the child plays to itself fairy tales that are more or less fantastic; staged in the nursery, the garden, or wherever player-and-audience happens to be for the moment. Continually the child is renewing the magical deed of the fairy who changes a pumpkin into a gilded coach. A little bench becomes a house; a piece of wood, a person; a tuft of grass, a bundle of carrots. It is difficult to decide how far the child believes in its own inventions. If we may generalise from the example of Spitteler, who has preserved exceptionally vivid memories of his own childhood, young folk retain a clearer realisation of fact than their elders sometimes suppose. But the child enters into the illusion quite enough to take it seriously for the nonce, quite as much as the audience at a theatre—and this is to go a considerable way, for many of us shed real tears at the fancied sorrows that are being played before us. The child's mythopeic faculty may help us to understand a good many things that children do. Consider, for instance, the apparent cruelty of a child. I knew a little boy who pulled off the wings of a butterfly, and who, when scolded for it, answered quietly: " I was transferring him from the air-force into the infantry." The kinship between the fairy tale and play is exceedingly close. We may say that the fairy tale is an imaginary and passive game, whereas a game is an active fairy tale. If we study the two phenomena, the love of fairy tales and the love of play, as expressions of instinct, we shall grasp the underlying rationale of their kinship. Karl Groos, whose books *The Play of Man* [1] and *The Play of Animals* [2] have become classics, has shown that play is an expenditure of surplus energy, stored up by instincts which have made their appearance before the individual really needs them. In like manner, the psychoanalysts have shown that the fantasies of adults (whether self-induced, or the reproductions of the imaginative creations of artists) give indirect satisfaction to instincts which have been repressed, because their full gratification is no longer expedient in the conditions under which we live. Is not this a very remarkable parallel? Does it not seem obvious that educationists must regard the need for fairy tales and the need for play as having an equal right to existence?

As far as play is concerned, the new education has definitely made its choice. No one denies that children must play; that play is a factor in the child's development; that play helps education, and does not hinder it. The modern school-room is a playroom, a room in which the pupils play games under the intelligent guidance of their teacher. Groos' biological interpretation of play justifies this trend of education. Similarly, we must agree that the biological interpretation of fantasy which psychoanalysis has supplied, justifies the use of fantasy as a method of education. If the latter inference is still disputed, there are two reasons for this. In the first place, the psychoanalytical explanation of fantasy is not yet generally understood. Secondly, in the fluid world of wonderland, the phenomena are less tangible than in the comparatively material domain of play.

We have still one objection to consider. Those who

[1] Die Spiele der Menschen, Jena, 1899; English translation by E. L. Baldwin, The Play of Man, New York, 1901.
[2] Die Spiele der Tiere, Jena, 1896; English translation by E. L. Baldwin, The Play of Animals. Chapman & Hall, London, 1898.

reprove us for telling our children fairy tales, continually recur to this point : " Parents must not tell lies."

But is a fairy tale a lie ? Nothing of the sort. A fairy tale is a myth, a dream, a work of art. The psychoanalysts have shown that day-dreams, the fantasies of waking life, are very closely allied to ordinary dreams. Herein we find the solution of our problem of conscience. If the child, after being told a fairy tale, should ask : " But is it true ? "— what can be simpler than to answer : " It is a dream " ? The child will understand perfectly what you mean. Furthermore, I speak from experience when I say that this answer will not destroy the child's pleasure in the tale. At a somewhat later stage, you will be able to pass from the notion of the dream to that of the legend. The pleasure will persist. The need for truth and the need for fiction are entirely distinct in the child's mind. Both are desirable, and both are worthy of cultivation. The former is the germ of the scientific spirit, and the latter is the germ of the artistic spirit. Coming back to Chalande [1] we have to admit that in this case the question of " falsehood " is somewhat more complicated than in the case of a fairy tale. But even here, there is no justification for talking of a lie. In all these ancient traditions we find symbols of eternal realities. As far as our present psychological knowledge enables us to interpret the legend of Father Christmas, it would seem that this myth concerning gifts brought silently during the night is a duplex symbol of the mute germination of nature beneath the snow and of that other germination (no less mute) of the treasures that slumber in the unconscious depths of our souls. As long as the child is still incapable of understanding the nature of a symbol, let us leave the ingenuous belief undisturbed. In due time, gently, and by degrees, we shall lead the child to understand the nature of

[1] The name of Father Christmas in Geneva.—E. & C. P.

the truth hidden beneath the fable. We need not perplex him, as yet, with the philosophical and folklorist implications of the myth ! But we can tell him that loving parents watch over his slumbers ; we can relate to him the pretty story of Bethlehem ; perhaps (why not ?) we can explain to him how, beneath winter's snows, the earth is rich with the promise of spring. If we know how to present the matter skilfully, I will go bail that the child's feelings will be touched, and that there will be no sense of loss when understanding replaces faith. Nothing could be simpler than to make the child see the value of the ritual according to which the gifts are placed on the hearth. It is a feast day, and that is part of the ceremony. Every child knows the meaning of a feast day, and its symbolism ; knows that the seven candles on the birthday cake represent seven years ; knows that the familiar neighbour, who figures dressed up in a procession, represents a historic personage. It resembles the child's own games. All art is like a game—the saying is an old one. These myths of childhood are the first steps in artistic education.

The child's education must be permeated with artistic education. There can be no real education without poesy. Moreover, those who would understand the child, and perhaps those who would be understood by the child, must be poets, as the child itself is a poet. Substantially this is what Pierre Bovet tells us.[1] Every true teacher has the soul of an artist. The teacher who is lacking in this respect can hardly—I say it unhesitatingly—be regarded as an expert in the profession.

[1] See his preface to Artus-Perrelet's Le dessin au service de l'éducation. Delachaux & Niestlé, Neuchâtel and Paris.

PART FOUR

ART AND CRITICISM

THE COMING POETRY

AN ESSAY ON THE TRENDS OF FRENCH POETRY IMMEDIATELY AFTER THE WAR. REALISM, SYMBOLISM, AND DYNAMISM [1]

(" La Nervie," Brussels and Paris,
January to May 1922.)

WE have been waiting for several years   It was impossible, we said to ourselves, that the war, the " great war," could pass across the world without (thanks to the noise it made) starting a flight of masterpieces. Would it not transfuse some red blood into our over-refined, morbid, Alexandrian art ? There had been such a universal shaking-up of things ; such an overplus of passion, suffering, and hope ; such a wealth of stimulating experiences. Our poetry had been wilting in a hot-house. More and more we were being haunted by our " terribly civilised old nerves."[2] The word of command had been issued : " For the novel, bar-barians are needed ! " Among our young writers there had

[1] This essay on The Coming Poetry was penned as a lecture which was delivered at Geneva in April 1921 and at Salzburg in August 1921. I have not attempted to expound the aesthetic theories of this or that poet. My aim has not been to define personalities or groups, but rather to sketch salient trends, of which the individuals selected for treatment are conspicuous representatives. But a personality is something very different from a pawn, and no one could be more fully convinced than I am that criticism which confines itself to the study of " movements " is both incomplete and shallow. This is but a minor part of the critic's task. Furthermore, I have deliberately restricted my outlook to that of a snapshot taken " immediately after the war." Obviously, therefore, I am far from claiming to offer a finished study. The chief place, too, is given, not to writers of established reputation, but to the youngest among our contemporary poets, and I have considered their reach rather than their grasp—for my design was, above all, to foreshadow developments, to describe the *coming poetry*.

[2] Théo Varlet, Villégiature, in Poèmes choisis, 1912.

171

sounded like an echo : " And for poetry, too, barbarians are needed ! " Emerson has told us that we are sometimes cursed by having our prayers granted !

In 1914 the barbarians came, bringing their barbarism with them. This barbarism made an end of Louvain ; it wounded Rheims and Venice. Secular works of art perished just as men perished. There was enough destruction to delight all the futurists on earth, to delight those who used to talk of " breaking up the Louvre." (Be it noted that these futurists did not sing hymns of rejoicing when the crash came. They were all " good patriots." Those who had been " renégats de toute paternité " were not even futurist enough to repudiate the " fatherland.") Thus did the great works of old perish ; but new works were long in coming.

They came at length ; and, behold, they did not sing the glories of war ! They did not sound a clarion call to the " Soldiers of the Year Two ! Wars ! Epics ! " They were anything but bellicose, these writings which issued from the war. They reeked of the trenches ; they portrayed the terrible desolation of the rain falling upon ground soaked with black blood. In 1917 appeared Barbusse's *Le feu*[1]—a revelation from the pit, a ray of light from the mud. There was no mistaking it ; this was a book of the war. The tone had been set. The more clear-sighted perceived it from the first. The thing awaited had come ! But like all great things for which people have been waiting —like love and like pain—how different it was from what had been expected ! What was the supreme revelation of *Le feu* ? It made people realise that the art which was to issue from the war would not sound a paean, but would fulminate a curse. It might, indeed, be epic ; but it

---

[1] Le feu, journal d'un escouade, Paris, 1916. For English translation, see Bibliography.

would be epic after the manner of the *Inferno*, and not after the manner of the *Iliad*.

The note which Barbusse voiced in prose, was sounded, likewise, by the poets. Mark the surly horror of Georges Chennevière's *Ravitaillement* :

> Sur la route qui s'élargit de jour en jour,
> Inonde les champs, et semble écarter les arbres,
> Sur la route défigurée aux trous boueux,
> Où croupit l'urine, où s'infusent des décombres,
> Le long des murs croulants et des maisons vidées,
> Auxquelles a mordu sans goût la dent du feu,
> Passent, éclaboussant les talus qui se fondent,
> Des files de camions chargés de viande humaine.[1]

> [On the road which widens day by day,
> Invading the fields, and seeming to thrust the trees aside ;
> On the road disfigured by muddy potholes
> Where urine stagnates, where garbage rots,
> Beside tottering walls and deserted houses
> Into which the tooth of fire has bitten remorselessly,
> There pass, splashing the crumbling slopes,
> Files of lorries laden with human flesh.]

Marcello Fabri has written an essay whose title and contents are equally characteristic of the art of our day. It is called *Essai sur l'œuvre d'art considérée comme une réaction* (An Essay upon the Work of Art regarded as a Reaction.)[2]

To summarise, he says that the work of art is a reaction to the environment of the day. The statement may seem somewhat categorical. Yet how true is the formula as far as the art of our own epoch is concerned. Even if it be not true of art in general, the art of the present time is a reaction, is a protest ; for, unquestionably, art is soul,

---

[1] Anthologie des poètes contre la guerre, Editions du Sablier, Geneva, 1920 ; Georges Chennevière, Poèmes 1911-1918, La Maison des Amis des Livres, Paris, 1920.

[2] " Revue de l'Epoque," Paris, October 1920.

and our age has no soul. This protest may be active or passive. In the active form, it is, says Fabri, an " aggression " ; in the passive form, it is an " evasion " or an " elevation." We learn from the study of biology that when a living creature is threatened by an enemy, either of two instinctive attitudes may be adopted : the threatened animal may take to flight ; or, on the other hand, it may stand at bay. The harsh realities of the years of war were hostile to the soul and to art. The soul and art were either in full flight from reality, or were at bay against reality. The poets of the time have adopted one of these attitudes or the other. As the outcome of the war, therefore, there have appeared two strongly marked and sometimes conflicting trends, which even before the war had been discernible among our poets. If we confine our attention to the main currents, if we ignore exceptions, and do not pause to gaze open-mouthed at the battalions of the mere spouters of verse, we may say that the poets of the new time can be classified as the " aggressives " and the " evaders." The former are the *Realists*, and the latter are the *Symbolists*. It is probable that most of our poets would refuse to accept these labels. Nevertheless, the terms are clear and simple, and I shall adopt them here in their widest signification, and not as the mere labels of a faction.

1. Whitmanesque Realism.

When I speak of Realists, I am not thinking of the successors of the Realist school of novelists, which flourished (or raged, if the term be preferred) during the latter half of the nineteenth century. My Realists are poets, who, not being novelists, certainly do not belong to this school. Nor, when I write about Realist poetry, do I want my readers to think of François Coppée, who wrote

realistic novels in verse. This form of poetry is preeminently
dangerous, for the verse is foredoomed to be prosaic unless
sustained by a vigorous inspiration. (Victor Hugo was
successful with his *Pauvres gens*—but perhaps his success
was a misfortune, for there have been many imitations of
Pauvres gens, poor ones, anything but successful.) The
Realists with whom I am concerned have nothing in common
with the paintings of the Dutch school, nor with Balzac's
" inventories " ; to play the auctioneer is not their vocation.
My meaning is, that their poetry deals with what we are
accustomed to speak of as reality, the real world—though
the inner world is no less real. But it would be superfluous
to define " reality " in contradistinction to the " dream " ;
in contradistinction to those wondrous images which,
hidden from others, pass by and disappear within the
mind of every one of us. When we speak of a Realist,
let us think of a man with windows open towards the world,
towards tangible reality, towards that which is flesh and
blood, substantial, common to us all. In this sense, the
most typical of realist poets is Walt Whitman :

> I say I bring thee Muse to-day and here,
> All occupations, duties broad and close,
> Toil, healthy toil and sweat, endless, without cessation.
>
> .   .   .   .
>
> This earth all spann'd with iron rails, with lines of steamships
>   threading every sea,
> Our own rondure, the current globe I bring.[1]

Without intending it, Walt Whitman founded a school,
for many of our younger poets proclaim themselves his
disciples. My " Realists " may just as well be named
Whitmanists. The " Unanimist " group, the poets of the
" Abbey," such as Duhamel, Romains, Arcos, and Vildrac,
form their centre. The innovation of the Whitmanists

---

[1] From Song of the Exposition, in Leaves of Grass.

finds expression, already, in the mere coupling of the two words " poetry " and " Realism." Almost always, hitherto, the domain of poetry has been an imaginary world ; whoever spoke of poetry, spoke, essentially, of fiction.[1] Before to-day, indeed, there has been Realism in Verse, but the verses were simply descriptive, and tended moment by moment to become unpoetical. The best of the descriptive poets were painters or sculptors in verse. I refer to the Parnassians.[2]

The modern Realists are not descriptive poets. They have an impetus towards the real, their inspiration is an arrow shot at the real ; what they depict is the trajectory of the arrow, not the target. If the actual object be described, it is shown as carried away by the impetus, as detached from the world to float upon the current of feeling. In descriptive poetry, on the other hand, the object is carefully arranged in its place among neighbouring objects. Realist poetry does not present things in a natural order, but capriciously, in a sequence determined by bursts of feeling. Let us hear Whitman once more :

You air that serves me with breath to speak !
You objects that call from diffusion my meanings and give
    them shape !
You light that wraps me and all things in delicate equable
    showers !
You paths worn in the irregular hollows by the roadsides !

    .   .   .   .

[1] We may recall that " poetry " is derived from ποιεῖν, to make ; and that " fiction " is derived from " fingere," to fashion. Thus the words are closely allied.

[2] " In the later sixties, with François Coppée, Sully-Prudhomme, Paul Verlaine, and others less distinguished, he (Heredia) made one of the band of poets who gathered round Leconte de Lisle, and received the name of ' Parnassien.' To this new school, form—the technical side of their art— was of supreme importance, and, in reaction against the influence of Musset, they rigorously repressed in their work the expression of personal feeling and emotion." Encyclopædia Britannica, eleventh edition, Vol xiii, p. 349. The names of Gautier, Baudelaire, and de Banville should be included in any representative list of the Parnassians.—E. & C. P.

You flagg'd walks of the cities! you strong curbs at the edges!
You ferries! you planks and posts of wharves! you timber-
   lined sides! you distant ships! [1]

All these images are realities, but the poet has no thought
of depicting a specific place which has been his model.
The contemporary Realist is not a copyist of the real.
He is in love with the real and he avows his love (or, as we
shall see, his hatred, which is akin to love). This is what
makes the Realist a poet. He is a poet because, instead of
slavishly following the order of reality, he regroups things
as fancy dictates. He takes the world to pieces, and uses
the pieces as a child uses toy bricks to build with; he
creates.

With an impetus towards things, the Whitmanist has,
above all, an impetus towards mankind—indeed, Iwan
Goll and others have proposed to term these poets
" Humanists." The Romanticists, and in especial the
Symbolists, whose energies are directed inwards, who are
enthralled by the rich hangings of imagery which curtain
the ancestral hall of the soul, live in a subjective and hidden
world. But outward reality, the teeming wealth which
the world offers so bounteously, this is the objective; this
is the heritage of us all; this, as René Arcos has phrased it,
is " the common good." The Romanticist and the
Symbolist have an aristocratic poise of mind; they have a
fastidious pride which makes them draw angrily away lest
their garments should be soiled by sacrilegious or evil-
smelling contacts. They are like a noblewoman who
withdraws into her oratory; a dignified gesture, which
may easily become ridiculous when it becomes the fashion.
(We need but recall the Romanticist manias; need but
think of the " grandes âmes," the " cœurs sensibles," and

[1] From Song of the Open Road, in Leaves of Grass.

the " âmes soeurs".) Whitman knows nothing of this fastidiousness or of this pride. He is of the people, and wishes to be of the people. He takes up his parable regardless of the barriers imposed by the amenities and the conventions. For him, the world is an inn, where we sit down as if at an ordinary to drink in the beauty of things. His poetry always seems to be laying a friendly hand on your shoulder and saying : "Camerado!" He loves to sing the friendship of comrades, to write of the travelling companion and the bedfellow. He wants to fraternise with all comers, with Man. All men are Man. The Whitmanists, like their master, sing comradeship and companionship. Since it is the common good which enthrals them—this world-alike-for-all which fascinates them—men, too, seem to them much alike. All men are eyes to see the world, hands to grasp it, lungs to breathe it in, a heart to love it, and a brain to understand it.

How cordial is the warmth which radiates from Marcel Martinet's verses :

> Frères vous combattez.
>
> Vous fuyez sous nos mains.
> —Avec toute ma vie je vous adjure,
> Je saisis vos mains,
> Je vous cherche dans vos yeux, dans vos âmes,
> Je m'attache à vous, je me livre à vous,
> Timidement, gauchement,
> Et avec une angoisse, une obstination brûlantes,
> Je vous appelle. . . .
>
> .   .   .   .   .
>
> Frères je vous adjure avec toute ma vie.[1]
>
> [Brothers you are fighting.

[1] From Frères, in Les temps maudits, Geneva, 1917; republished after the war by Ollendorff, Paris.

You elude our grasp.
—With all my life I adjure you,
I seize you by the hands,
I plumb to the depths of your eyes, of your soul,
I cling to you, I yield myself up to you,
Timidly, awkwardly,
And, with an anguish and a stubbornness which
        consume me,
I call to you. . . .

  .   .   .   .   .   .

Brothers, I adjure you with all my life.]

We are gripped by the same humanism in the poems of Luc Durtain. Man stands in the front rank ; nature is of value only through him and for him. One need but read *Toujours l'homme*, a poem whose very title is a manifesto, to be convinced of this :

Mieux que l'herbe le foin livre des odeurs ivres ;
Plus sacrée que la grappe est la saveur du vin ;
L'édifice pense plus haut que la montagne.
Mieux que l'oeuvre aux fixes limites vaut la face
Qui la scrute, lutte d'idées changeant de formes.[1]

[The hay gives off more intoxicating odours than the grass ;
The flavour of the wine is holier than the grapes ;
The building has loftier thoughts than the mountain.
Of more worth than the work with fixed limits is the face
Which scrutinizes it, a struggle of ideas, protean in form.]

In a way worthy of the subject, Durtain sings :

L'offre trop large du globe entier, dont pourtant nous sommes
Les vrais citoyens munis du regard comme d'un vote.[2]

[The too generous offer of the whole world, of which however
  we are
The true citizens, furnished with the right of inspection as if
  with the right to vote.]

[1] Luc Durtain, Le retour des hommes, Editions de la Nouvelle Revue Française, 1920.
[2] Durtain, op. cit., Le général.

This is the tone characteristic of Whitman ; or of Edward Carpenter, the great British Whitmanist, who speaks of a similar " democracy " (not civic but cosmic) as " the equality of men before life and before the world." Durtain's apostrophe *Aux soldats américains* forcibly evokes in us the same cordial glow of human fellowship that is aroused in us by the opening of many of Whitman's poems :

> Amis, compagnons, ô frères
> Comme si je pouvais vous saisir
> De ces mots (comme des mains tendues),
> Partis de là-bas, visage nature comme des mottes de terre,
> Avec du vrai vent d'air dans la poitrine,
> Et les quatre membres forts dont on se sert.[1]

> [Friends, companions, O brothers,
> If I could but clasp you
> With these words (stretched forth like hands),
> Come from over there, aspect racy of the soil,
> Chests filled with fresh air,
> And having four strong limbs which we turn to good account.]

Do we not catch the note of Whitman's " indifferentism," of his all-embracing comradeship—in such a phrase as the following :

Tout cela qui est nous mais certes fut vous-mêmes autant.[2]

[All this which is ourselves, but was certainly you quite as much.]

or in this :

> Quelqu'un quelconque,
> N'importe qui,
> Un homme est apparu sur ma route.[3]

> [Some one or other,
> No matter who,
> A man has crossed my path.]

---

[1] Op. cit., Aux soldats américains.   [2] Ibid.
[3] Op. cit., La vision de l'homme.—In The Varieties of Religious Experience, p. 86, William James lays stress on Walt Whitman's resolute attitude of " indifference."

The Romanticists made a mystical cult of Nature ; the Whitmanists make a mystical cult of Man. But these Realist mystics are rarely in a solemn mood. These lovers of Man are good fellows :

Car surtout y a de l'homme. . . .
Pleins les navires, les bars, les docks,
Vrai ça teinte tout. Yeux bleus, ces flaques bleues ?
Les odeurs sont anglaises ou turques ;
Tout le jaune est chinois, l'ombre est nègre.
Qu'on massacre ailleurs, qu'on enterre,
Par ici comme y a de l'homme, bon Dieu !
Comme y a de l'homme par le monde, comme y a de l'homme ! [1]

[There is man wherever you go. . . .
The ships are full of man, the drinking-bars, the docks,
Everything takes on a human complexion. Those blue puddles,
    are they blue eyes ?
The smells are English or Turkish ;
The yellow splashes are Chinese ; the dusky ones, nigger.
No doubt they are slaughtering and burying plenty of them
    elsewhere,
But here, good Lord ! what a lot of man there is !
How much man there is in the world, how much man !]

Durtain is certainly one of the most typical exponents of this Humanism. How could the notion that individuality is to be disregarded, be more forcibly expressed than by the words " there is *man* wherever you go " (not " there are *men* ") ? He speaks of " man " as if one could speak of " human meat," of " human matter." This hyperbole might seem somewhat distasteful if we were to contemplate it with the dry light of the intelligence.[2] But it springs— and this gives it its impetus—from an ardent need of the heart, from a need for human communion, from a need to break down all the artificial barriers (real enough, many

[1] Op. cit., Un port.
[2] Indeed, were it to become the fashion (and there is a risk that this may happen), it might be as absurd as the opposite fashion, that of the Romanticists with their undue isolation of the individual.

of them, however artificial) that divide men from their
fellows.

The barrier of national sentiment is one of the first to
be broken down : " the smells are English or Turkish." As
soon as these poets begin to exercise a rational control
over their instincts, they usually come to adopt the notion
of the brotherhood of the peoples, the community of mankind. Need we be surprised to find them practically unanimous in such convictions ? Their writings disclose an
ardent love for mankind—or perhaps it would be better
to say, an ardent and virile friendship for mankind. Their
temperament inclines them towards internationalism. They
have a sense of human unity, and this leads them to ignore
frontiers. It is easy to discern their attitude towards the
war ; they feel more keenly than most its tragical reality
and its unspeakable horror.

Théophile Gautier defined the poet as " a man for whom
the external world exists." This is certainly true of the
Realists, though of the Symbolists the very opposite is
true. The Realist poet is not merely one who is able
to see the outer world (which is all that Gautier
meant) ; he is one who is inspired with strong feelings
for or against things, men, and happenings ; he is one
who regards particular aspects of reality with love or
with hatred.

In this respect, our Realists differ from Whitman. The
American's writings form a hymn of love for the real,
they express approval of everything.

For Whitman, whatever is, is good, and could not be
bettered. Like God at the close of each of the days of
creation, from moment to moment throughout his life he
looks at the world and sees that it is good. Opposites
are equally beautiful, equally good. Everything is perfect
through the very fact of existence. Being is perfect. Being

is beyond good and evil. Being is absolute. This is unquestionably the climax of Realism.

In Verhaeren, likewise, we note at times this simultaneous
acceptance of opposites, of contradictories which (either
logically or morally) ought to be mutually exclusive, but
which the poet chooses to clasp in a single embrace, fervid
with the intoxication of the worshippers of Dionysus or Pan :

> Et vous, haines, vertus, vices, rages, désirs,
> Je vous accueillis tous, avec tous vos contrastes,
> Afin que fût plus long, plus complexe et plus vaste,
> Le merveilleux frisson qui m'a fait tressaillir.[1]

> [And you, hates, virtues, vices, rages, desires,
> I welcomed you all, with all your contrasts,
> To prolong, to render more complex and vaster,
> The wonderful thrill which made me quiver.]

But the poets who were young when the war broke out,
many of whom had to go to the front, could not retain this
intoxication. The realities they were compelled to face
were horrible realities. Being persons whose sensibilities
were keenly attuned to reality, they could not fail to suffer
intensely when confronted with such realities as these.
Hatred of the war, and sometimes a heretical cry of explicit
repudiation, were the dominant notes in their writings.

Such are the characteristics of most of the poets in the
Anthologie des poètes contre la guerre.[2] It is a remarkable
fact that these poets, who are linked by the feeling of protest
which is common to them all, should be linked also by
the way in which their protest finds artistic expression.
The similarity of style might incline us to suppose that
we are dealing with a formal " school," and yet there is
nothing of the kind. Indubitably there is a logical tie
between the form and the thought, and the nature of the

---

[1] Verhaeren, from La vie ardente, in Les flammes hautes
[2] Romain Rolland wrote a preface to this anthology.

tic emerges from what has already been said. When confronted with an appalling reality, an artist whose sensibilities are attuned to the real can react in no other way than " aggressively."

Two of the most aggressive are Marcel Martinet and Pierre Jean Jouve. In *Les temps maudits*, whose publication was forbidden in France while the war lasted, the former has given us a masterpiece of lyrical and denunciatory satire. Great lyrical satires are rare ; they presuppose in the writer an emotion which burns so fiercely that it is not chilled by enduring contact with irony. A fierce and a loving irony, but an irony which cannot quench either the fierceness or the love—this forms the substance of Martinet's poems. In their savage invective and their passionate impetus, they again and again recall the Hugo of *Les châtiments* and the d'Aubigné of *Les tragiques* :

J'ai douté, j'ai maudit, mais c'est alors, jeté
Plus haut que mon destin par la folle tempête,
Par l'ouragan funèbre à moi-même arraché,
Solitaire au milieu de l'oubli de mes frères,
Que moi-même glacé d'un tel isolement
Je me suis rechaufé de honte et de colère
Et que mon désespoir a fait jaillir ces chants.[1]

[I doubted, I uttered curses, but it was then, thrown
Higher than my destiny by the mad storm,
Dragged out of myself by the dismal hurricane,
Alone in the midst of my brethren's forgetfulness,
That I, chilled by this isolation,
Warmed myself at the fires of shame and of wrath,
So that my despair gushed forth in these songs.]

Jouve is both violent and gentle. In *Vous êtes des hommes*[2] gentleness predominates. We think of a Whitman grown

---

[1] From *Aux esclaves*, in *Les temps maudits*.
[2] Éditions de la Nouvelle Revue Française, Paris, 1915.

tender, one whose health is that of a convalescent,
one in whom love mostly takes the form of pity ; one who
is not now eager to embrace the crude integer of reality,
but chooses from out of reality like Tolstoy, and rejects
everything that is not instinct with goodness :

Qui que vous soyez, je m'approche de vous ;
Pour vous je me sacrifierais sans un regard en arrière.[1]

[Be you who you may, I draw near to you ;
For you I would sacrifice myself without ever looking backward.]

But there is another Jouve, who breathes anger and
irony.   This Jouve gives tongue in the biting sarcasm
of the *Danse des morts*.[2]   In this book, the macabre imagination of the Middle Ages dances devilishly amid the
horrors of our own day :

Je suis la Mort, la grande Mort à l'odeur forte.
Je suis la Mort, la grande Garce qui aime bien.
La planète entière, je l'ai.
Cette vermine à pensée
Dans un coin perdu des vies et des morts
Puait !
Je la nettoierai.[3]

[I am Death, great and strong-smelling.
I am Death, a great wench who loves well.
The whole planet is mine.
This vermin that can think,
In an out-of-the-way corner of lives and deaths
Has been making a stench.
I shall clean up the place.]

Among the cries against the war that were raised while
the war was still in progress, those of Martinet were perhaps
the loudest, and those of Jouve the most poignant.   In
these two writers we have the " aggressive " type of reaction

[1] From Sacrifice, in Vous êtes des hommes.
[2] Edition d'Action Sociale, La Chaux de Fonds, 1917.
[3] From La fin d'un monde, in Danse des morts.

in all its forceful or febrile vehemence. We must add
to their names those of the member of the Clarté group,
such as Noël Garnier and Vaillant Couturier—and also
the ardent Jean de Saint-Prix, who died young, " leaving
on our hearts a track of flame " (Romain Rolland).

Others are less violent in their denunciations, but their
work is none the less an eager affirmation. Jules Romains,
to whose work we shall return, sings his love for Europe the
fatherland, and his tone is confident :

> Europe je crie que tu es
> Dans l'oreille de tes tueurs.
>
> .   .   .   .   .   .
>
> Ils auront beau pousser leurs crimes ;
> Je reste garant et gardien
> De deux ou trois choses divines.[1]

> [Europe, in the ears of those who would slay thee,
> I cry aloud that thou still art.
>
> .   .   .   .   .   .
>
> Let them push their crimes to the uttermost ;
> Still I shall be trustee and guardian
> Of two or three divine things.]

We may term this Realism " negational," for it voices
a condemnation of extant reality. The negational quality
is a primary distinction between the French Whitmanists
and their American exemplar. The difference is in part
the outcome of current happenings, but in part it is racial.
Frenchmen find it difficult to discard their critical faculty ;
they are loath to adopt a Hegelian philosophy which accepts
and justifies all the real, without qualification ; they will
never renounce their right to revolt.

Even when they reject orthodox patriotism, our Realist
poets remain essentially French. Thus we become aware
of two additional characteristics whereby their spirit is

[1] Europe, Editions de la Nouvelle Revue Française, Paris, 1920.

distinguished from that of Whitman. I said just now that Jouve sometimes made us think of "a Whitman grown tender." Like qualifications have to be added in the case of the other French Realists. They lack the robustness of the great American writer; we do not hear in their song the rustle of virgin forests or the roar of huge cataracts. We have, instead, the delicacy of the French countryside, the fineness of one of our southern landscapes. Charles Vildrac, in connexion with whose work the names of Charles Louis Philippe and Francis Jammes rise in our minds, has a moving and piercing sweetness; he makes us think of a sky in which the sun is shining through a filmy haze :

> La chanson que je me chante
> Elle est triste et gaie ;
> La vieille peine y sourit
> Et la joie y pleure.
>
> .   .   .   .
>
> C'est, dans un jardin d'été,
> Le rire en pleurs d'un aveugle
> Qui titube dans les fleurs.[1]
>
> [The song I sing to myself
> Is both sad and merry ;
> The old grief is smiling in it,
> And joy is weeping there.
>
> .   .   .   .   .   .
>
> It is, in a garden during summer,
> The tearful laughter of a blind man
> Who walks with uncertain step amid the flowers.]

Georges Duhamel again, is one of those humanists to whom even the minutest details seem of moment. He identifies himself with all that is most trifling, most tenuous, in a petty human life. Thus in *La confession de minuit* [2]

---

[1] Chants du désespéré, 1914–1920, Editions de la Nouvelle Revue Française, Paris, 1920.
[2] Editions Mercure de France, 1920.

he depicts the romance of mediocrity, his aim being to interest us in, and to touch our emotions with, the most insignificant occurrences in the most inconspicuous of lives.   In some of his poems too, we find him, equally intent, bending over the microscope with which he is exploring a soul.   As long ago as 1912, he had written in *Compagnons* :

> Toutes ces douleurs misérables,
> Toutes ces joies faites de peu,
> Et ces longs moments sans joie ni douleur,
> Tous ces longs moments qui sont ta vie même,
> Tous cela peut-il m'être indifferent ?
>
> Et ces événements médiocres
> Qui charpentent ton existence,
> Qui te sont des événements considerables,
> Qui sont pour toi les seuls événements du monde,
> Les trouverai-je négligeables tout à fait ?
>
> —Je ne crois pas.[1]

> [All these petty griefs,
> All these joys made up of so little,
> And these long moments free from both joy and pain,
> All these long moments which are your very life,
> Can all this be indifferent to me ?
>
> And these trifling events
> Which form the framework of your life,
> Which to you do not seem trifling,
> Which for you are the only events in the world,
> Shall I find them altogether negligible ?
>
> —I do not think so.]

With the same subtle kindliness, in his *Elégies* [2] concerning the war, Georges Duhamel (who is a doctor by profession) auscultates the barely perceptible and delicate details

---

[1] From A un pauvre homme, in Visages (Compagnons, Editions de la Nouvelle Revue Française, Paris, 1912.)

[2] Editions Mercure de France.

which comprise the atmosphere of suffering. In the *Ballade de Florentin Prunier* [1] he describes how a mother watches by the bedside of her wounded son. Florentin struggles to live, struggles for twenty long days, for his mother does not want him to die. She has come from a long way off, from her little farm, " bringing with her a basket containing a dozen apples, and some fresh butter in a little pot." All day she sits by the dying man's bed— except when they tell her to leave him for a while because they are going to dress the wound in her son's shattered chest :

Elle resterait s'il fallait rester :
Elle est femme à voir la plaie de son fils.

Ne lui faut-il pas entendre les cris,
Pendant qu'elle attend, les souliers dans l'eau ?

Elle est près du lit comme un chien de garde
On ne la voit plus ni manger ni boire.

Florentin non plus ne sait plus manger :
Le beurre a jauni dans son petit pot.

[She would stay even then, if she had to :
She is not the woman to shrink from seeing her son's wound.

As it is, she has to listen to his cries,
While she waits, just outside, the water soaking through her shoes.

She keeps close to his bed like a watch-dog.
She no longer eats or drinks.

Florentin, too, can no longer eat :
The butter has turned yellow in the little pot.]

At last, one morning, after twenty days of vigil, and twenty nights passed in any odd corner, she was so tired that :

[1] Op. cit.

> Elle a laissé aller un peu sa tête,
> Elle a dormi un tout petit moment ;
>
> Et Florentin Prunier est mort bien vite
> Et sans bruit, pour ne pas la réveiller.
>
> [Her head drooped a little,
> And she dozed just for a moment ;
>
> And Florentin Prunier died very quickly,
> Very quietly, lest he should wake her.]

Most of the Realist poets are agreed in their notion of
rhythm. They all have a certain contempt for form, and
this is their weakness ; but the contempt is the outcome
of their active temperament, which makes them feel that
they have something to say, and that they must say it
forthwith. Assuredly, to have something worth saying,
and to say it without much regard for form, is better than
to cultivate forms of expression when there is no solid
kernel of matter. They have pity on the fair realm of the
world, and this draws from them, not a song, but a cry.
Had they waited to enchase their work in some richly
wrought specimen of the goldsmith's art, had they delayed
in order to write faultless sonnets after the Petrarchian
model, would they have still been the poets of this cry
" de profundis " ?

As with Pascal's " eloquence " (whose leading rule is
to be simple and natural)[1] their rhythm laughs at rhythm.
Martinet continues to write in the robust and carefully
chiselled verse which we have compared with that of
d'Aubigné and Victor Hugo. For the most part the rest
vie with one another in their scorn for regular and well-
marked rhythms. Sometimes, indeed, as in the case of
Jules Romains, they retain the use of verses that have an

[1] Pascal, Pensées (the " Thoughts on Style ").

equal, or nearly equal, length ; but, even then, they write in blank verse, in a verse that is unrhymed, and substantially free from assonance. Occasionally, all regular versification seems to be abandoned (Durtain, and from time to time Jouve). Then the verse becomes so " free," that at the first glance it may not seem to be verse at all. There is ostensible justification for the complaint of some of the critics that this free verse is not poetry, but only prose artificially printed in such a way as to give it the semblance of verse. In reality, however, there is nothing arbitrary about the subdivision into verses. Each verse comprises a pulse of emotion. The versification represents (if you like to phrase the matter thus) a sort of emotional punctuation superadded to the logical punctuation that characterises prose. The addition of this emotional punctuation suffices to distinguish free verse from prose. But we may agree that the distinction is thus reduced to a minimum—and that critics of the calibre of Molière's Monsieur Jourdain may naturally find it hard to see that there is any difference at all.

Since the Realist poets tend to abandon the use of verse as ordinarily understood, it follows that their poems cannot appeal chiefly to the ear. Their lines do not continue to ring in the memory, do not insist upon being read aloud as do the lines that appeal largely for their effect to rhyme and rhythm.

" Vildrac's free verse," writes René Schickelé,[1] " is by nature hostile to arioso ; it is even deliberately unharmonious that it may avoid a too obvious resemblance to music. Poets are apt to succumb to this temptation to write ' musical verse.' A dull and often uniform melody makes their verses rhythmical."

[1] " L'Art Libre," Brussels, March 1921.—The whole issue is devoted to Vildrac.

I agree, except that I dislike this reference to the desire to be musical as a " temptation," as if music were a sin. It makes a disagreeable impression when artists are praised for their negative qualities. Surely it would be better to praise them for what they are ; and frankly to point out their limitations, not as merits, but simply as limitations. The greatest have their limitations, and are none the less great for that. The poetry of our Realists could never wholly satisfy those endowed with musical sensibilities. Let us admit that melody is not their strong point, and let us neither praise them nor blame them on this account. Take them for what they are, and their rhythm for what it is. For they have a rhythm—intimate, and sometimes captivating. But what is this rhythm which is not made for the ear ? Beyond question, it is essentially muscular. It is a motor vibration. Besides being visualisers, these poets are " muscular " in their mode of perception, they are persons of active temperament. Need we be surprised, then, that their attitude is aggressive ? Here, I fancy, we touch the significance of their rhythmical endeavour. Muscular rhythm, the essential movement of reactive emotion, being detached from the audible rhythm which is its usual accompaniment, monopolises the artist's attention, and can thus be the better cultivated in isolation. Their art has its own peculiar characteristics, and must be appraised by itself, without comparison with alien forms of art. It is as wrong-headed to judge free verse by the standards of melodic verse, as it would be to judge music by the standards of sculpture or the dance.

Such are, to my mind, the most salient characteristics of the Whitmanesque Realists. There is nothing arbitrary in thus forming them into a group, seeing that they have so many points in common. They share a keen sense for the real, for the visible and tangible and solid world, which is plainly seen by all men, and is the common heritage of all. They are at one in their conviction of human fellowship, of that brotherhood in the flesh which is imposed by nature and sanctioned by the human mind. They all rise in rebellion against the war, though some of them rebel more fiercely than the others. They are all alike subject to Whitman's influence ; and most of them are inclined to reject formal versification in favour of a rhythm animated solely by the emotional movement which sets the muscles aquiver. These certainly comprise a sufficiency of traits to characterise a school or a literary trend.

For these poets, that which really and predominantly exists is man, modern man, with all his wretchedness which incites the strong towards revolt and towards love. Nature recedes into the background, and often disappears from the stage. Man with his towns overhung with smoke fills the picture and blocks the horizon. We see this in the vigorous woodcuts with which Frans Masereel [1] has illustrated several of the volumes published by the Realist poets. Behind the swarm of figures, radiating human warmth, struggling fiercely or clasped in brotherly embraces, we can hardly detect a square inch of sky. It is the gloomy art of a gloomy epoch, an art tinctured by all the intense physical suffering of the men of our day.

Sometimes however, nature, the limitless cosmos reappears. René Arcos lifts his eyes enough to follow the drama of the worlds :

Qu'importe la défaite,
Qu'importe la victoire ?
La bataille des hommes
N'est qu'un vain simulacre !

[1] Cf. Léon Bazalgette's noteworthy article on Masereel, in the " Revue de l'Epoque," Paris, April 1921. Bazalgette lays especial stress on the Whitmanesque character of Masereel's art.

Qu'un empire s'écroule, il restera la terre
Toujours prête et parée dans ses mêmes frontières.
Que la terre à son tour soit frappée dans sa course,
Il restera l'espace et ses grappes de mondes.

    •   •   •   •   •   •   •

Car le seul drame est la Passion de l'Univers.[1]

[What matters defeat,
What matters victory ?
The fight among men
Is but an empty simulacrum !

Though an empire fall, the world will remain
Always ready, and bounded by the same frontiers.
Though our world, in its turn, be shattered as it courses,
Space will still be there, with its clusters of worlds.

    •   •   •   •   •   •   •

For there is only one drama, the Passion of the Universe.

Jouve, too, has written :

Sirius vogue en son noir bleu.[2]

[Sirius floats in a blue-black sky.]

Nothing can be more thrilling, more exalting, than these fragments of eternity glimpsed as if through a sudden rent in the veil of human destiny.

This is the beginning of the break away. Other poets will aid us to break away more effectively.

2. The Symbolist Revival.

There are some who say, "After us, the deluge"; and there are others who say, "Before us, nothingness." The latter type is no less unpleasant than the former. Every innovation has its devotees, who make a point of repudiating as

[1] From La guerre des hommes, in Le sang des autres, Editions du Sablier, Geneva, 1919.
[2] From La bataille, in Heures, livre de la nuit, Editions du Sablier, 1919.

obsolete that which was the novelty of yesterday.   Sensible persons only smile at such childish vagaries.

Even though it be true that recent years have witnessed the rise of a Realist school which is new and virile and full of life, it would be absurd to think that all the earlier conquests of poesy have become valueless or outworn. To-day, among the youngest of our poets, there are Symbolists who may be looked upon as the direct heirs of the Symbolists of the last generation.

In a remarkably able study, *De Stéphane Mallarmé au prophète Ezéchiel et essai d'une théorie de réalisme symbolique*,[1] Edouard Dujardin makes a witty protest against the death sentence recently pronounced upon Symbolism :

" You are probably not aware that Monsieur Haraucourt, in a lecture given in 1916, wishing to insult the Symbolists, declared them to be under German influence :

" Here is his exquisite formula :

" ' Perhaps even more than the plastic arts, poetry had suffered from, or had at least been the first to experience, the intoxication of the breeze blowing from Germany. A poison gas was wafted across the Rhine. . . . Man had the symbol ; the Germans made a cult of Symbolism. So much the worse for them ! French poets took up this cult ? So much the worse for them—and for the world ! But I hope Symbolism is now dead and buried. . . .'

" Alas, Monsieur Haraucourt, you are exulting too soon. You have not yet heard the last of Symbolism, not by a long way." [2]

Nay more, we are entitled to expect, in the immediate future, a revival of Symbolist art. We have to recognise that, in general, art is modified by all the changes that occur in thought and in science. (The Realist novel was the

---

[1] Editions Mercure de France, Paris, 1919.
[2] Op. cit., p. 17

outcome of the psychological and sociological theories of an earlier day.) Now, one of the most remarkable among the achievements of contemporary science is the psychology of the unconscious, and, in especial, psychoanalysis, which has shown that the symbol is the most spontaneous form of thought ; that Symbolism is the spontaneous language of unfettered sensibility in the dream and the day-dream ; that, in a word, Symbolism is a natural method of expression welling up from the depths of our being. This theory is revolutionising a wide domain of psychological and medical science. How could it fail to influence art criticism, more especially in view of the fact that quite a number of authors have already been eager to show its bearing upon the science of aesthetics ? [1]

Symbolism is no mere passing fashion. It is not one of those crazy booths at a fair, in which a couple of humbugs, with a few idiots in their train, secure salvos of applause from a gaping crowd ready to admire any novelty, however foolish. No, it was the fruit of a brilliant intuition, which foreran science, but is now being substantiated by science. *Symbolism is an inspired endeavour to enable poetry to plumb the depths; to help art in its task of expressing the most intimate life of the soul—all that is most mysterious and most musical, all that surges up from the unconscious.* A bold endeavour, doubtless. Those who make it, run their risks ; but every fruitful innovation must rub shoulders with danger. "Nothing venture, nothing have," runs the proverb. The Symbolists have staked boldly, and their winnings are correspondingly large. Diving into the waters of the unconscious, they have done so at grave peril of being permanently submerged. Some of them have become

[1] Among them, the present writer. See Charles Baudouin, Psychoanalysis and Aesthetics (a study of the Symbolism in the writings of Emile Verhaeren), George Allen & Unwin, London, 1924.

esoteric, and are unintelligible to all but a few initiates. Moreover, in the case of one who makes a cult of his own ego, all the other persons in the world are non-initiates. A Symbolist who strives to give complete and integral expression to his inner self, is likely to produce something essentially incommunicable. (How striking is the contrast with the communicative ardour of the Realists!) Here, indeed, all attempt at expression seems futile. We touch the limit of Symbolism, and of all ultra-subjective art. Still, it is only the Symbolists of the first days of the movement, the revolutionary innovators, Mallarmé and his immediate followers, who approach this limit. Those who to-day are the heirs of the earlier Symbolists have thrown the windows wide in order to ventilate the stuffy room, and gusts of fresh air blow in from without. The dark corners in which phantoms were lurking are now flooded with sunshine.

Joseph Rivière's poems quiver with the light of southern France:

> La vie est là, sonore, et qui cogne à la porte
> A grands coups de poings de soleil.[1]

> [Life is there, sonorous, knocking at the door
> With great fist-blows of sunshine.]

In Nicholas Beauduin's *Rhythmes et chants dans le renouveau*,[2] all the voices of spring sound in chorus:

> Vois, je suis forte, ô mon amour,
> Et, d'un pas ferme,
> Je marche sur la route en fleurs des beaux demains.
> La myrtille fleurit, toute la plaine germe
> Et l'oiseau d'or du jour

[1] From *Tu rêves d'avenir*, in *En passant*, Editions Soi-même, Paris, 1917.
[2] Povoloshi, Paris, 1920.

Luit sur notre chemin.
La haie en fleurs frissonne ainsi qu'une épousée
Au baiser lumineux et doux du jeune avril qui passe
En secouant ses pieds blancs de rosée
Et son vêtement court tout poudré de grésil.

[See, I am strong, O my love,
And, with a confident tread,
I walk along the flower-decked road of the lovely to-morrows.
The myrtle blooms, the whole plain burgeons,
And the golden bird of day
Shines upon our path.
The blossoming hedge thrills like a bride
At the luminous and gentle kiss of Young April as he passes,
Shaking his feet that are white with dew,
And his tunic, powdered with hoar-frost.]

These unconstrained gestures have led some to believe (as even Beauduin is himself inclined to believe) that this author's verses, far from being part of the Symbolist succession, are a reaction against Symbolism. There is doubtless reaction, but there is also continuance. If we allow for the recoil, there is more kinship than difference. Edouard Dujardin expresses the matter very well :

" Let me quote something which Nicholas Beauduin published in 1913 ; it conveys admirably the views of the Symbolist poets concerning idealism. The amusing point is that these views, which are characteristically Symbolist, are presented to us by Monsieur Beauduin as a reaction against Symbolism. You will be inclined to think that, fine poet though he be, he is very little acquainted with his own elder brothers.

" Here is what he says—and it does not contain a word which would not have been endorsed by the young men of 1885

" ' The new poet is no longer the humble slave of his sensations ; he is as it were, *the master of the world*. This

poet discovers the universe by *an intuitive flash of insight.*
" We think the world," say the Paroxysts, " and that is
why, perforce, we recreate it in ourselves. . . ."[1] For us,
nothing exists outside the soul. . . . We have certainly
moved a long way from the idea of the Romanticist poet,
as Théophile Gautier understood that term : " a man for
whom the external world exists." ' "[2]

The style of several of our younger poets might be most
aptly described as a " ventilated Symbolism." Henri
Mugnier prostrates himself :

Devant les matins bleus peuplés d'âmes très blondes.[3]

[Before the blue mornings peopled with very fair souls.]

His dream is radiant with the light of the plains :

> La plaine !
>
> .   .   .   .   .   .
>
> Elle est,
> Qui prend l'espace entier de l'horizon,
> Elle est,
> Avec tous ses jardins et ses moissons
> Et ses rumeurs humaines.[4]
>
> [The plain !
>
> .   .   .   .   .   .
>
> It is there,
> Filling the whole horizon,
> It is there,
> With all its gardens and its harvests
> And its human noises.]

[1] The term " paroxysm," coined by Albert Mockel when writing of
Emile Verhaeren, has become a rallying-cry for Beauduin. Critics have
even spoken of a " Paroxyst School." Of late years, Beauduin seems
to have been a little influenced by the Futurists.

[2] Dujardin, op. cit., pp. 11–12.

[3] L'oasis dans la ville, Violette, Geneva, 1916.

[4] Henri Mugnier, La clairière automnale, Editions du Carmel, Geneva,
1917.

" Its human noises "—for the Symbolist, breaking away from the ego, becomes humanised ; from time to time he is as much concerned about the extant as any Realist writer can be. Henry Spiess, one of the most profound and clear-sighted of the Symbolist poets, devotes some impassioned stanzas to the agony of the world during the great war and the " peace " that has followed it :

> On nous avait dit on avait cru pourtant
> On avait espéré pourtant
> On avait cru la paix certaine
> On avait espéré la fin des haines
> Et cependant . . .
>   .   .   .   .   .   .
> Mes frères, quand serons-nous freres ? [1]

> [They told us, we had believed,
> We had hoped,
> We had fancied that peace would certainly come,
> We had looked forward to the end of hatred,
> And yet . . .
>   .   .   .   .   .   .
> My brothers, when shall we be brothers ?]

Thus emerging from themselves, the Symbolist poets have ceased to be esoteric. Their thought has been clarified. But we must avoid misunderstanding. The fact that they differ in certain respects from the earlier Symbolists must not hide from us the kinship between the earlier Symbolists and the later. We must not allow the later Symbolists to misunderstand.

Whether the name of " Symbolist " should be applied to these later Symbolists is of little importance. But this much is certain, that they have retained some of the essential characteristics of Symbolism, and notably its vigour.

[1] From the poem entitled " 1914–1921," published in " La Suisse," Geneva, December 31, 1920.

The Symbolists are poets who have broken away from
the real. Perhaps we may prefer to say that they have
broken away from external reality, and that each communes
with himself in the internal reality of his mind. Dujardin
writes that in their case we may invert Gautier's formula,
saying : " the world no longer exists," and " our soul is the
only living reality." In *La folie de l'homme*,[1] Marcello
Fabri has created the most typical of these poems of
" breaking away." Herein the cruel reality of the war is
not ignored, but it is transformed into a myth. It is an
image in a dream, a vision seen through a golden haze.
Divine beings are discussing man :

> En ce moment la terre est un charnier sans fin,
> Les hommes s'entretuent et se servent d'esclaves,
> De salpêtre et d'acier.

> [At present the world is a huge slaughter-house,
> Men are killing one another, and are using slaves,
> Saltpetre and steel.]

The last of the pictures is the only one that brings us
into direct contact with reality, revealing to us that we have
just been witnessing the dream of a man in whom this too
dreadful reality has induced a wondrous madness. (Is not
this madness the essential mechanism of the breaking away ?)
Pending the scene in which the author brings us back to
our footing in the real, we see landscapes of crystal and jade,
and the serene skies of an immaterial dawn. These skies
are fringed with " the first green bands of undying hope."
Here, in this realm of faëry, is unrolled a magical myth
of the redemption of man by a pure and simple being.
Redemption is not effected through the instrumentality
of poison gas. It is not the work of Scientia, who should
have been the servant of life, but whose services man has

[1] Editions du Carnet Critique, Paris.

of late so lamentably perverted to the work of destruction. Man has put out Scientia's eyes ! Nor does redemption come through the bleeding from a myriad wounds, through the piling up of corpses in desolate gullies, through the wasting of children by famine. The god of life, Bios the father of living men, is already lying in state—when he is reanimated by a miracle.

Thus the real loses itself in distant perspectives, where it is the mere symbol of an idea which subsumes vaster realities, and becomes philosophy. " Sirius floats in a blue-black sky," writes Jouve ; Sirius inaccessible in the cold night of the stellar universe. But in Fabri's vision we are watching the tumult of humanity from the vantage-ground of some Sirius ; we are contemplating the momentary from the standpoint of the eternal !

As I have written elsewhere, " flight from the real towards the dream has as its natural accompaniment a flight from the present towards the past." [1] He who flees the real, escapes into dreamland ; and the essential substance of the dream is the past, or sometimes the future. Whereas Whitman sang " the present and the real," sang them together, since they are coexistent, Marcello Fabri writes :

Vois-tu, enfant, ne crois jamais aux choses
Que tu verras.
Chasse les, enfuis-toi.
Il faut s'ensevelir
Dans le Passé, le Rêve ou l'Avenir ;
Toujours l'ont ainsi pratiqué ceux qui vécurent
Aux temps attiques des golfes bleus ourlés de blanc,
Ainsi qu'aux temps médiévaux des enluminures.

 · · · · · · ·

Ne crois pas aux présent ; l'avenir seul t'importe
Et plus tard le passé lui seul t'importera.

[1] Psychoanalysis and Aesthetics, p. 96.

[My child, never believe in the things
You actually see.
Drive them away, take flight.
You must bury yourself
In the Past, the Dream, or the Future ;
Thus always did those who lived
In Attic days, the times of blue bays fringed with white,
And in the Middle Ages, the days of illuminated manuscripts.

.   .   .   .

Never believe in the present ; the future is your sole concern,
And in days to come the past will be your sole concern.]

For the Realists, the actual moment and the real object
are crudely visible, detached from their surroundings,
nude, and free from any softening of the outlines by an
encircling haze. For the Symbolists, on the other hand,
the actual moment and the real object are merely images
through which other images are glimpsed, or upon which
other images are superposed in an ideal transparency. Or
we may say that for the Symbolists the object does not
consist of a " pure " note comprising a single series of vibrations ; it is a composite note whose quality depends upon
the superaddition of numerous harmonics. No matter
whether we prefer the visual or the auditory comparison,
the upshot is that, for the Symbolists, every object contains
something beyond its bare self, and becomes the symbol
of an idea. Symbolist art is like Helmholtz's resonators
which isolate the overtones of a musical note, and make
them perceptible in isolation. In like manner it discloses
the secret resonances which respond to the object in the
recesses of the perceiving mind.

In these respects the Symbolists of to-day are of the same
gens as those of yesterday. Without overstressing narrowly
conceived metaphors, which could only transfer the attention
from one object to another and leave it still unsatisfied,
they have a skilful way of partially disclosing infinite

perspectives resembling strains of music fading away in the distance. Thus, just now, in the imagery quoted from Marcello Fabri, the horizon at dawn was fringed with " the first green bands of undying hope."

One of the rules of what may be termed Symbolist syntax is to endow a word with an attribute which does not, strictly speaking, belong to it, but nevertheless belongs to one or more of the harmonics of which this word is the fundamental tone. The introduction of an ostensibly alien attribute makes us notice the overtones. In illustration, let me quote Marcello Fabri again :

> Et saurai-je jamais la moitié des enigmes
> Qui pendent aux rameaux de tes vergers divins ? [1]

> [And shall I ever solve half the enigmas
> Which hang on the branches in your divine orchards ?]

Here the imagery is so simple that it barely comes within the domain of Symbolism. Our harmonic is the emblem of the fruits ; it is these fruits, and not the enigmas, " which hang on the branches." The image is merely sketched ; it does not become materialised. Hence it readily undergoes spiritualisation into the idea of the rising sap, that of foison and of fertility—the living foison of the cosmos. The mind is impelled along a pathway, but is not brought to a halt anywhere ; an unending vista is opened. A dynamic image replaces a static image, and we shall see, ere long, how this bears on our conclusion.

Georges Périn expresses himself boldly :

> Temps, notre temps, visité d'espérance et cher
> Fluide carrefour de routes exaltées.

> .   .   .   .

> Belle magie où s'affermissait le réel
> Dans l'entrecroisement des vastes bienveillances.[2]

[1] La folie de l'homme.
[2] From Terre, published in " Le Carmel," No. 8, Geneva, 1916.

[Time, our time, full of promise, a dear
Fluid crossroads where embanked roads meet.

. . . .

Beautiful magic in which the real has affirmed itself
Through the interlacing of vast goodwills.]

The image becomes fluid even before it is formed. The
mind has no halting-place, but vibrates unceasingly. This
is what gives to Périn's verses their resemblance to a luminous
and opalescent mist.

Our modern Symbolists do not strictly keep Mallarmé's
rule that the poet should " expunge the word ' like '
[comme] from the dictionary."[1] The rule is too absolute.
Nevertheless, they act on this principle whenever they can
do so without becoming obscure. It would be interesting
to show how the Realists, even, are apt to employ the same
method of expression. It is, indeed, a form of speech
that is no longer confined to poetry, but tends to become
generalised.

The psychoanalysts have recognised that this language
in which a thing is called by the name of another and
somewhat similar thing, is continually being used in the
dream. Such Symbolism is preeminently spontaneous. But,
precisely because it speaks in this tongue, the dream has,
for our waking thought, a stupefying quality of incoherence.
The obscurity and incoherence of much of the writing of
Mallarmé and René Ghil can doubtless be accounted for
in the same way. The problem is, How can the natural
language of the imagination, while still remaining itself,
be adapted to the requirements of logical thought ? I
think the problem has been solved, often enough, by the
new Symbolists, who will neither sacrifice subtle suggestiveness to clarity, nor yet jettison clarity in the hope of en-
hancing suggestiveness.

[1] Quoted by Dujardin, op. cit., p. 21.

These poets are individualists. Is not this a logical out-come of their temperament ? Retiring within themselves that they may listen more intently to their own dreams, they naturally accord a supreme value to the ego. Re-pudiating the world, they affirm the mind ; and if the world be the " common good," the mind, on the other hand, is the private sanctuary. During the war, Joseph Rivière founded and conducted a review which bore the proud name of " Soi-Même." This was one of the most poetical acts performed in the France of that epoch. " Soi-Même " —what an expressive title. Side by side with poems, the periodical contained prose contributions dealing with theoretical problems. Among the most distinguished of its contributors was the great individualist Han Ryner, who is one of the leaders of this group. There was also a witty and pungent " Idealist Dictionary " (an " In-dividualist Dictionary," to say sooth !), penned by Gérard de Lacaze-Duthiers ; while Maunoury wrote in each issue under the caption " Considérations actuelles," the very title serving to remind us of Nietzsche's writings.

For, whereas the earlier Symbolists were disciples of Schopenhauer and Wagner, those of a later day have been mainly dominated by the shade of Nietzsche. These three names, Schopenhauer, Wagner, and Nietzsche, call up similar associations. Let us remember, however, in what re-spects the last-named severed himself from his two masters. He charged them with cowardice in the face of the real ; for his own part he wished to remain " faithful to the Earth." Symbolism, in its turn, has undergone the same evolution. The Symbolists, like Nietzsche, are unwilling to break away as completely as Schopenhauer and Wagner broke away ; they are loath to get out of touch with our world.

Still more do the Symbolists show their kinship to Nietzsche in their dogged individualism, in their admira-

tion for life and for fervour, an admiration which (like
Nietzsche's morality " beyond good and evil ") leads them
to laugh at moral restrictions :

Je ne veux point aux lourds anneaux de fer
Qu'a forgés la poigne sadique des morales
Emprisonner mon front libre sous le ciel clair.
J'ai soulevé le fard et déchiré le voile
Des idoles debout a l'entour de la salle
Où s'usine la glaise énorme du devoir.[1]

[I refuse to prison my free forehead beneath the cloudless sky,
Refuse to wear the heavy iron rings
Forged by the sadistic hand of moral codes.
I have cleared away the trappings and torn off the veils
From the idols placed at the entrance of the hall
Where is modelled the titanic clay of duty.]

Thus spake, not Zarathustra, but Joseph Rivière.
Oftentimes, the men of this group seemed to ignore the
war.   Or, without undue emphasis, they would show their
contempt for the war—as for all " duties " imposed by
social constraint, by " herd morality."

Les hommes sont partis vers un devoir qu'on leur apprit dans
les écoles, vers un devoir fait de mots en parade afin
qu'œuvrent en paix les fabricants de maximes et les
vendeurs de mitraille.[2]

[Men have marched forth to fulfil a duty taught them at school,
a duty performed at the word of command invented in order
that during peace time the manufacturers of maxim guns
and the vendors of grape-shot might keep their places of
business open.]

Occasionally, such poets may delight in solipsist fantasies.
Then for them, as for Max Stirner in his philosophical
vertigo, nothing exists but the self—the self become Brahma

[1] Joseph Rivière, from J'ai respiré la fleur des marronniers, in En passant.
[2] Joseph Rivière, from Avril, in En passant

in the solitude of a world which is no more than the lonely thinker's illusion. Thus Joseph Rivière writes :

Nous sommes seuls, tout seuls, immensément seuls sur la terre.

. . . .

Je n'ai jamais compris qu'il pût exister d'autres êtres que moi. Puisque je suis debout avec mon cœur qui bat et mon âme qui souffre, puisque je suis l'unique témoin de la tragédie qui se joue en moi, les formes qui passent, les couleurs qui chantent, les sons qui vibrent composent la redoubtable énigme à la porte de laquelle heurtent en vain mes poings mystérieux.

. . . .

Je regarde mes semblables si dissemblables avec des yeux qui ne comprennent pas. Sont-ils bien vivants ces autres puisqu'ils ne sont pas moi et qu'ils n'ont pas le même cœur que je nourris en moi ? [1]

[We are alone, quite alone, immensely alone in the world.

. . . .

I have never been able to understand that any other beings can exist besides myself. Inasmuch as I stand erect with beating heart and suffering soul, inasmuch as I am the only witness of the tragedy that is being played within me, the forms which pass, the colours which sing, the sounds which vibrate, comprise the formidable enigma at whose portals my wondering fists beat in vain.

. . . .

I contemplate those like me (those so unlike me), look upon them with eyes that do not understand. Are these others truly alive—for they are not me, and they have not the same heart that I nourish within myself ?]

The Realists attack the war in man's name, attack it because it gives off the halitus of shed human blood ; the Symbolists despise it because it taints the air with the stench of the herd. Thus towards the war, just as towards life in general, the attitude of the Symbolists is not unlike that of Nietzsche.

[1] From Seuls, in En passant.

Marcel Sauvage was one of Joseph Rivière's collaborators. To-day he is editor of an individualist weekly entitled " L'Ordre Naturel." From his pen came the brief prose poem *Damné*, an impressive tribute to Nietzsche :

" Quand le philosophe allemand fut mort, sa folie se dissipa comme un nuage sur une pipe et d'un bond son âme gagna le plus lointain des cieux :

" Vêtus d'éternel soleil les hallucinés de l'arrière monde, dans le cirque d'or et de cinabre. L'un dit :

" ' O, Nietzsche nous t'attendions malgré ta nuit ; assieds-toi donc parmi nous à la première des places.'

" Un autre continua : ' Tu as nié avec tant de force, que ta loi nous a sauvé et nous sommes ici par l'amour que tu nous enseignas de notre unique beauté.'

" Mais Nietzsche se mit à rire tant qu'on aperçut par delà les cieux en loques, d'or et de cinabre, d'innombrables splendeurs et d'autres cieux sans nombre."

[" When the German philosopher was dead, his madness dispersed like the cloud of smoke rising from a pipe, and at one bound his soul gained the most distant of the heavens :

" Clad in eternal sunshine, those who aforetime had been deluded backworldsmen were assembled in the amphitheatre of gold and cinnabar. One of them said :

" ' Oh, Nietzsche, we have been awaiting you, though your mind has been obscured ; take your seat therefore among us in the leading place.'

" Said another : ' So great was the force of your negation, that your law has been our salvation, and we are all here by the love you taught us, the love of our unique beauty.'

" But Nietzsche began to laugh so heartily that there became visible, beyond the tattered heavens, the heavens of gold and of cinnabar, innumerable splendours, and other heavens without number."[1]

[1] " Lumière," No. 6, Antwerp, January 1921.

We see that it would be foolish to suppose that Realism in poetry has dethroned Symbolism. Why, indeed, should any one wish that to-day should be the negation of yesterday ? It would be even more absurd to think that the Realists, by the adoption of rhythms as free as those of prose, have given verse its quietus. Those who would properly appraise an epoch will do well to look beyond the confines of a single country. We cannot fail, in this connexion, to think of a typical instance. Carl Spitteler, one of the greatest poets of our time, has given new vigour to German verse by modelling it on French Alexandrines. Is not this tantamount to saying that verse —even Alexandrine verse—is still very much alive ?

Here is a remarkable fact. Thirty or forty years ago it was the Realist poets of that epoch (the visualisers, the Parnassians) who wrote in extremely regular rhythms ; whereas the auditives, the Symbolists, introduced free verse. In the name of music, they said harsh things of rhyme, and substituted assonance. Our modern Symbolists have retained these innovations, but are now outdistanced by the new Realists. The apparent contradiction is not difficult to explain. Such poets as the Symbolists, in whose mode of cognition there is a predominance of auditory elements, need a rhythm at once supple and well modulated, one which is wedded to the thought and is at the same time gratifying to the ear ; and they have found this by liberating French verse from its old restraints. The visualisers, on the other hand, who do not look for a graduated melodious-ness in the phrase, readily accommodate themselves to the elementary and monotonous rhythms of that classical verse whose exalted immobility gives it the characteristics of great architecture; but they can accommodate themselves equally well to a freedom of versification kindred to the freedom of prose. They then pass from one extreme to the other.

In like manner they pass from the richly rhymed verse of the Parnassians to verse in which there are no rhymes at all. The Symbolist pendulum has not taken so wide a swing, for the Symbolists wish to make a stronger appeal to the ear, and are less easily satisfied. They therefore, in most cases, adopt a middle course in these matters of free verse and assonance. Their versification is freer than that of the Parnassians, but it is less unconstrained than that of the modern realists ; inasmuch as extreme strictness in the observance of the rules of prosody, and the complete disregard of these rules, are equally destructive as far as melody is concerned. Melody instinctively demands a fluid measure, which can sustain it without coercing it.

Thus we must not condemn the Symbolists, the revolutionists of yesterday, on the ground that they are reactionaries to-day, on the ground that they have failed to become as free as others have become. When we are considering the Symbolists and the Realists, we must never forget that they are offering us two distinct forms of art, whose laws cannot possibly be identical, any more than the drama and the novel can be subject to the same laws.

Poets who are also musicians are especially inclined to retain the use of rhyme and comparatively strict rhythm ; this is determined by the special characteristics of their artistic sensibility. Nay, more, a modern master of prose, Romain Rolland, who is also a musician, shows an increasing inclination to pack his prose with verse—Alexandrines, octosyllabic verses, assonances, and even rhymes. Just at the time when so many " poets " are abandoning the use of rhyme and formal rhythm, Rolland gives us *Colas Breugnon* and *Liluli*, as prose works which are unblushingly rhymed. This is because he is more of a musician than are the before-mentioned poets.

The Symbolists, too, are for the most part auditives. Continually they give us what the Realists so rarely give— " fine verse " which sings to us and which our memory cherishes.

Joseph Rivière tells of the trees in springtime :

> Où prie la chasteté
> De la chair évasée en fleurs d'éternité.[1]

> [Where is praying the chastity
> Of the flesh, burgeoning into flowers of eternity.]

and this is a " fine verse," for it enchases a lovely image in a perfectly finished musical phrase.

Henri Mugnier gives us music which is sweetly penetrating but a trifle weary, so that we think of Samain :

> Et des divans lourds de coussins et de fourrures
> Où des formes ont imprimé de belles poses,
> Et sur la cheminée un dieu de marbre rose
> Semble être là pour recueillir de frais murmures.[2]

> [And couches laden with cushions and fur-rugs,
> Where we trace the imprint of lovely forms ;
> And upon the mantel-piece a god in pink marble
> Seems to be there to gather up the artless whisperings.]

Sometimes, again, the music seems to surge, and to find its climax in a " fine verse " which is eloquent as well. Take, for instance, this close of an orgy :

> Et maintenant la nuit entière est bien passée,
> Et comme du matin se glisse un peu de jour,
> Dans l'atelier presque attristé, aveugle et sourd,
> Il semble qu'un grand rêve ait ses ailes cassées.[3]

---

[1] From J'ai respiré la fleur des marronniers, in En passant.

[2] Henri Mugnier, from Intérieur, in L'élévation voluptueuse, Ciana, Geneva, 1920.

[3] Henri Mugnier, from Orgie, in En passant.

[And now the whole night has passed away,
And when the first glimmer of morning steals
Into the studio, almost mournful, blind, and deaf,
It seems as if a great dream were standing there with
 broken wings.]

These Symbolists are less humanist than theWhitmanesque
Realists, but they are certainly more artistic.   Mankind and
art, you can take your choice ; they are mighty gods both.

Georges Armand Masson is one of the most melodious
of our poets, both when his fancy wanders off into legendary
perspectives, and when it broods ecstatically :

Sur le corps lumineux d'une dormeuse nue
. . . . qui d'une
Floconneuse vapeur à demi-revêtue
Semble sous le zénith mollement suspendue
Une vasque d'argent pleine de clair de lune.[1]

[On the radiant form of a nude woman asleep,
. . . . a form which,
Half-clad in mist wreaths,
Seems, beneath the zenith gently poised,
Like a silver bowl filled with moonlight.]

It is equally melodious when intoxicated by the panic
odours of the night :

Dans la nuit capiteuse où tournent les étoiles,
Dans la nuit de fête et de fièvre et de joie chaude,
Le vent qui a passé sur les collines mauves,
Le vent qui a baisé les joues des jeunes femmes,

 .   .   .   .

Le vent roule un flot d'or, de soie et de velours
Et dans la houle des feuillages qui bruissent

 .   .   .   .

Charrie de grands parfums maritimes et lourds
Comme de felouques chargées d'épices.[2]

[1] Décors, " Le Carmel," Geneva, January 1917.
[2] Parfums, " Le Carmel," Geneva, August 1916.

[In the heady night wherein the stars are spinning,
In the night of festival and of fever and of hot delight,
The wind which has passed across the mauve hills,
The wind which has kissed the cheeks of young women,

. . . . . .

The wind rolls, a flood of gold and silk and velvet,
And, in the swell of the rustling foliage,

. . . .

Bears with it huge and heavy sea-scents,
Like feluccas charged with spices.]

Listen to the suggestive harmony of these ultra-symbolist verses by Marcello Fabri :

Et par là c'est le lac où la candeur des cygnes
Sur la tristesse floue des algues et des eaux
Croise immaculément sous les dais d'or des vignes.[1]

[And over there is the lake where the whiteness of the swans
Upon the gentle sadness of the water-weeds and the waters
Criss-crosses immaculately beneath the golden daises of the
    vines.]

We may recall, finally, that *La folie de l'homme* has as its expressive sub-title "poème pour un musicien," thus modestly presenting itself as a foundation on which, perhaps, a musical superstructure may ultimately be upraised.

Another observation may be made apropos of this poem *La folie de l'homme*, which we have selected as typical of the new Symbolism. It trenches on the domain of myth. Indeed, unless the symbol moves in this direction it runs the risk of losing its way amid the trackless and impenetrable wilds of the inner self. The psychoanalysts, who interpret the dream as furnishing a spontaneous symbolical expression of the subject's most intimate feelings, regard the myth as a yet profounder dream wherein the affective life of the "collective unconscious" (Jung) is, in like

[1] From La folie de l'homme.

manner, symbolically portrayed. In other words, a myth is a symbol which has become impersonal, or suprapersonal. It is a road along which the symbol, without ceasing to be a symbol, can escape from the prison-house of the individual ego.

Such, indeed, was the royal road taken by Wagner. It is also the road along which, in a day nearer to our own, Carl Spitteler has moved.

But the fashioning of myth was a social and religious art. Now, as Jean Richard Bloch admirably shows, if Carnival is dead, it is because Lent died first of all. If our epoch has no great, no unanimous artistic expression, this is because it has no unanimity in anything. The era lacks a common faith ; it is a moral chaos. What society, what religion, can a myth beauteously typify to-day ? [1]

Monsieur Spenlé, professor at the University of Aix-Marseilles, in his study of Spitteler,[2] makes an attempt to reply to this contention, writing as follows :

" Outside the comparatively narrow limits of a particularist attachment to race and language, there exists a moral conception of the universal city, a wider fellowship of those who are guided by the same civilising thought, who are lighted by the same sun, who are grouped in the same Apollonian cult. As yet, doubtless, this is no more than an indefinable emotion, no more than the first lispings of a child—but from it there may one day grow new gods for mankind.

" That is what makes Spitteler's work so remarkably interesting to-day. It seems impossible to return to the artificial conception of literature which prevailed before the war. The emotions that have stirred our souls are too stupendous for such a relapse to be possible ; the horizons that have opened before our eyes are too vast. A cosmic poesy, no longer concerned with the subtle and quint-essential psychology of individual minds, but taking for its theme the universal human sentiments and the eternal human problems transfigured by a few myths, great, simple, and heroic—such would appear to be the aspiration of our epoch.

" This was the role of the old faiths. . . . This, too, will be the task of the poet in days to come. He will have to create round life an atmosphere that shall be once again serene, shall be luminous, shall be wholesome ; an atmo-sphere wafting an Apollonian spirit of freedom, clarity and order. He must fashion, as it were, a new Olympus, where these titanic emotions will revive in the form of victorious gods, visible and human."

Symbolist poetry, therefore, which already to-day is aerating itself in the breezes of nature and life, will end by objectifying itself through its trend towards myth. While remaining faithful to nature, it will cease to wander in the hidden recesses of a soul that has lost contact with real life. The Sleeping Beauty in the Wood will awaken, will open her eyes to look upon the world.

3. Towards a Synthesis : Dynamism.

Thus Symbolist art has likewise been influenced by the great current of " humanism " which, as we have already seen, bears the Whitmanesque poems along. The trend is not new. Some of the poets of the previous generation—Paul Fort, Emile Verhaeren, and Paul Claudel—were exemplars of a Symbolism that had undergone expansion and clarification.

Need I insist upon the supreme lucidity of Paul Fort ?

Even if it be true that Symbolism has a Teutonic colouring, this writer was fully competent to adorn it with the exquisite and limpid tints of the Ile de France. In his work we find the " dove-coloured " skies of which he is so fond, and no poet could be more typically French. Paul Fort tells us that he had learned from Moréas " to ventilate his verses " ; and his poetry is, indeed, open to all the winds that blow.

Verhaeren, a poet of vast range, is both Symbolist and Realist. That is why so many of our younger poets look upon him as their master, seeing that both schools can claim to follow his example. But, like all the headstrong, he must be wholly one thing or wholly the other. His development may be divided into three phases. The first is preparatory ; he is a Realist, a Parnassian Realist ; he writes *Les flamandes* (1883) and *Les moines* (1886). Then he becomes the most abstruse, the most introverted of the Symbolists ; he is a master of the new school, and gives us the dread poems *Les débâcles* (1888) and *Les flambeaux noirs* (1891). At length his mind is reopened to the outer world and to a revived Realism, the change being so great that Verhaeren has even come to be regarded as the Whitman of the French-speaking world. His plays, indeed, retain a Symbolist undertone ; but the Symbolism has an objective trend, and in *Hélène de Sparte* (1912) it tends to assume the characteristics of classified myth.

As for Paul Claudel, his poetry, with its framework of pious legend and its stained-glass Symbolism, does not find Realist and substantial details unworthy of notice. By his use of biblical " versification," this author especially reminds us of Whitman's rhythms. His topics, sometimes, are frankly Realist. But we must not be led astray by this. In one way or another he always remains a Symbolist. His poems remind us of the dreams Bergson describes (I quote from memory) as dreams " in which everything that happens appears perfectly natural, and through which, none the less, there somehow seems to resonate a note of eccentricity." In Claudel, this note is the symbolic resonance of the real. As an example it will suffice to recall *Le pain dur* when, at the close of the first act, the father, Turelure, conversing with Sichel in the quiet room at eventide, hears his son's carriage drive through the sleeping street and stop at the door. He utters the simple words : " I am afraid of death." The carriage is essentially real. Everything that happens is perfectly natural, and yet we shudder in sympathy with the father as if the real were sinking into a nightmare, and as if the carriage which has pulled up at the door were bringing Destiny in person.

Whereas the evolution of Symbolism may be described as a march towards the real, that of Realist poetry exhibits a movement in the opposite direction, a movement towards the subjective and the symbol. A meeting between the two trends would therefore seem to be imminent.

When we compare the Parnassian Realists of half a century ago with the Whitmanesque Realists of our own day, the extent of the movement is obvious. The Parnassian projected himself into the object, and in this object his own ego became merged. The Whitmanesque Realist, as previously explained, no longer describes the object, but describes merely his own impetus towards the object. Although the modern Realists are concerned with the same world of reality, they are much less objective than were the earlier Realists, and that is why the poets of the Whitmanesque school have moved so far away from the " ivory tower " [1]

---

[1] Tour d'ivoire. This is equivalent to " l'art pour l'art "—art for art's sake. The Parnassians held that the artist must hold aloof from social strife, and must shun having any moral aim in his art.—E. & C. P.

of the Parnassians. Between them and the Parnassians there is all the distance separating contemplation, which reflects the world, from action, which remoulds it. Thus the evolution of the Realists is in the direction of subjectivity. But if we consider the Whitmanesque poets only, we see that this movement, of which they represent the last stages at the present date, is continuing in them, so that they tend increasingly to become Symbolists of a kind.

Jules Romains has sometimes been acclaimed the leader of the Unanimists. But Victor Hugo, chief of the Romanticist poets, was—ironically enough—the least Romanticist of them all, or was at any rate a poet whose writings could not easily be fitted into the Romanticist framework. Perhaps something like this always happens in the case of those who are hailed as leaders of schools ? This much is certain, that Jules Romains appears to be the most Symbolist among the Realists. Mischievously, and yet good-humouredly, Dujardin (op. cit.) quotes stanzas written by Romains in the style of Mallarmé.[1]. In *Europe*, we may find quite a number of Symbolist passages. Take, for instance, the following lines, which close one of the poems :

> Tandis que, passion et défaite des yeux,
> Le lac sonnait midi d'un tel coup de lumière
> Que l'eau même semblait une forme de feu.

> [While, passion and defeat of the eyes,
> The lake struck noon with such a blow of light
> That the very water seemed a kind of fire.]

Still more striking, in this respect, is the following brief poem :

> Il y eut vers le nord de la plaine d'Europe,
> Dans un pays d'étangs que serrent les forêts,
> Au carrefour de deux canaux voués à l'âme,
> Un village, comme le cri d'un oiseau triste.

[1] Dujardin, op. cit., p. 28.

Il y eut, le matin du Dimanche en octobre,
Des barques qui menaient les familles frileuses,
Lentement, vers une maison pareille aux autres
Où l'on chante à plusieurs voix la gloire du Père.

[Towards the north of the great plain of Europe,
In a country full of ponds encircled by forests,
At the intersection of two canals consecrated to the soul,
Was a village like the cry of a sad bird.

On a Sunday morning in October,
Boats laden with shivering families
Were moving slowly towards a house like the others,
Where many voices were raised to the glory of the Father.]

Finally, in his latest works, Romains takes a decided turn towards legend (this implying a movement in the direction of the symbol). *Le bourg régénéré* has as its subtitle, " Petites légendes," and *Cromedeyre le vieil* often makes us think of the weird Claudel of *L'annonce faite à Marie.* *Cromedeyre*, doubtless, is much harsher, sturdier, rougher, than Claudel's work ; much less legendary and mystical. The reader must not understand more than 1 mean to say ! Beyond question, however, a comparison between the two authors is irresistible at times. Moreover, whereas a Symbolist trend is especially salient in Romains' case, in some of the other Realists we find passages which seem strongly Symbolist when compared with the work of their master, Whitman. Sometimes we even find that the strained methods of expression characteristic of the early Symbolists have found their way back by a devious route. Jouve, whose *Vous êtes des hommes* is extraordinarily limpid, becomes comparatively obscure in one of his later works :

> Il ne serait plus là
> Qu'une bête avec deux narines
> Pour être égal à l'odeur
> Des résines de la nuit,
>
> .   .   .   .

Qu'une bête ayant un cœur
Pour éprouver toute la terre
Avec le sang d'un amour.[1]

[Nothing would be there
But a beast with two nostrils,
To be equal to the smell
Of the resins of the night,

. . . .

A beast having a heart
To test the whole earth
With the blood of a love.]

He is not afraid to lapse into mythology:

Les tarasques des forêts,
Egarant les voyageurs
Se retournent dans le ciel
Avec un grand bruit étoilé.[2]

[The tarasques [3] of the forests,
Leading travellers astray,
Spin round in the sky
With a great starry noise.]

What could be more natural than that the advocates of
" direct expression " should exhibit such a trend ?   Psychological considerations have shown us that direct expression
is, before all, symbolical expression ; and that, when we
carry direct expression to its limit, we are likely to become
symbolical.   Anyone who wishes to be perfectly spontaneous, anyone who (like Jules Romains) shuns the
" discursive expression " which is the method of logical

[1] From Les vues du soleil levant, in Heures, livre de la grâce, Kundig,
Geneva, 1920.
[2] From Les vues du soleil levant, in Heures, livre de la grâce.
[3] A " tarasque " is a mythical monster, an amphibian supposed to have
dwelt of yore in the forests of the lower Rhone, and at times to have preyed
upon human beings.   At Whitsuntide, and on St. Martha's day, July 29th,
images of this creature are carried about in some of the towns of southern
France, and especially at Tarascon—the town having been founded by
one of the slayers of the tarasque.—E. & C. P.

thought, must, willy-nilly, adopt symbolical expression, which is the method of the affective life. Some of these writers may reject it on systematic grounds ; but the most straightforward among them will accept symbolical expression when it rises out of the depths of their unconscious.

No one will ask me to speak of contemporary verse from an entirely detached outlook, to consider it as it might be considered by a critic living in the year 2000. I am endeavouring to understand and to sympathise with the various trends. (Indeed, my conception of criticism is that it is a sincere attempt to sympathise, culminating in the straightforward statement : " I am able to sympathise up to this point. . .") I shall not be expected to furbish up an objectivity of view which could only be simulated, inasmuch as, myself a writer of verse and belonging to the same generation as the poets under discussion, I must necessarily have feelings of my own towards the poetry of our day. We were speaking just now of " humanism." When human beings meet, they do not expect from one another a learned treatise on literature, but a causerie in which each one says what he thinks. Probably, in the course of my exposition, you will have already asked yourself what my own preference might be, and you may already have foreseen that I cannot make a choice. Like a child asked which of two sweets it would like best, I am greedy enough to want both ! My " choice " is a synthesis, one that already looms on the horizon. Unconsciously, perhaps, the Realists and the Symbolists are drawing together. I am in full agreement with Dujardin, who looks forward to a " Symbolist Realism." He conceives the possibility of poetry which would have the tangible Realism and the comprehensive suggestiveness of the prophet Ezechiel, in conjunction with the judicious simplicity and far-reaching cordiality of André Spire :

Pauvres,
Qu'est ce que j'ai à vous dire ?
Je vous aimais.
Mes livres, mon Dieu, m'avaient parlé de vous.
Je suis parti vers vous pour vous porter ma force.
Mais j'ai vu vos dos ronds, vos genoux arqués,
Vos yeux de chiens battus qui guettaient ma main.
Qu'est ce que j'ai à vous dire ?
Il y a votre paume creuse entre nous.[1]

[You poor,
What can I say to you ?
I loved you.
My books, indeed, had spoken to me of you.
I set out towards you to bring you my strength.
But I saw your rounded backs, your bent knees,
Your eyes watching my hand like the eyes of a whipped dog.
What can I say to you ?
Your hollowed palm comes between us.]

In *Les époux d'Heur-le-port*, which bears the subtitle "légende du temps présent," Dujardin has given us a fine work which corresponds to his own formula, a work in which the real is reflected in symbols and in which the most perfect simplicity is wedded to the broad sweep of biblical versification. I am in full accord with this desire for a synthesis.

Indeed, in my own *Baptismales* I formulated what might be regarded as the catechism of the perfect Realist :

Car la réalité suffit et il n'est pas besoin de l'emphase.
Il n'est besoin de nul amphigouri, de nulle enflure pour faire
    épanouir la fleur rare de l' exstase.
Il me suffit de la réalité de cet enfant et du pli grassouillet de
    ses membres.

[1] André Spire, quoted by Dujardin, op. cit., p. 30.

[For reality suffices, and stress is superfluous.
There is no need for literary flourishes, no need for bombast,
    to make the rare flower of ecstasy expand its petals.
Enough for me the reality of this child, the folds of its plump
    little limbs.]

Two critics, writing without collusion, have mentioned
the name of Whitman in connexion with two of my books.
(I do not plume myself on the fact, for a literary work may
recall the style of one of the masters, even the greatest,
without being any the better for the comparison. Nay,
it may suffer thereby.) But I have translated Spitteler
into French, and I have written *Hantises légendaires*.
" Le Carmel " (founded by me in 1916, in conjunction
with Henri Mugnier) aimed at being a sanctuary, the Holy
Mountain, rather than an arena. The works of the new
Realists, Martinet's *Les temps maudits* and Jouve's *Danse
des morts*, appeared in its columns. But it likewise gave
hospitality to such Symbolists as Georges Armand Masson,
Georges Périn, and Henri Mugnier ; and a young poet,
Serge Milliet, made his debut here, publishing verses inspired
by Verlaine and Baudelaire.

Among our elders and masters, men differing as widely
as Emile Verhaeren, Romain Rolland, Carl Spitteler, Han
Ryner, and Paul Brulat, found a common platform in
" Le Carmel "—just as our admiration and affection went
out to them one and all. My aim in this periodical was,
I think, rather towards " breaking away " or towards
" elevation " than towards " aggression " ; but beyond
question my aim was to achieve a synthesis. I simply
record the fact, without comment, in order to show that,
in myself as in others, the two tendencies converge and seek
a confluence. But I do not wish to dwell on a matter
which is perhaps unduly personal. There may be vanity
in speaking of oneself, but I should certainly have been

hypocritical to say nothing about myself in this connexion. The need for frankness must serve as my excuse.

What is the nature of this confluence towards which our poetry is moving ? First of all, we may ask ourselves what points of contact already exist between the two trends. Realism and Symbolism are, perhaps, less remote one from another than they seem at first sight. Things which, when looked at from close at hand, appear to contrast strongly, may fuse into a comprehensive harmony when viewed from afar. Thus do mountains, fissured by precipitous chasms and roughened by tumbled rocks, assume, when seen from a sufficient distance, the unified aspect of a huge blue rampart.

Those able to appraise our epoch with the requisite aloofness will, beyond question, be mainly impressed by the traits we share. Let us try, for our own part to grasp these common characteristics.

One of the most striking of the common traits, I think, is the need for movement, for continuity and impetus, which is manifest in all our poetry, in that of the Realists no less than in that of the Symbolists. A name is needed for this trait, and we may perhaps describe it as *Dynamism*. The word has been proposed in various quarters ; and, having been put forward, it may well be accepted, even by those who would not have chosen it in the first instance. We do not choose our own Christian names, and an epoch seldom has the privilege of making such a choice. The name Romanticism was first applied derisively, to be subsequently adopted by the Romanticists as a challenge.

Dynamism lies at the heart of our age. It is part of our daily life. We see it at work in the growing inclination

15

towards movement and speed ; we see it, for good or for ill, in the fever for action. Man, who aforetime was " attached to the soil," now launches himself through space like a meteor. To one who looks from the window of a moving train, the whole countryside seems to be in a whirl. He no longer sees things, but only movement, the movement of warp and woof in a working loom. This Dynamism marks its impress on all the sciences. Since Darwin wrote, there have no longer been fixed species, but an evolving Life which scatters species as it flies. Freud applies a similar principle to the human psyche, deriving all the feelings from the primal " libido " which manifested itself first of all in instinct. Physical science resolves the atom into " centres of force." Einstein makes us dizzy by showing us that time is but a stupendous relation ; and that absolute dimension is a dimension moving with the velocity of light. Even philosophy follows in the wake of this movement, and at times actually runs ahead. For Nietzsche, it is the will-to-power ; for the pragmatists it is " action " ; for Bergson, who holds that " there is no being but only becoming," it is fluidity, continuity, " vital impetus." To Bergson, indeed, most of our poets are indebted for this great idea. How could it fail to have repercussions in art ? Upon the very stone, Rodin impresses a quivering tension, which suggests the unceasing energy of running water, the latent force of the panther crouching for the leap.

Need we be surprised that our poetry, likewise, is dynamic, or is tending to become so ? At the first glance, Dynamism exhibits two aspects. I mentioned them a moment ago : the unceasing energy of running water ; and the latent force of the panther crouching for the leap. The former aspect is that of continuity ; that of perceiving things and life as a flow, wherein there is neither beginning nor end, but universal evolution. The latter aspect is that of the force which impels to this continuous evolution; it is impetus and action. We find both aspects represented in Bergson's philosophy. When he is speaking of the inner life, which is a "melody" whose every note "trembles on the brink of the next note" and merges into it, he is contemplating the aspect of continuity. When he is speaking of the "vital impetus," he is contemplating the aspect of force.

The first, Aristotle would have said, is the form and the purpose of the movement; the second is its substance and its cause. Among the poets, the Symbolists have retained the former aspect; the Realists, the latter. Let me add that form and purpose have always been regarded by philosophers as the "categories" of the work of art, and we shall see how natural it is that the Symbolists have seemed to us to exhibit more "artistic finish," whereas the Realists, though often with less perfection, supply us with a greater quantity of concrete substance. Just now, the contrast between the two aspects became plain to us. Here we grasp their unity of origin and their unity of significance. This unity is Dynamism.

Thus we have no reason for astonishment that two trends which are so closely connected should achieve a confluence. We may congratulate ourselves that variety will never die out among poets, and that some of these will be more inclined to depict the aspect of flux, whilst others, differing in temperament, will be more inclined to depict the aspect of impetus. But, if they turn their attention towards the movement which underlies both the flux and the impetus, they will gain a more synthetic outlook. The synthesis will be the motive power of our art. Bergson's philosophy realised the same synthesis in another domain than that of art, and this, doubtless, was why his philosophy proved so influential at a particular phase in the evolution of thought.

The new poetry is a kinetic art. It was natural, therefore, that in such an innovator as Jean-Bard, the new poetry should have instigated the remarkable endeavour which he himself has named "dynamic interpretation." On the stage, Jean-Bard interprets poetry by the gesture accompanying the verse, as the bass of a piece of music sustains the melody and marks the rhythm. This unexpected resurrection of one of the principles of the Greek chorus is quite in the line of development of the most modern art. Effective gesture cannot but serve to prolong and reinforce the inner movement which is suggested by the rhythm of the poem.[1]

The meaning of Futurism,[2] for everything has a meaning, is to embody the most exaggerated form of the Dynamism towards which all our art aspires. But the Futurist formula is febrile, jerky, and illogical. To be so impetuous as to repudiate all the past, is to make a fetich of impetus. This is a fine aspiration, perhaps, even though it be impossible of fulfilment. But to repudiate all the sentiments of yesterday, while at the same time exalting the primitive and quasi-bestial instincts which form the biological foundation of all the sentiments, exalting these latter because they represent impetus—this is contradictory, for it is to accept wholesale what has just been refused when offered retail. The gravamen of the charge against the Futurists is that they are not what their name implies But they have certainly had some substantial and potent intuitions, which come within the Dynamist scheme :

[1] See below, " Jean-Bard and Dynamism," and " The Dynamic Interpretation of Poetry."

[2] In so far as the movement is sincere.

" Literature has hitherto glorified thoughtful immobility, ecstasy, and sleep; we shall extol aggressive movement, feverish insomnia. . . ."[1]

Before Einstein's physics had become famous, Marinetti's aim as poet was to suppress time and space so that nothing but speed should remain. Herein we find a remarkable resemblance of ideas, and one highly significant of contemporary trends:

" We stand upon the extreme promontory of the centuries! . . . Why should we look behind us, when we have to break in the mysterious portals of the Impossible? Time and Space died yesterday. Already we live in the absolute, since we have already created speed, eternal and ever-present."[2]

Again, there is indisputable greatness in the following challenge:

" 'Let us go, friends,' I say; ' let us set forth! Mythology and the mystical ideal have at length been surpassed. We are about to witness the birth of the Centaur, and we shall soon see the first of the Angels start their flight! We must shake the doors of life, in order to test the hinges and the screws. Let us set forth! Behold, upon the earth, the first glimmer of Dawn! What can equal the splendour of her red sword, which flashes for the first time upon our secular darkness? ' "[3]

Brave words! But what is really being created, the Angel or the Centaur? We are all familiar with the wise

[1] Initial Manifesto of Futurism, 3. [The English translation will be found prefixed to the catalogue of the Italian Futurist Painters' Exhibition at the Sackville Gallery, London, in March 1912. It is signed F. T. Marinetti.]

[2] Initial Manifesto of Futurism, 8.

[3] Initial Manifesto of Futurism. Preamble. [The preamble is not given in the English translation previously quoted. The Italian original may be read in Marinetti, I manifesti del futurismo, 4 vols., Istituto Editoriale Italiano, Milan, 1920, Vol. iv, pp. 9–27.]

and monitory saying, " He who tries to make an angel, makes a beast."

The Futurists err in their attempt to launch new gods. Without being aware of it, they are merely unchaining the most ancient instincts of the old Adam. Therein they neither serve the future nor negate the past.

Some of the Futurists exhibit the tribal pride of a Redskin chief. Marinetti glorifies " War, the only health-giver of the world " [1]—this being Nietzsche turned upsidedown !

(I apologise to Marinetti, who has written some fine verses ; but in certain respects, Futurist though he deem himself, he is " Pastist," hopelessly out of date.

Precisely because Futurism aspires to be impetus and nothing but impetus, it cannot possibly be reflective. Marinetti exalts intuition and categorically asks us to " hate intelligence." [2]

Bergson exalts intuition without asking us to despise intelligence, and herein lies his superiority to the Futurists. If we surrender ourselves to what we call intuition while rejecting the guidance of intelligence, we shall soon find ourselves enslaved by crude instinct. In actual fact, intelligence is the crown of evolution. The ecstasy, the mythology, and the mystical idealism which are supposed to be overcome by those who give themselves up to instinct, have themselves come into existence only that they may over-come instinct, which is the least Futurist of forces. As Tolstoy says : " A man may make use of the telephone, and yet be a barbarian." In like manner, we may thrill to the vibrations of a motor, and may intoxicate ourselves with speed so that the world flashes past our eyes, and yet

[1] Initial Manifesto of Futurism, 9.
[2] Les mots en liberté futuriste Edition futuriste, Milan, 1919, p. 25.

all the time be less "evolved" than the Christian ascetics.

Moreover, we are not innovators merely because we frisk about and shake ourselves vigorously. A dog does as much when he first comes out of the water. Contemplative immobility may at times be infinitely more Dynamist, more truly Futurist, than the shaking of a whole town as by an earthquake.[1]

Just as the musician can perceive as music things that produce very little sound, and even silence itself, so the Dynamist poet can perceive as movement that which is not moving in a material sense. To make music with that which is already music (bird song, for instance), or to make Dynamism with that which is already movement (motors, for instance)—this is the alphabet of art, and is as little praiseworthy as is, to quote Harpagon, the talent of "making good cheer with plenty of money." The artist in poetry, like the culinary artist, is one who knows how to "make good cheer with very little money," and how to make Dynamism with that which does not ostensibly move— with all the light of the world.

Futurism is action, just as the faith of many believers is sentiment. It is action to such a degree that it may be unable to remain intelligence ; that it may even, as we have seen, come to hate intelligence. Futurism cannot be argued with, any more than blind faith can be argued with. Even if such a formula may impel to splendid flights, we can foresee that it will never satisfy those who are unwilling to surrender their faculty of judgment. Let us, therefore, avoid the cruelty of passing judgment upon Futurism, and let us be content to understand its historical significance. We are indebted to it because, by its very intoler-

[1] The new theories of the will, assign more importance to the intellectual part of the voluntary act than to its motor and muscular elements. (William James, and the New Nancy School.)

ance, it has focussed attention upon kinetic art, and because it has thus paved the way for a more human form of Dynamism.

The most definite manifestation of Dynamism is in the domain of rhythm. The creation of free verse by the Symbolists, and the yet more thorough freeing of verse by the Whitmanesque Realists, have a dynamic bearing. The aim of the former is to avoid brusque interruptions in the continuity of feeling. The aim of the latter, who have rejected even melodic cadence, is to mark off more sharply the articulations of the movement, the pulses of the impetus. What will count henceforward in rhythm is movement. Dujardin, searching for the rhythmical formula which shall best suit the new poetry, culminates in biblical versification. The methods of Claudel and Dujardin are practically identical. The use of biblical versification does not necessarily imply the complete and final rejection of the classical types of verse, which may exist side by side with the other. Unquestionably, however, the effect of the movement in favour of biblical versification will be to widen and ventilate verse yet more. Dynamism needs fresh currents of air, and biblical versification gives especial scope for this. It is certainly remarkable that two men as different from one another as Whitman and Nietzsche, two writers whom the groups we have been considering acclaim as their respective masters, should both have come to adopt a quasi-biblical versification—Whitman, in *Leaves of Grass*, and Nietzsche, in *Also sprach Zarathustra*.

Another characteristic common to the poets of both groups is the antagonism displayed by most of them towards the brutality of the present. Whether their attitude be one of aggression or one of breaking away, they are all hostile to the present. In the age of iron they raise the protest of the soul.

In this respect, our epoch is certainly one of a revived Romanticism—the fact has been pointed out by more than one author.

Thus, Paul Colin writes : " An epoch without splendour and without frenzy—every century knows an epoch characterised by thoughtfulness and timidity. Some such have been famous, and I blush to cite here the name of Werther. Our century opened with a crisis similar to the Wertherian. It was not finished when the war broke out, and the war has not put a term to it." [1]

In *Pays du soir*,[2] René Arcos has finely expressed the other aspect, the positive and creative aspect, of this contemporary " Romanticism." " The peculiarity of the strong in soul is that they know how to provide a light for themselves even in the thickest darkness. ' The day of misfortune is least of all the day on which I should dream of repudiating life,' cries the hero of Senancourt's *Obermann* in the hour of his greatest need. He adds : ' Resistance awakens the soul and gives it a more stalwart attitude.' Not by chance do I quote the words of one of the most sombre among our Romanticists, for the sadness which weighs to-day upon youth, disillusioned and discouraged, is akin to that which bowed men's spirits after the Napoleonic wars.

" Let the soul awaken at length. On all hands, claims are being voiced—for a better standard of life, for higher wages, for the right to scandalous wealth, for the old privileges of the master, for the new demands of the slave, for the dividing up of the land, and so on, and so on. But who will voice the claims of the soul ? "

[1] " L'Art Libre." Brussels. March 1921 (the number devoted to Vildrac).
[2] Editions du Sablier, Geneva, 1920.

Some of us have had the bitter joy of living in the retirement of a voluntary exile, among the upper valleys of Switzerland or on the shores of her lakes, above the pestilential atmosphere of a gangrenous Europe. Political opposition was not congenial to us. We rendered unto Cæsar the things which were Cæsar's, and were content with the humble endeavour to cherish the goods of the spirit. We had an inward conviction that we were not alone. We did not, indeed, know as yet how many comrades we had among the vigorous younger Frenchmen, for they were still constrained to silence ; we did not yet know the remarkable unanimity of the poets. But Romain Rolland was among us. The Upper Engadine still seemed to echo to the footsteps of Nietzsche, who had come there when he contemptuously shook off the dust of the brutalised and self-satisfied Germany of 1870—the monstrous birth which was to grow into the Europe of to-day. We had with us, too, the memory of our great forefathers, the French refugees from the First Empire, whose descendants have come to regard them as incorporating the very spirit of France. I am writing close to Madame de Staël's place of exile, the Château of Coppet with its rose-coloured walls and its green shutters, closed, and thick with dust—the Château which broods over its memories, amid great trees, beside the peaceful waters of the lake. How similar was the history of the spirit then and to-day !

There is an essay of Lamartine's which is read too rarely, an essay entitled *Les destinées de la poésie.* Let me quote :

" It was in the days of the Empire. None but those who have lived through those days can realise their arrogant sterility.

" It was the diabolical smile of a genius from the nether pit who had been able to degrade a whole generation. Cunning and force, figures and sabres—everything was there ! . . . Nothing but figures was acceptable. Since figures do not reason, they are an apt instrument for tyranny. . . . The military chief of those days wanted no other missionary, no other criminal agent ; and this agent served him well. Throughout Europe, there was not an idea but was crushed beneath his heel, was not a mouth but was gagged by his leaden hand. . . .

" Two great geniuses whom tyranny watched with uneasy eye stood alone in their protest against this sentence of death upon the soul, upon intelligence, and upon poesy— Madame de Staël and Chateaubriand."

Shall we not soon be reading everywhere, and even (oh, banality !) in manuals of literature, that Romain Rolland in our own days played the saviour like Staël and Chateaubriand ? As for us of the younger generation, it is not our business to pose as Lamartines. But it is a fact that Romanticism, which was the essence of the poetic life of a century ago, was born of a protest against the brutal reality of the Empire, and that our own generation of poets has grown to manhood while making a similar protest. It is in this respect that we revive the Romanticist tradition.

How does the new Romanticism differ from the old ? It is, or at least aspires to be, more fully conscious. Genuine Romanticism does not know where it is going ; it is a chaos. In the field of ideas, it wants to be simultaneously, though without any clear understanding of the fact, individualist and socialist. These two trends neutralise one another within the Romanticist, but their conflict will persist when Romanticism has had its day. In poetry, Romanticism is both painting and music, both reality and dream. Here, likewise, a severance occurs ; and we see the Parnassians in opposition to the Symbolists. The double opposition continues to find expression in the art and thought of our own day, wherein we may discern individualist and communist leanings, Symbolist and Realist poetry.

But the most remarkable feature of the contemporary artistic movement is that these two forms of poesy are moving towards a confluence. Does not this amount to saying that the individualist and communist trends which these schools of poetry respectively represent, and between which the conflict is so real, are confusedly endeavouring to make common cause and to complete one another within us ? There can be no doubt that our epoch will not attain stability until a perfect union shall have been achieved, in full awareness. This harmonious conjuncture is already fore-shadowed in certain minds. All Romain Rolland's energies are working in this direction, and that is why so many of us take him as guide. Though indomitably individualist, he is an individualist through love, and only retires into himself that he may serve mankind better :

" Every man who is truly a man must learn how to remain alone amid the multitude, how to think alone for the multitude—and, in case of need, against the multitude. To think sincerely, even if it be against the multitude, is still to think for the multitude. Mankind needs that those who love their fellows should be able to hold their own against their fellows, and to revolt against them if needs must." [1]

In a word, and to speak in the Hegelian manner, after the Romanticist thesis, and after the ensuing antithesis wherein Symbolism runs counter to Realism and the individualist spirit runs counter to the communist spirit, it would seem that we are moving, at long last, towards a new synthesis. In the synthesis we find the same elements as in the thesis ; but whereas in the thesis they were in a state of confusion, in the synthesis, thanks to the period of

[1] Romain Rolland, Clerambault, Ollendorff, Paris, 1920, Introduction.

opposition, they are being arranged in orderly fashion and have grown self-conscious.

Our synthetic art will, therefore, be more fully conscious. Are we too bold in saying that it will be more intelligent than Romanticism—the enfant terrible, so free-handed, so young, so simple, so appealing ?

" I detest figures," wrote Lamartine,[1] who regarded figures as synonymous with tyranny. This is the quintessence of Romanticism, which is hostile to precision and to science. This, as Brunetière points out, is its supreme weakness, and a mark of its great simplicity. Romanticism shuns the truth, and its idealism always rings false. That is why the most outstanding intelligences of the last century, such as Stendhal and Mérimée, dismissed it with a smile.

No doubt our own literary epoch has its faults, but at any rate it has escaped this one. We no longer loathe figures. The contemporary poet is willing, as Goethe was willing, to be a scholar. To say nothing of Romain Rolland, who has been described as a living encyclopaedia, many of our poets have scientific leanings. Dujardin is professor at the Sorbonne, where he lectures on the history of religion. Durtain and Duhamel are doctors. One of the members of the Unanimist school is said to have just published, under a pseudonym, a treatise on physiological optics.

" After a lengthy period of patient analysis," writes Rolland, " the new age is fired with an imperious need for synthesis." [2]

I read, moreover, in an article by Jacques Duvaldizier entitled *Les tendances nouvelles de la poésie moderne* : " Alike for rhythmical purposes and for the choice of images and words, not merely has verse been completely enfran-

---

[1] Op. cit.
[2] Empédocle d'Agrigente et l'âge de la haine, Editions du Carmel, Geneva, 1918.

chised, but fresh combinations and new riches are offered, like a string of jewels, to the cultivated artist. He needs nothing but a synthetic spirit to make him the universal beneficiary of the analytical discoveries of his predecessors." [1]

We shall become aware both of this chaotic tumult and of this need for synthesis, if we turn over the pages of some such young and lively periodical as Marcello Fabri's " Revue de l'Epoque " (Paris), or Roger Avermaete's " Lumière " (Antwerp).

This poetic synthesis which is striving for realisation within us is, first of all, a union of the various arts which are incorporated in poetry ; imagery and melody, reality and symbol. It is also, despite the Futurists, a union of art and thought. Dynamism is well fitted to become the foundation of so comprehensive a synthesis, for a kinetic art is preeminently a synthetic art. As I shall show in fuller detail subsequently,[2] every sensation gives rise to a motor reaction, or at least to the sketch of one. But whereas we have as many different kinds of sensation as we have sense organs, only one kind of motor reaction is possible. Perhaps the general similarity of motor reactions furnishes the sole adequate explanation of the remarkable similarities the mind sometimes perceives between sounds, colours, other sensations of light, sensations of touch, weight, etc., so that we speak of a " clear tone," a " colourless voice," a " piercing cry "—to say nothing of the phenomena of coloured hearing.

Bergson writes :

" As the same motor reaction may follow many different recollections, it is not a definite recollection which is evoked by a definite bodily state ; on the contrary, many different recollections are equally possible. . . . They are subject to

---

[1] " Revue de l'Epoque," No. 15, Paris, March 1921.
[2] Infra, The Dynamic Interpretation of Poetry, pp. 270 et seq.

only one common condition—that of entering the same
motor frame : in this lies their ' resemblance,' a term
which is vague in current association theories, but which
acquires a precise meaning when we define it by the identity
of motor articulations." [1]

I may add that this is of supreme importance to those
who wish to understand the likeness between the sensations
felt by means of the different sense organs, to those who wish
to understand the common foundation which underlies the
various arts. The common foundation is to be found
in motor reactions, in a kinetic art. Furthermore, an idea,
like a sensation, initiates motor reactions ; and it is in
this direction that we must look if we wish to discover the
foundation for a synthesis of ideas and sensations, of thought
and art.

A true and living synthesis must never be conceived as a
static assembling of fragments, but as a living organism, a
Dynamism in fact, through which the various parts are
enabled to secure mutual interpenetration.

" The generations to which we belong," writes Canudo,
" are affected with the restlessness and the pains of travail.
An art, vaster than could ever have existed before, is now
in the throes of being born. It will be an art that will give
supreme expression to these generations, just as ecstasy
was the supreme expression of Christianity, and as the dance
was the supreme expression of paganism. It bears the
name of Dynamism, being more spiritual than the dance
and more fleshly than ecstasy." [2]

Too often, poetry has aimed at rivalling music in the
matter of melody, painting in the matter of imagery,
logical prose (and even philosophy and science) in the matter

[1] Bergson, L'énergie spirituelle, Alcan, Paris, 1919, pp. 212–213 ; the
quotation in the text is from the English translation by H. Wildon Carr,
Mind-Energy, Macmillan, London, 1920, p. 198.
[2] Cent versets d'imitation, " Revue de l'Epoque," No. 15, March 1921.

of thought. The combat has ever been unequal. All that poetry can legitimately aspire to, is to be a brief synthesis of music and painting, of sensation and thought. In this respect, no other art, no other mental discipline, can compete with it ; for whereas each of the other arts can serve better than poetry to satisfy some of our faculties considered in isolation, poetry alone can give harmonious, though abbreviated, expression to the human spirit in its entirety. Now, Dynamism will be of great help to poetry in this harmonising and cultural role, in this role of becoming a point of convergence for all the roads of the senses and the spirit ; just as, beneath the shadow of a wayside cross, the men of a dozen hamlets come together on feast days to rejoice and to pray.

But is there not a certain futility about this attempt to forecast the direction in which the art of an epoch will move ? May it not come to pass that to-morrow there will arise a new genius who, affirming his masterful individuality regardless of the prevailing trends of the time, will falsify all our anticipations ?

Indubitably, the work of genius is always a creation. Every great artist reveals himself, in the art of his day, as a figure that is unexpected, as a figure that is essentially new. He gives an unforeseen turn to the furrow that time is tracing. Nevertheless the fresh turn is given to a furrow which was being traced before his influence made itself felt. His work is always the resultant of two forces : that of the time in which he lives ; and that which is peculiar to himself. Even the most refractory of geniuses, even the one who seems most in revolt against his environment, is none the less, whether he like it or not, the child of his own day. Would not the genius be greater still if he could be exclusively himself—though it were probably at the cost of remaining unrecognised ? I think not ; for, though originality is essential to art, sympathy is no less indispensable. Does not Guyau tell us that sympathy is the most vital element of art ? It is through sympathy that a great artist is always part of his own epoch, even though, in virtue of his originality, he can detach himself from and can dominate that epoch.

A few pages back we were considering the case of Victor Hugo, who in this respect is typical. Fundamentally, no one could be less a Romanticist than he, if the Romanticist soul be mainly characterised by pessimism and by intense subjectivity. Nevertheless " the sonorous echo " of his artist's sympathy enabled him to understand the Romanticist trend of his time, and to understand it so well that he became its herald and its guide. But he soon sloughed the spirit of René,[1] laid aside the doleful garb which ill became the ruddy complexion of his triumphant health. Our masters are those who are, in this fashion, permeated with the time spirit, and who are yet able to absorb it instead of being absorbed by it. This time spirit is for each one of them, the promontory from which will begin a flight peculiar to himself. Now, though we may be unable to foresee the purely individual elements in the impetus that will animate the movements of the geniuses of the new day, we can none the less outline the promontory, whence will begin the joyous curve of their unforeseeable flight.

[1] The hero of Chateaubriand's novel of that name, the counterpart of Werther, Obermann, Childe Harold, etc.—E. & C. P.

COPPET,
March 1912.

MARCEL MARTINET

1. Les Temps maudits.

(" Le Carmel,"
August 1917.)

Les temps maudits, though during the war it was exiled
to Switzerland by the censorship, is the work of a French
poet. The author is a typical Frenchman, in his ardour,
his animation, his wit, the warmth of his sympathies, and
his genuine love for France in its concrete and palpitating
actuality.

Already before the war Marcel Martinet was a socialist,
one of the most sincere and the most human, and was on
the staff of " L'Effort Libre." He knows the workers,
loves and understands the people, is himself of the people ;
and some of his sallies recall Jehan Rictus, author
of *Le Cœur populaire*. As a true Frenchman, he
unmasks hypocrisies and satirises idols ; and, as a man
whose heart is of the people, he unmasks and satirises in
the vein, not of Voltaire, but of Hugo.

Les temps maudits continually recalls *Les châtiments*.
I do not hesitate to say that these poems signalise the revival
of lyrical satire : the satire which Hugo evoked with the
cry, " Muse Indignation, viens " ; that which spontaneously
surges up in fervent hearts during troublous times in the
history of the nations ; that of which, long ago, Isaiah was
the mouthpiece. I do not say that Martinet equals Hugo.
Still less do I wish to convey the impression that he imitates
Hugo. Although some of his verses ring like those of

Les châtiments, the form of *Les temps maudits* is very different, and is extremely individual. These poems are written in free verse. But, though they are unrhymed, they are for the most part rhythmical, the pulses of the rhythm communicating to the reader the buffetings endured by the poet. From time to time this rhythm gathers its forces, in proportion as the author's feeling becomes condensed and concentrated. Then we have splendid Alexandrines, almost classical, full of fire, and weighted with anguish and restrained horror. They are virile, these verses; they are vigorous and great. Consider, for example, the following strophe from the opening poem, *Aux esclaves* :

Peuple, grand peuple, ...

     .   .   .   .

A l'heure où je vous vis panteler et mourir,
Pour une cause, hélas ! qui n'était point la vôtre,
O hommes de mon sang, compagnons de ma race,
Frères de la patrie que nous devions bâtir,

A l'heure où je vous vis dans ce noir Paris morne,
Femmes des ouvriers qui partaient en riant,
Vous depuis si longtemps rompues aux sacrifices,
Sangloter puis sourir pour un dernier adieu,

     .   .   .   .

Peuple, peuple trahi par tous ceux qui parlaient,
Du fond de ma douleur, du fond de ma colère,
O peuple déchiré, je t'ai jeté ces cris.

[People, great people . . . .

     .   .   .   .

At the hour when I saw you panting and dying
For a cause, alas, which was not yours,
O men of my own blood, companions of my own race,
My brothers in the fatherland which it behoved us to upbuild,

At the hour when I saw you in this dark and gloomy Paris,
Wives of working men who were going to the front with a smile,
You women who for so long have been inured to sacrifice,
When I saw you weeping, then smiling in a last farewell,

.   .   .   .

People, people betrayed by all those who talked,
From the depth of my sorrow, from the depth of my anger,
O lacerated people I uttered to you these cries.]

Consider, again, in the poem *L'agonie* whose refrain is
" Grande pitié que est au royaume de France," the
following apostrophe to the people of France :

Oui, tu aimais la vie, et tu savais aimer,
Et sachant bien aimer tu savais bien haïr ;
C'est par là qu'ils t'ont prise, avilie et trompée,
Ceux qui ont pour métier de savoir bien mentir.

Tu avais tant souffert, tu allais tant souffrir !
Pour porter ta douleur, pour porter ta misère,
Pour renier ta vie, il fallait bien haïr ;
Peuple partout dupé, tu t'es haï toi-même.

.   .   .   .   . O mon peuple de France,
C'est le crime des crimes, ils ont pourri ton âme.
Après la mort des hommes et la mort de la terre,
Si ton âme était saine, il restait l'espérance,

Mais ton âme, ô mon peuple ! où retrouvera-t-elle,
O grand peuple aveuglé, la lumière perdue ?
Mendiera-t-elle encor la divine étincelle
Dans les cœurs apostats de ceux qui l'ont vendue ?

[Ay, you loved life, and you knew how to love,
And, knowing well how to love, you knew well how to hate ;
Thereby were they enabled to snare you, to degrade and betray
    you,
Those whose trade it is to be successful liars.

You had suffered so much, and had still so much to suffer!
To endure your pain, to endure your wretchedness,
To deny your life, you needed to hate well ;
People, deceived in all things, you hated yourself.

. . . . . . O my people of France,
It is the crime of crimes that they have corrupted your soul.
After the death of men and the death of the land,
If your soul were healthy, hope would still be left,

But your soul, O my people, where will your soul find again,
O great blinded people, the lost light ?
Will your soul be able to beg back once more the divine spark
From the apostate hearts of those who have sold it ?]

Amid these vigorous outbursts we have interludes
whose delicate and captivating grace moves us profoundly
by its contrast:

> Petit matin d'octobre
> Tendre, frais et limpide,
> Ta lumière est légère
> Sur les derniers feuillages
> Et sur la calme Seine
> Où la brume est fondue
> Et sur ces doux nuages
> Qu'un un peu de brise aère.[1]

> [Early October morning,
> Tender, fresh, and limpid,
> Your light falls softly
> On the last leaves,
> And upon the tranquil waters of the Seine
> Where the mist-wreaths are scattering,
> And upon the flimsy clouds
> Drifting before the breeze.]

In this book there are many instances of carelessness in
matters of form, and a good many repetitions. These
things are natural under stress of emotion, but they would
tend to weary us in the long run, were not the poignant
and impassioned strophes sustained throughout by so
vigorous an impetus. But, as I have already pointed out
(supra, p. 184), the power to write lyrical satire is a sign

[1] From Petit matin d'octobre, in Les temps maudits.

of a sovereign emotion—of such an emotion as breathes through Martinet's verses :

> L'incendie gagne, bonnes gens,
> Et la bête lachée ravage
> Au mépris des règles du jeu,
> Au-delà des bornes prescrites,
> On tue les blessés et les femmes,
> On mutile les prisonniers,
> On affame les petits enfants,
> Alors vous sursautez, Tartufes,
> Et vous criez avec effroi :
> Halte-là ! ce n'est plus la guerre,
> Ce crime n'est plus patenté,
> Voici les frontières du crime
> Délimitées par nos décrets,
> Ce n'est qu'à l'intérieur du cercle
> Qu'est reniée l'humanité.[1]

> [The fire gains, good folk.
> The unchained beast is ravaging
> In defiance of the rules of the game,
> And far beyond the bounds that have been set.
> The wounded are being killed ; women, too ;
> Prisoners are being mutilated ;
> Children are starving.
> Now, Tartufes that you are, you are horrified.
> In alarm, you exclaim :
> Stop, stop ! This is not the way to make war !
> There is no warrant for that particular crime !
> Here are the bounds set to crime
> By the statutes we have drawn up !
> You must not deny humanity
> Except within the charmed circle !]

Les temps maudits, then, is a true lyrical satire. This suffices to make it a magnificent book, one upon which, in better days, France will pride herself.

[1] From Droit des gens, in Les temps maudits.

2. La Maison à l'Abri.[1]

Marcel Martinet has been one of the revelations of the war epoch.   Moreover, he shares with the other true writers of this period the characteristic of producing work which is the very opposite of bellicose.   " The Sheltered House " is a novel of anger and pity, and a great love breathes through the anger no less than through the pity.

But anger, revolt, is the key-note.   This is the note that sounds so fiercely in the strains of *Les temps maudits*, but the tension of these poems cannot be persistently maintained.   The lyrical hour is followed by an hour of prose ; it is followed by an hour of realism as pitiless, as disillusioned, as circumscribed, as the poor lives of men ; an hour full of the loathing and the heartache inspired by the prevalent lethargy, but also full of a cordial sympathy for all that is human.   Such is *La maison à l'abri*.

The book contains the story of a Parisian household during the war—a household just like other households, " for the duration of the war."   Sheltered ?   Pitiful irony !   Death enters, none the less ; death comes, to bring mourning and misery in its train.   All the war is disclosed to us within the narrow space bounded by the four walls of this " sheltered " house.

The war is itself the real " person of the drama " : the war, and the house ; for this latter is likewise a living personality.   We must not grumble because the other dramatis personae are silhouettes, are nothing more than silhouettes which we follow for a brief space until they fade away.   They only exist in virtue of their relationships with the wartime house.   It is just as well that they should have no independent existence, that they should be

[1] Published by Ollendorff, Paris, 1919.

obliterated and crushed by the great and tragical superposed entity, for this obliteration of the individual, of
individual suffering, is the painful dramatic reality of our
time. That is what Martinet portrays for us.

Nevertheless the silhouettes live, for they are skilfully
drawn by a consummate artist. " A plump little fellow,
wearing a flower in his buttonhole ; self-important, but with
an ingratiating smile ; bald and clean-shaven, with a
blue chin and pink cheeks "—he seemed like a doll, with a
shining but cruel face, this puppet who came unconcernedly
on his official mission to tell a woman that her husband had
been killed at the front. Here is one of the most fleeting
sketches in the book, and yet how vivid it is ; and many of
the others, more detailed, are more vivid still. There is
Madame Blin, the concierge, the incarnate soul of the great
house, its mother, as it were ; Pensiot, the poor old chap
with an impediment in his speech, who is becoming doited ;
Professor Dumont, who has faith in virtue and in the Repub-
lic, whom the war robs of his son, his all, and who has then
nothing left to live for except his obstinate hatred ; Madame
André Maury, the young widow of a painter who has fallen
in the war, remains maternal in spirit, and is an embodiment of all the grief of those days. Marcel Martinet has
the skill of the born novelist ; he knows how to put himself
in the place of his various characters, and how to espouse
their ideas instead of inflicting his own on them. His
outlooks are disclosed plainly enough by the totality of
his vision, but he does not put his private opinions into
the mouths of the persons he depicts.

The style is excellent, straightforward, and to the point.
It might have been bettered by a little more condensation.
The author has a fondness for repetitions, partly instinctive
and partly deliberate, in this reminding us of Péguy. " Lui
perdu au loin de la mer dorée, de la mer lointaine, elle

retournée sur la terre, elle terre-à-terre, sur la pauvre terre détrempée par le sang et par les larmes." [" He, lost in the depths of the golden sea, of the far-off sea ; she, her eyes turned back earthward, of the earth earthy, gazing upon the poor earth, drenched with blood and with tears."] Sometimes there is actual tautology. " Ne pouvaient presque pas supporter, endurer, tolérer cette voix." Such repetitions are characteristic of the linguistic rhythms used by persons suffering from obsession, by persons who are obstinately convinced. Martinet is obsessed by what his characters live through and by what they say. That is his excuse. But the mechanism forces itself unduly upon our attention, and therefore becomes wearisome at times.

Martinet, however, is not so much concerned with writing as with expressing, and with doing this latter as humanly as possible. Above all, he is human. He resembles Whitman in the way in which he takes to his arms all human suffering, all the life of mankind, each and all, separately and collectively. " Chaque cas est le plus exceptionnel et le plus terrible." [" It is always a special case, and always the most terrible."]

So, too, each instantaneous glimpse of life is the only true picture at that particular moment. No matter that a different picture may conflict with it to-morrow. That is why, by turns, Martinet will give fervent expression to contradictory sentiments. Sometimes he shows us his disdain for supinely accepted and uninspired suffering, which lacks even the element of nobility that belongs to great and lyrical afflictions : " All that now remained was despair. . . . In the infinite and universal discouragement, nothing was left but the foul and irremediable fact of being man." Anon, however, in spite of everything, the marvel of being alive and aware fires his imagination ; he is filled with the sense of wonder and admiration of which Verhaeren made an evangel, and which is always the poet's gospel. Such a sentiment continually recurs in Martinet on the morrow of intense disillusionment : " How lovely was the world, even the poor town world, this day in late autumn !"

P. J. JOUVE

I

Poème contre le grand Crime. [1]

("Le Carmel,"
September 1916.)

P. J. JOUVE is one of the rare spirits who have been bold enough to voice sentiments discordant with those of the European chorus. Even persons who differ from him, should at least acclaim his courage and sincerity. In 1915 he published the first of his books to be inspired by the world catastrophe. This was entitled *Vous êtes des hommes.*[2] His new volume, *Poème contre le grand crime,* voices the same inspiration. Comparing the second book with the first, we find that an all-embracing pity has become even more comprehensive and more intense in the heart of the poet ; that his thought is more steadfast and more undaunted than ever ; and (so he seems to imply) that for these developments he is indebted to Romain Rolland. The form of the new book is adequate to the thought it conveys ; there is no superfluous ornament. Rhyme is discarded throughout. The rhythm, founded rather upon the tonic accent of the words than upon their syllabification, is that of a rhythmical prose, of a prose whose rhythm is determined by the pulses of emotion, by the systole and diastole of feeling. There is no pose of isolation. Jouve proclaims himself a disciple of Tolstoy, and he is a disciple

[1] Editions de Demain, Geneva.
[2] Editions de la Nouvelle Revue Française, Paris.

y

y
y
y
y

to the core. He does not, as do so many, merely profess
the master's doctrines outwardly and verbally ; he relives
Tolstoy's very life. He visualises the Russian in the familiar
attitude, leaning against an oak, hands thrust into the belt
of a well-worn blouse. Jouve sees Tolstoy as vividly as
the Christian mystics used to see Christ ; Jouve is permeated
with Tolstoy's faith, his love, his thirst for martyrdom,
and his humility. The world is traversing a period of confusion like that of the opening centuries of the Christian
era. Now, as then, our spiritual life is in a ferment. Jouve's
books are among those in which this invisible fermentation
can be felt. They must be read much as we read the Acts
of the Apostles. Then only can we understand them.

II

Danse des Morts. [1]

("" Le Carmel,"
February 1919.)

The dance of the dead, all the dead : those of the trenches ;
those of no-man's land, whose ragged corpses hang limply
among the barbed wire entanglements ; and those of the
rear (described by Marcel Martinet as "" live men colder than
the dead ""), the gorged, the profiteers, whose souls are
dead, who bleat sanctimonious amens over others' sacrifices ; those who are gassed and blinded by the mephitic
exhalations of "" public opinion "" ; and those, likewise,
who are dead to themselves—men of science, men of letters,
churchmen, and statesmen. All these figures file past, and
Death makes them dance a jig : Death who alone is intelligent, clear-sighted, chuckling at the omnipresent absurdity ;
Voltairian and sceptical Death, whose outbursts of laughter

[1] Editions des Tablettes, Geneva, 1917 ; second edition, éditions de
l'Action Sociale, La Chaux de Fonds, 1917.

sound the note of despair. Then we see the heart of the
poet, in whom faith still lives, a faith obstinately upbuilded
upon the universal ruin, and in defiance of Death's mockeries.
Such are the characteristics of this work, breathless with
the rapidity of its movement—a nightmare book, sombre
and puissant, resembling (so Jean de Saint-Prix phrased it
to me) " that of a medieval monk fulminating maledictions."
Martinet's poems were lyrical satire ; Jouve's *Danse des
morts* is tragical satire.

Vous êtes des hommes and *Poème contre le grand crime* were
works in a different vein ; they were placid and lyrical.
From one point of view, I prefer the last-named to the
Danse des morts, for there is more literary finish in the
Poème. In the *Danse*, the emotion boils over ; anger
tears the rhythm to tatters. There is no longer a song but
a cry ; we are at or near the verge where art becomes
impossible. This may do credit to the author's sensibility,
but it does harm to his work. The *Danse* is no longer suggestive, as was the *Poème* ; though the feeling that animates
the *Danse* is more ardent, it does not communicate itself
to the reader so effectively, *and will hardly communicate
itself except to those who have previously and spontaneously
experienced it.* That is what differentiates an " effusion "
from a work of art. Here, in the *Danse*, we have an effusion,
one might almost say an explosion. But those who are
already in sympathy with the author, who share his feelings
but have not always ventured to avow them, will find that
the book makes a strong appeal, that it is moving and stirring.
Now there are many of us who, in essentials, share the
author's *feelings*, though they may not necessarily follow
all his *thoughts* to their logical conclusion. For those of
this way of feeling, artistry is superfluous. Thus the book
is appropriate to its time.

Moreover, the work is a deed. Others have felt

indignant, like Jouve, but have kept silence. The publication of the *Danse des morts* is a bold undertaking. Here
we must salute the author, without more ado.

Finally, the *Danse* is typical. It typifies the period of
chaos through which we are passing ; it has chaos within
it ; its chaotic rhythm (chaos being the negation of rhythm)
does not set an example to be followed—and yet is perhaps
the best for this particular work. In such an epoch, the
poet may cease to be an artist, and nevertheless remain a
poet in the strongest sense of the word, may remain a
creator. His song is a clarion call, a deed, a stroke with the
pickaxe in the hands of one who is digging the foundations
of the city of the future ; it is like Amphion's song, which
endows the stones with life, and makes of them a rampart.

THE DIARY OF A FRENCH PRIVATE [1]

(" Le Carmel," December 1917.)

THIS is a good war-book. There are so few of them, that they are worth greeting when they come. It is a work based upon living experience, and it has historical importance.

The author gives us a record of daily happenings, of impressions noted without prejudice, and without any aim at systematisation. Nevertheless, these scattered impressions are not so interesting on their own account as because of the conclusions which the writer goes on to draw from them. The diary does not make its mark through the force of imagination, through vigorous draughtsmanship, or by brilliancy of colouring. Not that it is wanting in picturesqueness. Nothing could be better visualised than the arrival of the convoy of Russian prisoners in the fortress where the Frenchmen are confined. In bold outline we are shown the overflow of sympathy, the ludicrous failure of the French and the Russians to understand one another, the use of dumb show, the prostrations of the Muscovite bears to kiss their benefactors' footsteps, the brotherly exchange of képis for fur caps swarming with lice. Substantially, however, Gaston Riou is not to be classed among the visualisers, and the chief merit of the book is not to be found in the pictures it presents.

Its main excellence, I think, lies in the clarity of its reasoning. The writer has a well-balanced mind, is full of good sense, and never lets himself be carried away by his emotions. Though a patriotic Frenchman, he wants to understand the enemy. Though he suffered, suffered

[1] Gaston Riou, Journal d'un simple soldat, Hachette, 1916 ; English translation by Eden and Cedar Paul, George Allen & Unwin, 1916.

much, at the hands of the Germans, his suffering never aroused in him a feeling of blind hatred.

Afflicted by the tortures of underfeeding and by the weariness of his exile, he is none the less able to do justice to his " gaoler," the commandant of Fort Orff near Ingolstadt. Indeed, all the prisoners were fond of the commandant, and were sad when he left. They presented him with a formal address on this occasion. It was penned by Riou, and read by him to the baron :

" Mon commandant, to every one of us your departure is a matter of personal regret. You are an enemy, but never has any one had a more courteous enemy.

" You have treated us as soldiers, with perfect frankness ; we have treated you as the true gentleman that you are.

" We, the French prisoners at Fort Orff, differ upon many points. But there is one matter upon which, when we return to France, we shall all agree, namely, that Commandant Major Baron von Stengel deserved and gained the affection and admiration of those towards whom for three months he had to fill the position of gaoler.

" Accept our thanks, mon commandant. God have you in his keeping."

The book is interspersed with admirable psychological reflections. Consider, for instance, Riou's account of the working of persistent hunger :

" Imprisonment is, above all, hunger, chronic hunger. Those only who have experienced it can understand the effect which chronic hunger speedily exercises even upon an active brain. At first it induces hallucinations. With terrible realism, the sufferer recalls meals eaten before the war, some particular dinner, such and such a picnic. The nerves of taste and smell, exasperated by the scanty regimen, are visited by memories of odours and tastes. The man thinks of nothing but eating. Literally he is nothing but a clamorous stomach. He will lie awake the entire night thinking only of this : What can I do to-morrow morning to secure a supplementary loaf ? "

Seeing that Riou possesses both the qualities disclosed in the foregoing extracts—a capacity to understand the enemy, and a keen psychological insight—he is obviously well fitted to sketch the psychology of the common people of Germany, with whom he rubbed shoulders during his imprisonment.

The common folk seem to him good people, kind-hearted, greatly concerned about domestic matters, and quite uninterested in politics. To them, the Kaiser and the political Olympus appear inaccessibly remote. They accept the doings of persons in authority as they accept hail or rain or sunshine. Active in private life, the German is extraordinarily passive in public life. One might almost say that public life does not exist for him. Thus the Germans allow themselves to be led by the nose. Though hatreds and enthusiasms can be artificially imposed upon him, at bottom the German is not a patriot. " Ubi bene, ibi patria." The mere contact with the French prisoners serves to dull both his hatreds and his enthusiasms ; his eyes are opened ; he sees the man in the enemy. To this man he confides his miseries, his overwhelming desire for peace, his animosity towards his leaders. Nevertheless, he remains passive; and although there has been a revolution in his heart, it finds no means of translating itself into action.

Such are the characteristics of the German common people, seen without distortion or idealisation, contemplated unemotionally by Gaston Riou, a true Frenchman. He gives us a very different picture from the conventional one due to systematic misunderstanding. We no longer hear the customary wild-beast cries.

17

JEAN-BARD AND DYNAMISM

(" Revue de l'Epoque," Paris,
January 1921.)

SOMETHING, perhaps, has already been heard in France of
the achievements of Pitoyeff and his company; and my
compatriots know of Jaques Dalcroze's attempt to accommodate rhythmic movement and gesture to the curve of melodic phrases. But my main object in this article is to discuss
Jean-Bard's " Dynamism." The Genevese stage has been
worthy of close attention for some years past. Whereas
the Parisian theatre has been becoming philistine in its
routine, the French theatre of to-morrow would seem
to be undergoing elaboration in Geneva.

Jean-Bard is a young actor whose boldness is worthy of
all admiration. At a time when we are dogmatically
told that lyricism is out of place on the boards, and when the
critics seem almost inclined to appraise the scenic value of
a play more highly in proportion as it is free from lyricism
(I might even write, in proportion as it is prosaic and com-
monplace), Jean-Bard takes the Boeotian bull by the
horns, and proposes to give us pure poetry in the theatre.
Do you understand? Not poetic drama, but pure poetry.
What is more, he has succeeded. In Geneva, in Prague,
and in many other towns, he has been enthusiastically
applauded for his " dynamic interpretation " of some
of Verhaeren's poems. I was present, recently, at one of
his performances, and came away assured that this is likely
to be a fruitful development of art.

We must not jump to the conclusion that the works of

every poet can be interpreted in this way with equal success. But Verhaeren's poems are addressed to the motor sense quite as much as to sight and hearing. Indeed, Jean-Bard tells us that he was led to originate the idea of "Dynamism" by the reading of Verhaeren's poems. These poems made his muscles thrill, giving rise to "physical fatigue"; and he has merely to allow the vibration to continue within himself and outside himself, in order to create expressive gesture. On the stage, the poems are recited by one person or by several, and are at the same time acted by one person or by several. Without the addition of a single word, the poem thus becomes a drama. How enormously better this is than a dull recitation by a man in evening dress, his arms dangling at his sides, or with one hand upon the heart, or holding a roll of paper to keep himself in countenance.

The recital comprised from eight to ten poems, and the audience displayed a breathless interest throughout.

We may be told that this interpretation is extremely subjective. Perhaps so, but even then the objection means no more than that we have to do with an independant form of art superadded to that of the poet. But the interpretation is much less subjective than might have been supposed. On several occasions I found that I had anticipated the gesture, the dramatisation, which actually came. I should myself have interpreted the poem in the same way; and this signifies that the artist's intuition had secured a certain objectivity, had effected one of the "correspondences" of which Wagner and Baudelaire and Rimbaud have spoken.

Of course the performance was not quite free from blunders, the penalty of a bold innovation. Some of the critics have pounced upon these. Here, preeminently, criticism is easy and art is difficult; but I am convinced that there is an art in the method of presentation.

Even if we were inclined to regard this effort as a mere feat, an exploit bordering on the impossible, and one whose success had been purely accidental, still the exploit would remind us of a truth people are apt to forget. Lyricism can be staged ; and all the more, therefore, a drama can be scenic while still remaining lyrical. The truth is as old as the plays of Aeschylus, but it is one which the modern stage (despite Wagner) tends stupidly to ignore.

Whatever we may think of the attempt on general grounds, " Dynamism " will at least serve to jostle the complacency of our pettily realist stage. Jean-Bard smilingly upholds the following paradox : " I do not like action on the boards." If I understand him aright, he means that action may be wholly internal ; that the movement of the feelings of one person may suffice to animate the scene.

Aeschylus had the same idea when he wrote *Prometheus*. The chorus in all the Greek tragedies is nothing more than a dynamic expression of the flux and reflux of emotions. Thus " Dynamism " would seem to round off Wagner's effort, and to be bringing the theatre back towards a form more closely akin to that of the Greek tragedy. There can be no doubt that this form is loftier, more civilised, more plastic, more artistic, than our modern drama, whose trend often is towards the worst sort of cinema and towards Grand Guignol.

DYNAMIC DRAWING

("La Feuille," Geneva,
February 15, 1920.)

A DRAWING is not a servile copy. Primarily it is a method
of expression. It expresses sentiments, ideas, memories,
and plans. Generally speaking, the child makes use of
drawing for these purposes. So much, where children
are concerned, is drawing an active form of self-expression,
so little is it a mere copy of what is drawn, that the youthful
artist, when depicting natural objects, inclines to represent
only those parts of persons or things whose active and
practical utility a child can understand. These useful
parts are depicted even when they cannot be seen in the
model. A child will often draw two eyes upon a face
viewed in profile, or will equip the front of a house with a
chimney which is really placed at the back. The child is
not an impressionist, being by no means satisfied with the
reproduction of the sensations of the moment. The new-
born infant, doubtless, sees the world after the impressionist
manner, as a moving mosaic, a kaleidoscope of sensations.
But by the time a child begins to draw, its whole being
tends towards action. The impressionist, in fact, has
become an expressionist.

Originally, drawing must have been as spontaneous
a method of expression as speech. Drawing is expression
directed towards the eye, and speech is expression directed
towards the ear. As in so many other respects, we civilised
adults have lost part of what primitive men possessed, and

of what our own children still possess. We have retained only the latter of these two forms of expression. For, now that we no longer use ideographic writing, our writing is merely a means of registering speech ; just like the phonograph, which may tend, in days to come, to replace writing in many cases. If we believe writing to be a method of expression directed towards the eye, we are victims of a fallacy. We have gained certain advantages by substituting an audible method of expression for a visible one ; but the change involves a corresponding drawback, inasmuch as we risk the decay of a precious faculty. Trains and trams are convenient for getting about ; but it is unwise to use them so exclusively that our legs atrophy. Now, writing is to drawing what a railway train is to our legs.

The new education is opposed to our allowing either legs or arms to atrophy. Manual work has become part of the regular curriculum in a modern school. The study of William James' *Talks to Teachers on Psychology* has shown us that this manual work is not simply a " branch." It is the persistent corollary of mental instruction. By manual work, the child is able to express and to verify what it knows. Manual work is expression and reaction ; it is the natural sequel of the impression produced on the brain by knowledge, just as reflex action is the natural outcome of sensation. But we may, and should, say exactly the same thing of drawing. This, likewise, is expression and reaction ; this, likewise, is the touchstone of certain elements of knowledge. It must not, any more than manual work, be cultivated as a separate branch. As Madame Artus-Perrelet happily phrases the matter, drawing must be " at the service " of all departments of education. Being both artist and teacher, this author arrives, intuitively in many cases, at the conclusions which have been reached by the most advanced among educationists and psychologists.

We shall do well to consider for a moment the book in which she has condensed the substance of a course of lectures delivered at the Jean Jacques Rousseau Institute.[1]

1. MOVEMENT.

It is a general principle of the new education that active movement on the pupil's part should replace the passive immobility prescribed by the educationists of the old school. Madame Artus-Perrelet applies this principle in the drawing lesson. This is correlative to the conception of drawing as a reaction to the most diversified impressions. The draughtsman no longer designs merely with the hand, but with the whole body. The child, when drawing, will not be satisfied with being a spectator, but will become an actor. It will walk all round the objects, will handle them, will look at them alternately from close at hand and from a distance, will make them its own, will imitate them. Paradoxical as the phrase may seem, the pupil will do quite a lot of gymnastics during the drawing lesson. The youngster will learn the meaning of " horizontal " by stretching the arm out horizontally, by lying down, by various games in which these positions are assumed. After such games, the child will spontaneously draw pictures of the horizontal. If we want to make the child understand the notion of the line as a succession of points, we may play with our pupil the drama of Tom Thumb, who drops pebbles to mark out his road. Then the child will draw (always on the blackboard, so that the movements shall be expansive) the line which represents the road, and the dots which represent the pebbles. At the first glance, some may be inclined to think these motor preliminaries trivial, but their value will be proved by results. A line, a drawing, which has

[1] L. Artus-Perrelet, Le dessin au service de l'éducation, with a preface by Pierre Bovet, Delachaux & Niestlé, Neuchâtel and Paris.

thus been lived through to begin with, will be achieved with far more vigour and ease.

2. THE FUSION OF THE ARTS.

Through grasping the motor foundation of drawing, Madame Artus-Perrelet was led, almost simultaneously, to another important principle. Motor activity lies at the foundation, not only of the plastic arts, but of all the arts. In the arts which appeal to the ear, we can even trace the connexion more readily, for these arts have a time dimension, and movement is a function of time. In the plastic arts, on the other hand, movement is immobilised ; the observer has to make a certain effort to detect it. But when we have done so, we shall be impressed with the notion of the kinship of all the arts, for we shall have traced them back to their common source. Madame Artus-Perrelet does not expound the logical nexus that we have been disclosing, but she grasps it implicitly. Having, as a part of her peculiar originality, a keen motor sensibility, she divines at one and the same time the motor foundation of drawing and the kinship of the arts. She rediscovers the Wagnerian idea that the arts must render one another mutual service. Thus, children will sing their drawings ; will play them on the piano ; will be continually trying to express the same state of mind by recitation, by music, and by drawing. No doubt we have moved a long way from the Wagnerian fantasies of some of the aesthetes. The " correspondences " with which we are here concerned are those which children can grasp spontaneously ; just as, in current parlance, we spontaneously refer to a " clear note," a " sharp note," a " ponderous drawing," a " warm colour." The motor disturbance reacts in various directions ; discharges itself in visual images as well as in auditory ones. If we accept

William James' principle that complete reactions are necessary, there can be no apriori objection to Madame Artus-Perrelet's plan of "singing a drawing." Drawing is a reaction; but the reaction is not complete until the drawing has been sung, recited, reacted through all the senses.

3. THE MEANING OF FORMS.

Another logical tie leads us to another of Madame Artus-Perrelet's masterly notions. In her method all the parts are interconnected, even those parts that are presented as separate. "A logical tie," I said. I might just as well have written "an organic tie," for the unity is the unity of life.

There is a connexion, a sort of equivalence, between such and such a line, and such and such a sound, so that the line and the sound may, to some extent, replace one another as means of expression. The artist will tell us that in his eyes they have the same signification. What is this signification? What is the idea, or what is the sentiment, which these various perceptible forms, be they lines, or be they sounds, etc., symbolise?

This meaning, this link between various perceptible forms, must necessarily be a matter of interest to any one who has come to recognise in motor reactions the intimate unity of these forms. But motor reaction is only the bodily unity, and what we are now in search of is the mental accompaniment. Inasmuch as a motor disturbance may be either active or passive, it may be accompanied by a mental state belonging to either of two kinds. Thus the perceptible forms may have two kinds of meaning, one being active or practical (utilitarian, if you like), whereas the other is emotional and sentimental. Madame Artus-Perrelet reaches this conclusion, although not by the road of abstract reasoning. She looks for two kinds of meaning in lines, and aims at making her little pupils consciously aware of these two kinds of meaning.

Consider, for instance, the simple curve of a vase or a bird's nest. Here we have a containing, a protecting line. Throughout nature, this line has been utilised in the same sense ; turn a bird's nest upside down, and you have a savage's hut. This is a good example of the practical significance of a line.

If, on the other hand, we say that a horizontal is a line of repose (the line of the body of a sleeper or of the expanse of a calm sea), we have an example of emotional signification.

The meaning of lines, whether practical or emotional, is not the learned discovery of some abstruse devotee of Symbolism ; it is a thing which is readily understood, intuitively perceived by the child. When children are helped to grasp the meaning of lines, they are being shown the way to the very heart of drawing, and drawing becomes a sovereign method of expression. The teacher is also furnished with repeated opportunities for giving vivid object lessons, as we have just seen in the case of the bird's nest and the savage's hut.

4. SIMPLE FORMS.

The fact that Madame Artus-Perrelet is on the look-out for the meaning of forms, no doubt explains her predilection for simple forms, and especially for geometrical forms, since in the case of these latter it is easy to make a sort of dictionary of significations. The author advises us to begin with simple forms before going on to the study of the more complicated forms of life. She encourages her pupils to analyse and systematise the shapes of living beings so as to represent them in simple forms. A goose becomes an ovoid on feet. The method would seem to be justified by results. But I think there is a misunderstanding involved, an error from the theoretical outlook, although Madame Artus-Perrelet corrects it in practice thanks to her vivid methods of instruction. Tolstoy, in his writings on educational subjects, points out the same error in Froebel's method. Froebel, too, corrected it in practical work; but disciples, who follow the method too literally, are likely to overlook the correction. Froebel and Madame Artus-Perrelet wish to progress from the simple to the complex. But this is not the way in which the child's mind works. In the first instance, a child grasps living creatures as integers; and the progress from the simple to the complex is that of the abstract intelligence, working in a very different way from spontaneous perception, which proceeds intuitively. Kuhlmann's experiments [1] have shown that children take longer to classify geometrical forms than biological forms. This might have been anticipated. Probably, too, it will be found that a child cognises volume before superficies, superficies before lines, and lines before points. The analysis of the living being into simple forms would certainly seem, therefore, to correspond to the march of the child's mind; but the theoretical explanation of this is the converse of that given by Madame Artus-Perrelet. It does not seem to me that the start is made from simple forms, from such analytical elements as the point. The child has to be brought to these by analysis, and to take a fresh start therefrom.

5. PERSONIFICATION AND INTERNALISATION.

The child, we have learned, will draw with its whole body; it will understand the meaning of lines. In this

[1] " American Journal of Psychology," 1904.

way it will endow with life the objects which it draws, and, in the end, it will personify them. By encouraging children to personify objects, Madame Artus-Perrelet shows her profound knowledge of the child mind, and also of the psychology of the artist.

" This shadow which is cast is a friendly messenger. It says to the table : ' Your trusty friend the bowl is there.' The table answers : ' The bowl can count on me ; I shall support it firmly.' "

Such little fables give movement and life to this instruction in the meaning of forms, an instruction which would otherwise seem cold and abstract, like a dictionary.

The counterpart and complement of this personification is the internalisation or introjection of the child into the forms of objects. The child will not merely personify the object but will identify itself with the object. If the expression be permissible, it will put itself inside the object's skin. By movements of its own body, the child will imitate the movements it cognises in the object. Lines only acquire a meaning because we humanise them. Madame Artus-Perrelet wishes children to humanise them more completely, in full awareness.

The reader will have realised that this method, though markedly original, is no more than one manifestation of the general trend of the new education. But the foregoing exposition may have presented it from an unduly abstract and systematised outlook. The method is eminently, almost incredibly, alive. Everything is made by it to stir, to leap, to dance. Inanimate objects come to life, as in a fairy tale. And, conversely, just as in a fairy tale, children are transformed into inanimate objects. A wave of the enchanter's wand, and they become children once more. Then the children see before them the object which they have been for a time, and which to some extent they still are. The drawing the child has made is a memento of the metamorphosis. Thus the child does not so much draw an object, as participate in the creation of an object.

It would almost be superfluous to stress the fact that Madame Artus-Perrelet's book has aesthetic bearings as well as educational bearings in the narrower sense of the term. The author is continually appealing to aesthetic postulates, to Symbolism, to the interpretation of the before-mentioned metamorphoses, to personification, and so on. Now, if an educational system based upon such postulates prove successful, does not this show that the postulates are sound? May it not be that, in the teaching of art to children, we have a criterion by which we can appraise theories concerning art—a criterion which may prove of great value to artists?

THE DYNAMIC INTERPRETATION
OF POETRY

(" Rassegna Internazionale," Rome,
November 1921.)

FOR some time I have had thoughts and wishes concerning
an expansive poesy, a poesy as wide in its scope as that of
the Greek chorus, a poesy which should no longer be the
Cinderella of the arts, shame-faced, stay-at-home, and
bedraggled. While I was toying with these thoughts and
wishes, without as yet having given them definite shape,
the prince who was to set Cinderella free, the renovated art
of gesture, was at hand. I do not know what fairy god-
mother sent him athwart my path.

Jean-Bard, a young artist whose sincerity makes a strong
appeal to me, showed me the bearing of this movement,
as Diogenes of old proved the existence of movement in
general—by moving. Jean-Bard's " dynamic interpretation " of Verhaeren's poems was enough to convince me of
the existence of a new art, an art of the future. Moreover,
Verhaeren's verse was especially suitable for this dynamic
interpretation.

The very words, the images, are often, in Verhaeren,
movement and muscle. But even when the words and the
images are not this, the rhythm always is. We have rhythm
in action—shock, stir, impetus. Stefan Zweig, one of the
ablest of Verhaeren's commentators, aptly characterises
this poet's rhythm as something which one feels physically,
muscularly. The same statement doubtless applies, in
some degree, to every artistic rhythm ; but it is especially
true of the rhythms of Verhaeren.

Furthermore, I consider that " dynamic interpretation " is in conformity with one of the most notable trends of modern poesy. Dynamism is not merely a method of interpretation ; it is also a method of creation. The name " Dynamism " has been more than once suggested to denote the work of our younger poets, and it seems likely to secure acceptance. But the name matters little. The actual fact is that for the last forty years our poets have been trying by various methods to reveal the Dynamism of the poem, and this has been the essential significance of one innovation after another.

The earlier Symbolists inaugurated free verse, their aim being to give spontaneity and suppleness to this inward movement. In our own day, towards the close of the same evolutionary period, the Unanimists (Whitman's pupils, visualisers for the most part) are little concerned with the " music " which the Symbolists prized above all, and they are at odds with the Symbolists upon many matters. But when they disregard music, it is only to cultivate the more assiduously another kind of rhythm, a muscular and motor rhythm. I have myself felt justified in maintaining [1] that the search for Dynamism is the inspiration of all poetry, although, according as the poets' temperaments vary, the Dynamism may assume either of two very different forms. Some poets, musical by temperament, pay heed above all to the continuity, the flux, of the inner life. Others are more sensitive to vital impetus and to force. But continuity and vital impetus (the conjuncture of these two concepts in Bergson's philosophy is no chance matter) are but the form and the substance of one and the same reality— movement.

The art of movement is a synthetic art, competent to

[1] Vide supra, The Coming Poetry.

express that which is common to the other arts. A simple instance from the realm of physiological psychology will suffice to show the possibility of such a synthesis.

It has long been noticed that relationships exist between certain sounds, certain colours, and certain shapes. In ordinary speech we are not afraid to indicate such associations by speaking of a " clear note," a " ponderous shape," a " loud colour." Since the days of Wagner, and since scientific observers have recorded more or less pathological instances of " coloured hearing," artists have been ready to turn this knowledge to account. Baudelaire wrote a sonnet entitled *Correspondances*.

Les parfums, les couleurs, et les sons se répondent.

Rimbaud, in another noted sonnet, has the line :

A noir, E blanc, I rouge, O vert, U bleu, voyelles. . . .

It is a mistake to go very far upon such a search, for any precise relationship which we might discover would be illusory, or extremely subjective. But there really is a relationship.

We have, then, to ask ourselves, when we find that two distinct sorts of sensation—one visual and the other auditory, for example—seem to us to correspond, what their subjacent unity can consist of. The nature of the tie remains enigmatic, unless we appeal to a physiological connecting link. But this latter, it seems to me, is not difficult to divine. A sensation is a centrepetal affair ; but every sensation unleashes a centrifugal reaction, or at least the sketch of one. Such is the nature of the alternate play of the sensory and the motor nerves. But, whether the sensation be visual or auditory or tactile, and whatever sense organ it enters by, the reaction is always and simply motor. We have only one kind of motor reaction as a response to various kinds of sensibility. It may be inferred, therefore that sensations entering by different sense organs will appear to "correspond" when they unleash kindred motor reactions.

It may be inferred, likewise, that the art of gesture is really a disclosure of the common principle which underlies the other arts, namely movement. Painters speak of the movement of a line ; musicians, of the movement of a melody. Both painters and musicians are in these cases aware of the motor reaction which the organism is sketching. The art of gesture searches out this reaction, amplifies it, and prolongs it, so that what was nothing more than the sketch of a movement becomes a complete movement. Movement is a function of space and time. An art whose main substance is movement, participates simultaneously in the plastic arts, which are space, and in music, which is time. Hence its synthetic force and its universal value.

There is, then, a region of mutual comprehension, a language common to the different arts. To educate this "motor sense" which the art of gesture brings into play, is doubtless to acquire a fuller, a more human sensibility. Every one of the other arts can and must gain thereby.

It is, above all, because the art of gesture effects such a synthesis, that this art, I think, must draw near to poetry and must collaborate with poetry. For poetry embodies an analogous synthesis.

We are told that poetry has sometimes tried to rival music in respect of melody, the plastic arts as a means of depicting things seen, philosophy or science as an instrument of thought. In all these fields, the combat has been unequal. But where poetry can triumph is in a rapid and vigorous synthesis of all these scattered forces, one or other of them being stressed as the poet's temperament may dictate. While incapable of giving full expression to any one of our faculties taken in isolation, poetry is privileged to express these faculties jointly—to express the human mind as an integer. That is its harmonising and cultural role. In such an age as our own, when the mind suffers from its dissection into a thousand specialities occupying water-tight compartments, when unity is so desirable, when even art and science have ceased to wrangle, when the scattered fragments of the body of Osiris are seeking re-union—least of all, in such an epoch, can poetry repudiate its synthetic role.

But in poetry these various elements, music and vision and thought, may seem to be merely juxtaposed rather than truly combined. The intimate unity we desire is to be found in movement. I consider, therefore, that a motor accompaniment of the poem furnishes the best way of achieving a synthesis, and of making it intuitively perceptible. Thus poetry can indeed take possession of us from all sides at once, without any subdivision of the impression. In this way the ocean takes possession of us through every channel of sense. Its colour and the music of its waves, its vastness, its smell of iodine, its bitter taste, and its moist breath, combine to induce one all-absorbing ecstasy.

BIBLIOGRAPHY

ABDUL BAHA. Translations of most of the works mentioned in the text can be obtained from the Bahai Publishing Society, 508, Dearborn Street, Chicago, Ill., U.S.A. ; and many of them from Burnside, Ltd., Beaconsfield Terrace Road, West Kensington, London, W. 14.

Anthologie des poètes contre la guerre, Le Sablier, Geneva, 1920, with a preface by Romain Rolland.

ARCOS, René, Le sang des autres, poèmes, 1914–1918, ornés de huit bois hors-texte par Frans Masereel, Editions du Sablier, Kundig, Geneva, 1917.

ARTUS-PERRELET, L., Le dessin au service de l'éducation, with a preface by Pierre Bovet, Delachaux and Niestlé, Neuchâtel and Paris.

AUBIGNÉ, Théodore Agrippa d', Les tragiques.

BAHA'U'LLAH. Translations of most of the works mentioned in the text can be obtained from the Bahai Publishing Society, 508, Dearborn Street, Chicago, Ill., U.S.A. ; and many of them from Burnside, Ltd., Beaconsfield Terrace Road, West Kensington, London, W. 14.

BARBUSSE, Henri, Le feu, journal d'un escouade, Paris, 1916 ; English translation by Fitzwater Wray, Under Fire, the Story of a Squad, Dent, London and Toronto, 1917.

BAUDOUIN, Charles, Baptismales, Editions du Carmel, Geneva, 1919.

BAUDOUIN, Charles, Hantises légendaires, poems published in various periodicals, not reissued in book form.

BAUDOUIN, Charles, Le symbole chez Verhaeren, essai de psychanalyse de l'art, Mongenet, Geneva, 1924.—English translation by Eden and Cedar Paul, Psychoanalysis and Aesthetics, George Allen & Unwin, London, 1924.

BAUDOUIN, Charles, Psychoanalysis and Aesthetics, see Le symbole chez Verhaeren.

BAZALGETTE, Léon, Article on Frans Masereel, " Revue de l'Epoque," Paris, April 1921.

BEAUDUIN, Nicholas, Rhythmes et chants dans le renouveau, Povoloski, Paris, 1920.

BERGSON, Henri Louis, L'énergie spirituelle, Alcan, Paris, 1919 ; English translation by H. Wildon Carr, Mind-Energy, Macmillan, London, 1920.

BLOCH, Jean Richard, Carnaval est mort, Editions de la Nouvelle Revue Française, Paris, 1920.

BONDAREFF, Timothée M., Léon Tolstoï et Timothée Bondareff, Le travail, traduit du Russe par B. Tseytline et A. Pagès, Marpon et Flammarion, Paris.

BOVET, Pierre, Preface to Artus-Perrelet's Le dessin au service de l'éducation.—See ARTUS-PERRELET.

BREUER, Josef, and FREUD, Sigmund, Ueber den psychischen Mechanismus hysterischer Phänomene, " Neurologisches Zentralblatt," Nos. 1 and 2, 1893.

BREWSTER, David, Memoirs of the Life, Writings, and Discoveries of Sir Isaac Newton, Edmonston & Douglas, Edinburgh, second edition, 2 vols, 1860.

BRITTINGHAM, Isabella D., The Revelation of Bahä-Ulläh in a Sequence of Four Lessons, The Bahai Publishing Co., Chicago, 1902.

CANUDO, Riciotto, Cents versets d'imitation, " Revue de l'Epoque," No. 15, Paris, March 1921.

CHATEAUBRIAND, François René de, René.

CHENNEVIÈRE, Georges, Poèmes, 1911–1918, La Maison des Amis des Livres, Paris, 1920.

CLAUDEL, Paul, L'annonce faite à Marie, fifth edition, Paris, 1913.—English translation by Louise Morgan Sill, The Tidings brought to Mary, Chatto & Windus, London, 1916.

CLAUDEL, Paul, Le pain dur, Editions de la Nouvelle Revue Française, Paris, 1918.

CUREL, François de, Souvenirs sur Carl Spitteler, Mercure de France, 1919.

DESFEUILLES, P., Le poète suisse, Carl Spitteler, " Revue de l'enseignement des langues vivantes," Didier, Paris, 1915.

DREYFUS, Hippolyte, Le Béhaisme, son histoire, sa portée sociale, Leroux, Paris.

DREYFUS, Hippolyte, Le livre de la certitude de Béha-Oullah, Leroux, Paris, 1904.

DREYFUS, Hippolyte, Les paroles cachées de Béha-Oullah, Leroux, Paris.

DREYFUS, Hippolyte, The Universal Religion, Bahaism, its Rise and Social Import, Cope & Fenwick, London, 1909.

DUHAMEL, Georges, Compagnons, Editions de la Nouvelle Revue Française, Paris, 1912.

DUHAMEL, Georges, Elégies, Editions Mercure de France, Paris, eighth edition, 1920.

DUHAMEL, Georges, La confession de minuit, Editions Mercure de France, 1920.

DUJARDIN, Edouard, De Stéphane Mallarmé au prophète Ezéchiel et essai d'une théorie de réalisme symbolique, Editions Mercure de France, 1919.

DUJARDIN, Edouard, Les époux d'Heur-le-port, Paris, 1919.

DURTAIN, Luc, Le retour des hommes, Editions de la Nouvelle Revue Française, 1920.

DUTHIERS, see LUCAZE-DUTHIERS.

DUVALDIZIER, Jacques, Les tendances nouvelles de la poésie moderne, " Revue de l'Epoque," No. 15, Paris, March 1921.

ELLIS, Henry Havelock, The Psychology of the English, " Edinburgh Review," April 1916.

ESSLEMONT, J. E., Bahā'U'llah and the New Era, George Allen & Unwin, London, 1923. [This work contains an excellent bibliography.]

FABRI, Marcello, Essai sur l'œuvre d'art considerée comme une réaction, " Revue de l'Epoque," Paris, October 1920.

FABRI, Marcello, La folie de l'homme, Editions du Carnet Critique, Paris.

GROOS, Karl, Die Spiele der Menschen, Jena, 1899; English translation by E. L. Baldwin, the Play of Man, New York, 1901.

GROOS, Karl, Die Spiele der Tiere, Jena, 1896; English translation by E. L. Baldwin, The Play of Animals, Chapman & Hall, London, 1898.

HUGO, Victor Marie, Dieu.

HUGO, Victor Marie, La légende des siècles.

HUGO, Victor Marie, Les châtiments.

HUGO, Victor Marie, Les pauvres gens (La légende des siècles).

JAMES, William, Talks to Teachers on Psychology, and to Students on some of Life's Ideals, Longmans, 1899.— French translation, Causeries pédagogiques, Payot, Lausanne and Paris.

JAMES, William, The Varieties of Religious Experience ; a Study in Human Nature, Longmans, London, 1902.

JOUVE, Pierre Jean, Danse des morts, Edition d'Action Sociale, La Chaux de Fonds, 1917.

JOUVE, Pierre Jean, Heures, livre de la grâce, Kundig, Geneva, 1920.

JOUVE, Pierre Jean, Heures, livre de la nuit, Editions du Sablier, Kundig, Geneva, 1919.

JOUVE, Pierre Jean, Poème contre le grand crime, Editions de Demain, Geneva, 1916.

JOUVE, Pierre Jean, Vous êtes des hommes, Editions de la Nouvelle Revue Française, Paris, 1915.

KLUTH, Otto, Carl Spitteler et les sources de son génie épique, Sonor, Geneva, 1918.

KUHLMANN, F., Experimental Studies in Mental Deficiency, "American Journal of Psychology," July 1904.

LACAZE-DUTHIERS, Gérard de, Dictionnaire idéaliste, in the review "Soi-Même."

LAMARTINE, Alphonse de, Les destinées de la poésie.

LARIVIÈRE, Pierre, Au temps des sous-hommes.

MOEDER, Alphonse, F. Hodler : eine Skizze seiner seelischen Entwicklung und Bedeutung für die schweizerisch-nationale Kultur, Zurich, 1916.

MARINETTI, Filippo Tommaso, I manifesti del futurismo, Istituto Editoriale Italiano, 4 vols., Milan, 1920.

MARINETTI, Filippo Tommaso, Initial Manifesto of Futurism, prefixed to the catalogue of the Exhibition of Works by the Italian Futurist Painters, Sackville Gallery, March 1912.

MARINETTI, Filippo Tommasi, Les mots en liberté futuriste, Edition futuriste, Milan, 1919.

MARTINET, Marcel, La maison à l'abri, Ollendorff, Paris, 1919.

MARTINET, Marcel, Les temps maudits, poèmes 1914–1918, Geneva, 1917 ; after the war, republished by Ollendorff, Paris.

MASSIS, Henri, Romain Rolland contre la France, Floury, Paris, 1915.

MASSON, Georges Armand, Décors, "Le Carmel," Geneva, January 1917.

MASSON, Georges Armand, Parfums, "Le Carmel," Geneva, August 1916.

MAUNOURY, Considérations actuelles, in the review "Soi-Même."

MEISSNER, Carl, Carl Spitteler, Diederichs, Jena, 1912.

MUGNIER, Henri, La clairière automnale, Editions du Carmel, Geneva, 1917.

MUGNIER, Henri, L'élévation voluptueuse, Ciana, Geneva, 1920.

MUGNIER, Henri, L'oasis dans la ville, Violette, Geneva, 1917.

NICOLAI, G. F., Die Biologie des Krieges, Betrachtungen eines Naturforschers den Deutschen zur Besinnung, Orel Füssli, Zurich, 1917 ; English translation by Constance A. Grande and Julian Grande, The Biology of War, Dent, London and Toronto, 1919.

NIETZSCHE, Friedrich Wilhelm, Briefwechsel mit Franz Overbeck, Insel-Verlag, Leipzig, 1916.

NIETZSCHE, Friedrich Wilhelm, Der Fall Wagner, ein Musikanten-Problem, 2nd edition, Leipzig, 1889 ; the English translation, The Case of Wagner, is in vol. viii of Oscar Levy's edition of the complete works ; Foulis, Edinburgh and London.

NIETZSCHE, Friedrich Wilhelm, Die Geburt der Tragödie aus der Geiste der Musik, Leipzig, 1872, subsequently renamed Die Geburt der Tragödie, oder Hellenismus und Pessimismus ; English translation by William A. Haussmann, The Birth of Tragedy or Hellenism and Pessimism, being vol. i of Oscar Levy's edition of the complete works.

NIETZSCHE, Friedrich Wilhelm, Ecce Homo ; the English translation is vol. xvii of Oscar Levy's edition of the complete works.

NIETZSCHE, Friedrich Wilhelm, Menschliches, Allzumenschliches, ein Buch für freie Geister, 2 parts, Chemnitz, 1878–9 ; English translation of Part I by Helen Zimmern, with an Introduction by J. M. Kennedy, Human, All-Too-Human, a Book for Free Spirits, being vol. vii of Oscar Levy's edition of the complete works, Foulis, Edinburgh and London, 1909.

NIETZSCHE, Friedrich Wilhelm, Zur Genealogie der Moral, eine Streitschrift, Leipzig, 1887; English translation by Horace B. Samuel, The Genealogy of Morals, a Polemic, being vol. xiii of Oscar Levy's edition of the complete works, Foulis, Edinburgh and London, 1910.

PASCAL, Blaise, Pensées.

PÉRIN, Georges, Terre, " Le Carmel," No. 8, Geneva, 1916.

PHELPS, Myron H., Life and Teachings of Abbas Effendi, A Study of the Religion of the Babis or Beha'is founded by the Persian Bab and by his Successors Beha Allah and Abbas Effendi, with an Introduction by Edward Granville Browne, Putnam, London and New York, second, revised, edition, 1912.

RAGAZ, Spittelers Prometheus und Nietzsches Zarathustra, Chur, 1912.

RAGOZIN, Zénaide A., Chaldea, " Story of the Nations " series, Fisher Unwin, London, 1887.

RANDON, Gabriel, see RICTUS.

RICTUS, Jehan (pen-name of Gabriel Randon), Le cœur populaire, poèmes, Paris, 1920.

RIOU, Gaston, Journal d'un simple soldat, Hachette, Paris, 1916 ; English translation by Eden and Cedar Paul, The Diary of a French Private, George Allen & Unwin, London, 1916.

RIVIÈRE, Joseph, En passant, Editions de Soi-Même, Paris, 1917.

ROLLAND, Romain, Au-dessus de la mêlée, Ollendorff, Paris, 1915.—English translation, Above the Battlefield, with an introduction by Richard Roberts, Friends' Peace Committee, London, 1915 ; another English translation by C. K. Ogden, Above the Battle, George Allen & Unwin, London, 1916.

ROLLAND, Romain, Colas Breugnon, Ollendorff, Paris, 1918 ; English translation by K. Miller, Holt, New York, 1919.

ROLLAND, Romain, Empédocle d'Agrigente et l'âge de la haine, Cahier du Carmel, Geneva, 1910.

ROLLAND, Romain, Clerambault, Ollendorff, Paris, 1920.

ROLLAND, Romain, Jean Christophe, 10 vols., Ollendorff, Paris, 1904–1912.—English translation by Gilbert Cannan, Heinemann, London, 1910–1913, Holt, New York, 1911–1913.

ROLLAND, Romain, Liluli (with woodcuts by Frans Masereel), Le Sablier, Geneva, 1919 ; Ollendorff, Paris, 1920.— An English translation appeared in " The Nation," London, September 20 to November 29, 1919 ; in book form, Boni & Liveright, New York, 1920.

ROLLAND, Romain, Les Précurseurs, L'Humanité, Paris, 1919.— English translation by Eden and Cedar Paul, The Forerunners, George Allen & Unwin, London, 1920 ; Harcourt, Brace, & Howe, New York, 1920.

ROLLAND, Romain, Vie de Tolstoï, Hachette, Paris, 1911.— English translation by Bernard Miall, Tolstoy, Fisher Unwin, London, 1911.

ROMAINS, Jules, Europe, Editions de la Nouvelle Revue Française, Paris, 1920.

ROSTOVA, Natasha, article in " Le Carmel," No. 8 for 1917.

RYNER, Jayme Hans, dit Han, né a Nemours (Algérie) en 1861. (His earlier works were published under the name of " Henri NER.")

RYNER, Han, Comment te bats-tu ? " Le Symbole," August 1917.

RYNER, Han, La philosophie, " Revue de l'Epoque," Paris, 1919.

RYNER, Han, La tour des peuples, Paris, Figuière, 1919.

RYNER, Han, Le cinquième évangile, second edition, Paris, Figuière, 1911.

RYNER, Han, Le fils du silence, Figuière, Paris, 1911.

RYNER, Han, Le livre de Pierre, Paris, 1917.

RYNER, Han, Les apparitions d'Ahasvérus, Figuière, Paris, 1920.

RYNER, Han, Les chrétiens et les philosophes, Librairie française, Paris, 1906.

RYNER, Han, Les pacifiques, Figuière, Paris, 1914.

RYNER, Han, Les paraboles cyniques, Figuière, Paris, 1912.

RYNER, Han, Les voyages de Psychodore, Cahiers humains, Paris, 1903.

RYNER, Han, L'homme-fourmi, roman, Maison d'art, Paris, 1901.

SAUVAGE, Marcel, Damné, " Lumière," No. 6, Antwerp, January 1921.

SCHICKELÉ, René, Article on Vildrac in " L'Art Libre," Brussels, March 1921.

SENANCOURT, Étienne Pivert de, Obermann.

SPENLÉ, J. E., Carl Spitteler, l'homme et le poète, Comité de relations avec les pays neutres, Marseilles, 1916.

SPIESS, Henry, 1914–1921, " La Suisse," Geneva, December 31, 1920.

SPIR, African Alexandrovich, Denken und Wirklichkeit, Versuch einer Erneuerung der kritischen Philosophie, 2 vols., Neff, Stuttgart ; original edition, 2 vols., Leipzig, 1873 ; French translation by A. Penjon, Pensée et réalité, Alcan, Paris.

SPIR, African Alexandrovich, Esquisses de philosophie critique, Alcan, Paris.

SPIR, African Alexandrovich, Nouvelles esquisses de philosophie critique, précédées d'une biographie de l'auteur [by Hélène Claparède], Alcan, Paris, 1899.

SPITTELER, Carl, Balladen, Müller, Zurich, 1896.

SPITTELER, Carl, Conrad der Leutnant, eine Darstellung, Vita, Berlin, 1898.—Now published by Diederichs of Jena.

SPITTELER, Carl, Extramundana, Diederichs, Jena, 1885 and 1905.

SPITTELER, Carl, Friedli, der Kolderi, Müller, Zurich, 1891.

SPITTELER, Carl, Der Gotthard, Huber, Frauenfeld, 1897.

SPITTELER, Carl, Glockenlieder, Gedichte, Diederichs, Jena, 1906.

SPITTELER, Carl, Gustav, ein Idyll, Müller, Zurich, 1892.— French translation by E. Desfeuilles, Gustave, Georg, Geneva, and Crès, Paris.

SPITTELER, Carl, Imago, Diederichs, Jena, 1906.

SPITTELER, Carl, Lachende Wahrheiten, Gedammelte Essays, Diederichs, Leipzig and Florence (now Jena), 1898.

SPITTELER, Carl, Literarische Gleichnisse, Müller, Zurich, 1892.

SPITTELER, Carl, Die Mädchenfeinde (Gerold und Hansli), eine Kindergeschichte, Diederichs, Jena, 1907.

SPITTELER, Carl, Meine Beziehungen zu Nietzsche, " Süddeutsche Monatshefte," Munich, 1908.

SPITTELER, Carl, Meine frühesten Erlebnisse, Diederichs, Jena, 1914 ; French translation by H. de Ziegler, Premiers souvenirs, Payot, Paris and Lausanne.

SPITTELER, Carl, Olympischer Frühling, 5 Bücher in 2 Bänden, Diederichs, Jena, 1900, etc.

SPITTELER, Carl, Paroles au jubilé de Genève, " Journal de Genève, ' October 9, 1915.

SPITTELER, Carl, Prometheus und Epimetheus, ein Gleichnis, Diederichs, Jena, new edition, 1920. (First published in 1880–1881).

SPITTELER, Carl, Schmetterlinge, Gedichte, now published by Diederichs of Jena ; the first edition was published at Hamburg in 1889, under the pseudonym of F. Tandem.

SPITTELER, Carl, Unser schweizer Standpunkt, Rascher, Zurich, 1915.—French translation by Catherine Guilland, Notre point de vue suisse, Rascher, Zurich, 1915.

TAGORE, Rabindranath, Nationalism, Macmillan, London, 1917.

TOLSTOY, Leo, Childhood and Youth.

TOLSTOY, Leo, Comte Léon Tolstoï, Journal intime, 1895–1899, French translation by Natasha Rostova and Marguerite Jean-Debrit, Preface, etc., by Paul Birukoff, Portrait by Frans Masereel; Jeheber, Geneva, and Flammarion, Paris, 1917.

TOLSTOY, Leo, Lettres à Bondarev, Cahiers du Carmel, Geneva and Paris, 1918.

TOLSTOY, Leo, Pensées de Tolstoy, and Nouvelles pensées de Tolstoy, collected and translated into French by Ossip-Lourié, Alcan, Paris, 1898, etc.

TOLSTOY, Leo, The Journal of Leo Tolstoi, 1895–1899, translated from the Russian by Rose Strunsky, Knopf, New York, 1917.

TOLSTOY, Leo, Travail, see BONDAREFF.

TOLSTOY, Leo, Work, see BONDAREFF.

VARLET, Théo, Poèmes choisis, 1912.

VERHAEREN, Emile, Les débâcles.

VERHAEREN, Emile, Les Flamandes.

VERHAEREN, Emile, Les flambeaux noirs.

VERHAEREN, Emile, Les flammes hautes.

VERHAEREN, Emile, Hélène de Sparte.

VERHAEREN, Emile, Les moines.

VILDRAC, Charles, Chants du désespéré, 1914–1920, Edition de la Nouvelle Revue Française, Paris, 1920.

WHITMAN, Walt, Leaves of Grass.

ZLINCHENKO, Tolstoï et le mouchard, " Cœnobium," Lugano, August, 1916.

ZWEIG, Stefan, Der Turm zu Babel, " Vossische Zeitung," May 8, 1916 ; French translation, " Le Carmel," 1916 ; English translation by Eden and Cedar Paul, " The Workers' Dreadnought," 1917.